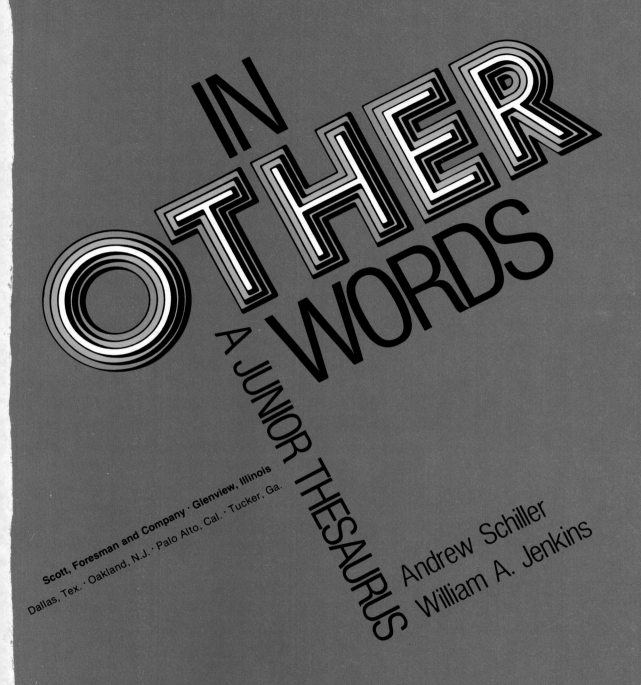

IN OTHER WORDS

A JUNIOR THESAURUS

Scott, Foresman and Company · Glenview, Illinois
Dallas, Tex. · Oakland, N.J. · Palo Alto, Cal. · Tucker, Ga.

Andrew Schiller

William A. Jenkins

Contents

Introduction 3

Entries 19

Index 417

Answers to Questions 446

ISBN 0-673-10266-1

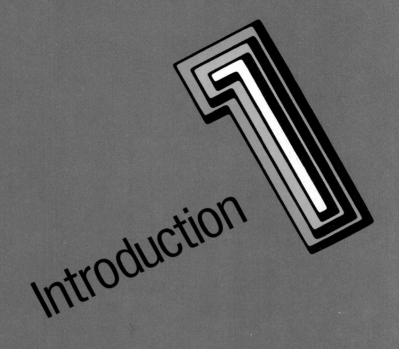

Introduction

FIRE!

The forest fire began early one evening. Luisa and Romana were camping with their Uncle Pablo when they saw the fire in the distant mountains. All three watched anxiously as rangers left the campground and headed for the burning forest. Fortunately, though, a heavy rainstorm helped the rangers put out the fire before it spread very far.

A few days later Luisa, Romana, and Uncle Pablo drove to the mountains so they could get a closer look at the area that was burned by the fire. When they returned to the campground, Luisa and Romana wrote letters to their parents about the forest fire they had seen.

Luisa wrote: "It was really an *appalling* thing to see. The *tremendous* fire *demolished* part of a *stately* forest. Now I know what a *misfortune* forest fires are. I can't describe the *astonishment* I felt when I saw the *harm* done to giant pine and fir trees."

Romana wrote: "It was the most *frightful* sight I had ever seen. The *immense* flames *destroyed magnificent* trees. When the *disaster* was over, I looked with *awe* at the *damage* done to trees that had been growing for more than a hundred years."

Luisa and Romana showed their letters to their uncle before mailing them. After reading the letters, Uncle Pablo said, "You both have seen the same forest fire and you have told the same story—but you chose different words to describe it."

Have you ever noticed how two people can describe the same event and never use the same words?

One of the most exciting things about the English language is its wealth of words. It possesses all kinds—words that stretch, words that shrink; some that crawl and some that soar; silly ones and boisterous ones and melancholy ones; words to make you laugh or cry.

4

Whoever learns to use words well can use them as precisely as a surgeon uses a scalpel, as delicately as a violinist uses a bow, and as powerfully as a lumberjack swings an ax.

This Book

This book is a thesaurus. The dictionary defines the word *thesaurus* as a book of words; a storehouse; a treasury. *Storehouse* and *treasury* are words for a place in which you can store or save things. You would put furniture, old newspapers, empty bottles, or machinery in a storehouse. But you would put money or jewels or bars of solid gold in a treasury.

In this thesaurus you will find over 300 words that you know and use every day. Many of these words are worn out from overuse. You will also find more than 2000 very good words that you can use instead of the worn-out ones.

This book is a storehouse for your tired words. It is also a treasury filled with good, vigorous, new words. Welcome to the treasury! You will find gold in every corner. Come in. You're invited to browse among words that will make your language more precise and powerful.

But while you are browsing, remember that a thesaurus is not a dictionary. You will never be able to throw away your dictionary and use this book instead. This thesaurus contains only synonyms, related words, and antonyms. You'll never learn from this book how to pronounce a word. You won't even find every meaning of a word. And there are thousands of words you won't find here at all. Now, let's see exactly what you *can* find in a thesaurus.

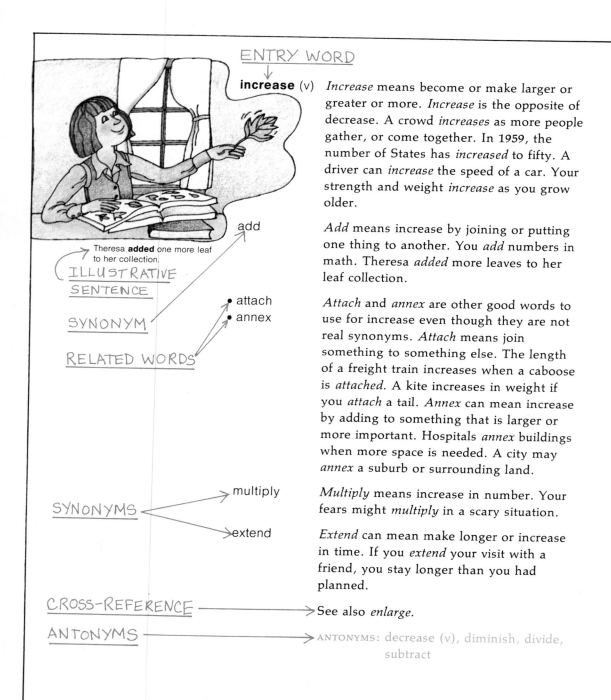

ENTRY WORD

increase (v)   *Increase* means become or make larger or greater or more. *Increase* is the opposite of decrease. A crowd *increases* as more people gather, or come together. In 1959, the number of States has *increased* to fifty. A driver can *increase* the speed of a car. Your strength and weight *increase* as you grow older.

Add means increase by joining or putting one thing to another. You *add* numbers in math. Theresa *added* more leaves to her leaf collection.

Attach and *annex* are other good words to use for increase even though they are not real synonyms. *Attach* means join something to something else. The length of a freight train increases when a caboose is *attached*. A kite increases in weight if you *attach* a tail. *Annex* can mean increase by adding to something that is larger or more important. Hospitals *annex* buildings when more space is needed. A city may *annex* a suburb or surrounding land.

Multiply means increase in number. Your fears might *multiply* in a scary situation.

Extend can mean make longer or increase in time. If you *extend* your visit with a friend, you stay longer than you had planned.

See also *enlarge*.

ANTONYMS: decrease (v), diminish, divide, subtract

Theresa **added** one more leaf to her collection.

ILLUSTRATIVE SENTENCE

SYNONYM

RELATED WORDS

add

• attach
• annex

SYNONYMS

multiply

extend

CROSS-REFERENCE

ANTONYMS

Entries

Look at the sample entry on the opposite page. Think of it as a map that will show you which direction to take as you find your way through your thesaurus.

1. What is the entry word? (Notice that it is printed in **heavy, black type.**)
2. What word do you see printed in *italic type* in the paragraph next to the entry word?
3. What do the first two sentences in the paragraph tell you about *increase?*
4. Read the other sentences in the paragraph. What do they show you?
5. What are the synonyms of the entry word **increase?** (Notice that they are printed in a lighter type than the entry word and that they are listed in a column under the entry word.)
6. Each synonym also has a paragraph next to it. How do these paragraphs help you in choosing synonyms for *increase?*
7. What are the related words?
8. Why are they called related words? (If you read the paragraph next to *attach* and *annex,* you'll find out.)
9. Suppose *attach* and *annex* did not have the label "related words." How could you tell that they are related words and are not real synonyms?

You're halfway through the sample entry now. Once you know your way around it, you'll be able to find your way through other entries in this book any time you feel like browsing. By the way, all of the entries are listed in alphabetical order.

10. What does the cross-reference tell you to do?
11. Why do you think you might need to use a cross-reference?

12. Where can you find the list of antonyms in this entry?
13. What are the antonyms in this entry?
14. What has been done to the antonyms to make them look different from the rest of the words in the entry?

Next, find the picture and the illustrative sentence under it.

15. What is the girl in the picture doing?
16. What describes what she is doing?
17. Which word is in **heavy, black type** in the sentence?
18. Where else in the entry can you find a similar sentence?

That's it! You've found your way through your first entry. Look at some other entries on pages 36, 97, 119, and 124 to find the ways in which they are alike or different from the entry for **increase** (v).

19. What things in the entry for **increase** (v) did you *not* see in the entry on page 36? page 97? page 119? page 124?

All you need is a little more know-how and then you can browse among all the words that your thesaurus has been saving for you.

Synonyms

Now it's time for some more know-how. Here's a sentence using the word *run.*

If you *run* to the bus stop, you won't miss the bus.

Turn to pages 315 and 316 in your thesaurus and look at the entry for **run** (v).

1. Which synonyms could you use in place of *run* in the sentence?

Now, think about the word *run* and its synonyms *gallop, flow, operate, jog,* and *flee.* Would you say—

The Mississippi River *gallops* into the Gulf of Mexico

or

Sandy's new calculator *jogs* on batteries

or

I *flee* around the block at 6:00 every morning

or

I don't like to ride a horse when it *operates*

or

Rudy dreamed that he was trying to *flow* from a riderless motorcycle?

2. Do any of these sentences make sense? Why or why not?

Each synonym for *run* means almost the same as *run,* yet each has its own special meaning.

3. Turn back to pages 315 and 316 and look at the entry for **run** (v). Read the paragraphs next to *gallop, jog, flow, operate,* and *flee* and then decide in which of the above sentences each of these synonyms makes sense.

Some synonyms show differences of degree. The way in which you use them depends on how strong they are when compared to the entry word. Turn to the entry for **hate** (v) on page 194.

4. Which synonym means "disapprove of something" and is not as strong a word as *hate?*
5. Which synonym is a very strong word that means "detest"?
6. Decide which synonyms listed in the entry for **hate** (v) best fit in each of the following sentences. The first one is done for you.

Sometimes I *dislike* rainy days. If it isn't raining very hard, I _____ my raincoat and usually don't wear it. But when I have made plans to play ball or go swimming and it rains very hard, I _____ rainy days. I like the feeling of the fresh air after it rains, but I _____ and look with disgust at the worms that I see on the sidewalk.

You still need a little more know-how in choosing synonyms. Remember *attach* and *annex* in the sample entry? If you don't, take a minute to check back and refresh your memory. . . . All set?

Even though related words are not real synonyms of an entry word, they must be chosen with as much care as synonyms. Turn to pages 413 and 414 and find the entry for **yell** (v).

7. What tells you that the words listed in this entry are related words and not synonyms of *yell?*

Here are three sentences, each using a related word for *yell.*

"Don't walk on the new grass!" I *exclaimed.*
The audience *roared* with laughter when the magician pulled a chicken, and not a rabbit, out of a hat.
Our dog *whines* when it wants to come back into the house.

8. See if you can find other related words in the entry for **yell** (v) that can be used in place of the related words used in these sentences.

Here's one important thing to remember about synonyms. Usually one fits better than any other. That's why you'll browse through this book—to find the one that best suits your needs.

Antonyms

Are you ready for some more know-how? Well, let's get going so you can begin to browse.

An antonym is what a synonym isn't. No doubt you know that an antonym is a word that means the opposite of another word. These are as easy to remember as stop and go and up and down.

There are many antonyms in this book, but not all that might have been included. You may think of some good antonyms that aren't in this book. The fact that you can think of them so easily may be the very reason they were left out. Another reason you may not find antonyms in some entries is that some words simply do not have antonyms. Have you ever tried to think of an antonym for *history* or *duel?*

Just as two synonyms for the same word can mean completely different things, two antonyms in one entry can have different meanings. Turn to page 301 and find the antonyms at the end of the entry for **real.**

1. What are the antonyms listed at the end of the entry for **real?**

Next, find the synonym *genuine.* One of the sentences in the paragraph next to *genuine* is "His beard was not *genuine.*"

2. Which antonyms could you use in place of "not *genuine*" in the above sentence?

Now you can see that not every antonym of *real* can be used as an antonym of *genuine.* If you say "His beard was imaginary," what happens to the meaning of the sentence? If you were wearing an imaginary beard, would anyone see it?

Wait! Don't browse just yet. There's more know-how to come.

Tired Words

There are some words that you use over and over in speaking or writing. These poor words have become tired and need a long rest. Now you need to know where to find these words. It's as easy as turning to page 58 and finding the entry for **big.**

1. How is this entry different from the other entries you have seen?
2. What other words are you told to look up?

As you read entries such as this, you will find refreshing and vigorous words to replace the tired and worn-out ones that you have used and used and used.

Idioms

Idiom—how's that for a valuable treasury word? An idiom is made up of two or more words and has a different meaning than the words within it. Find the entry word **act** (v) on page 23.

1. What does *act* mean? What do the idioms *act for, act on,* and *act up* mean?
2. In the sentence, "The firefighter *acted* quickly to put out the fire," could *acted for, acted on,* or *acted up* be used in place of *acted?* Why or why not?

There are also phrases that have slightly different meanings from the words in them. Find the synonym *honor* (in the entry for **honesty**) on page 203.

3. What does *honor* mean? "hold in *honor*"? "uphold the *honor*"?

Formal and Informal Words

Suppose you were talking to a friend.

1. Would you be more likely to say "I *purchased* some roller skates" or "I *bought* some roller skates"? Why?

Suppose you were buying tickets at a theater.

2. Would the price sign say:

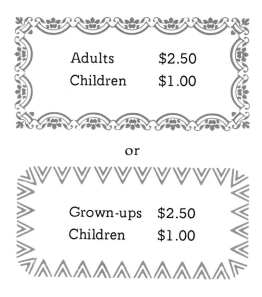

Adults $2.50
Children $1.00

or

Grown-ups $2.50
Children $1.00

Why?

Purchase is a more formal word than *buy,* and *grown-up* is a more informal word than *adult.* Read the paragraph next to the synonyms *buy* and *purchase* on page 260. Then read the paragraph next to the synonym *grown-up* on page 29.

Formal words sound dignified and may be seldom used in everyday speech. You would probably hear formal words at ceremonies or in formal speeches or see them in writing. But some words are not formal enough to use on certain occasions. You might use an informal or a slang word in everyday speech that you wouldn't use when you were talking to someone you didn't know.

Here are some sentences using formal and informal words.

A *mob* of people lined the streets to see the parade.
(**crowd** (n), pages 101–102)
The space flight *commenced* at 6:07 A.M.
(**start** (v), pages 354–355)
What kind of sandwich do you *desire?*
(**want** (v), page 395)
Let's *swap* skateboards today.
(**trade** (v), pages 384–385)

3. Decide whether *mob, commenced, desire,* and *swap* are formal or informal words. If you look up the entries that are given after the sentences, you'll quickly find out which of these four words are formal and which are informal.

As one would formally say, you have just acquired an additional skill that will aid you in utilizing your thesaurus to the utmost degree. In other (informal) words, that means you've just been given some more know-how that will help you use your thesaurus in the best possible way. You're almost ready to browse. Let's move on, or, more formally, "Let's proceed."

Parts of Speech

In case you've been wondering about the (v) in entries like **run, yell,** and the sample entry, you're going to find out about it now. You probably know that (n), (v), (adj), and (adv) stand for noun, verb, adjective, and adverb. Look at pages 69 through 71.

1. How many entries do you see for **calm?**

Here are three sentences, each using *calm* in a different way.

No one could *calm* Melvin during the thunderstorm.
It was hard for Leona to feel *calm* during the mystery movie.
Calm can be felt in the air before a tornado strikes the ground.

2. To get the know-how you need, follow these three steps:
   1. Look at the way *calm* is used in the sentences in each entry.
   2. Decide in which entry for **calm** each of the above sentences could be used.
   3. Choose synonyms from the appropriate entry that could be used in place of *calm* in each sentence.

16

Index

This is it! This is the last bit of know-how you will need before you can begin your browsing.

Every entry word, synonym, related word, and antonym used in this book is listed alphabetically in the Index at the back of the book. So you always begin using this thesaurus from the back. When you look up a word that you have been using too often, the Index will direct you to many vigorous, new words.

Here is part of an Index page.

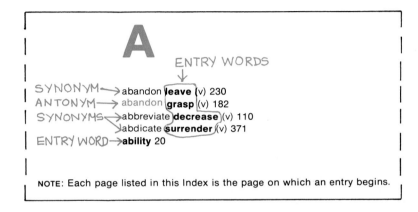

NOTE: Each page listed in this Index is the page on which an entry begins.

1. Read the first word under A. What kind of word does the label tell you it is?
2. In what entry will you find *abandon?*
3. On what page does that entry begin?
4. What is written at the bottom of the sample Index after the word NOTE?
5. Will you always find the synonym you want on the page where the entry begins? Why or why not?
6. What helps you identify related words in the Index?
7. Which word is an antonym? Suppose it wasn't labeled "antonym." How would you know it is an antonym?

8. Under which entry will you find abandon as an antonym?

9. What is the entry word that is listed by itself?

Here are some things to remember. Every entry word, synonym, related word, and antonym in this book appears in the Index as many times as it is listed in the entries. Any word in the Index that is not printed in blue or in **heavy, black type** is a synonym or related word. Each related word has a black dot in front of it. Some abbreviations for parts of speech are included in the Index to help you decide where to look when you need a particular word. For example, since *love* and *hate* can be nouns or verbs, the (n) and (v) tell you which is which. But some words, like *lovely* or *beautiful*, are only adjectives and need no abbreviations.

If a word is listed as a synonym or an antonym for two or more entry words, it is because the word has different meanings. If you can't tell from the entry words which meaning you want, it's a good idea to read all the entries. Just for fun, take a look at *calm* in the Index.

10. How many times is it listed?

Now you have all the know-how you need and you can begin to use your thesaurus. What are you waiting for? It's time to browse!

Entries

A

ability

Ability is being able to do something. You can be born with an *ability.* You can also develop an *ability* by learning to do something and then practicing it. For example, some people are born with an *ability* to carry a tune. Even if they never take singing lessons, they can sing. But no one is born with the *ability* to ski. Skiers must develop the *ability* to keep their balance and control their skis.

talent

Talent is some special ability that you are born with. A musician or a painter has *talent.*

skill

Skill and *dexterity* are abilities that you must develop. You develop the *skill* to do something by learning how it is done, and then by doing it over and over until you can do it easily and well. Typing is a *skill.* A good typist can type a letter easily and well.

Skiers must develop the **ability** to control their skis.

dexterity

Dexterity means skill in using your hands cleverly and gracefully—without fumbling or dropping things. For instance, a typist shows *skill* in typing accurately and fast. Carlos shows *dexterity* when he changes the typewriter ribbon.

ingenuity

Ingenuity is cleverness in inventing or designing things and in seeing new uses for everyday objects. It also means the ability to see, do, say, or use something in a different way. Amelia used a lot of *ingenuity* in designing a costume from an old curtain.

ANTONYM: inability

accomplishment

An *accomplishment* is something that has been accomplished, done, or completed. An *accomplishment* requires knowledge and, usually, hard work. When you have solved a hard math problem or learned to skate, you can be proud of your *accomplishment.*

achievement

An *achievement* is the accomplishment of something unusually dangerous or difficult. Because courage and effort are needed to achieve, an *achievement* is always admirable. The first space flight was a great *achievement.* The discovery of the polio vaccine was a great *achievement* in the fight against disease.

deed

A *deed* is anything that is done. You might call any kind or helpful or useful act that someone does a good *deed.* Some people try to do good *deeds* by helping others.

accomplishment continued on page 22 ▶

A

feat
exploit

A *feat* and an *exploit* are accomplishments. A *feat* requires more courage and strength than a deed. Climbing the mountain was a *feat* of skill and daring. An *exploit* is an accomplishment that requires even greater daring and heroism than a *feat.* Have you read any books about the *exploits* of Nellie Bly, the first woman news reporter?

ANTONYM: failure

account (n)

An *account* can be any description, explanation, or record of facts or real events. It is not a made-up story. It may be spoken or written. A charge *account* is a record of purchases. The eyewitness gave an *account* of the plane crash.

• article

An *article* is a written account of something that has happened or is going on. Newspaper and magazine *articles* keep the public up-to-date on current events.

• report

A *report* is a detailed account that is drawn up after some thing or situation has been carefully examined or investigated. The medical *report* showed that the patient would soon be released from the hospital. Mary's book *report* was so detailed that we don't have to read the book.

• version

A *version* is an account given from just one point of view. Your *version* of an incident

Mary's book **report** is so detailed that no one will have to read the book.

might be different from someone else's *version.* Each of the girls gave her own *version* of how the window had been broken.

A *story* can also be one kind of account. A newspaper *story* is an account that tells what happened. It may also tell who, when, where, and why. A magazine article often tells a *story* but sometimes includes whatever the writer thinks about the *story.* A *story* made up to entertain someone or even to deceive that person is not an account—it is a different kind of *story.* Leon told us an interesting *story* of his adventures in Africa.

See also *history, story, tale.*

• story

Leon told an interesting **story** of his adventures in Africa.

act (v)

Act means do something or cause something to happen. The firefighter *acted* quickly to put out the fire. Bubbles were produced when the acid *acted* upon the powder. *Act for* means do something in place of someone else. I will *act for* you while you are on vacation. *Act on* means follow through on something. The secretary *acted on* the boss's suggestion

act (v) continued on page 24 ▶

act (v) continued from page 23

and typed the letter. *Act up* means disobey or not act properly. The dogs sometimes *act up* when they have to stay in a kennel.

behave

Behave means act in a certain way. Usually when you *behave* yourself, you are good and act the way you should. They *behaved* very nicely during the movie.

perform

Perform means act or do something. The plane *performed* perfectly on its test flight. *Perform* can also mean act or take part in a play or show. The dolphin *performed* some unusual tricks for the crowd.

function

Function can mean work properly or act as something else. The car *functioned* perfectly. Sometimes a football player *functions* as a coach.

See also *pretend, work* (v).

The dolphin **performed** some unusual tricks for the crowd.

action

Action means several things that are done or events that occur one right after the other. The fast *action* of a hockey game is hard to follow. A Western movie has lots of *action*.

act

An *act* is only one thing that has been done or accomplished. Throwing a ball is an *act*, but the *action* in a ball game is everything that happens during the game. An *action* is made up of a series of *acts*.

activity

Activity means action, often over a long period of time. The *activity* of the thief escaped the notice of the detective. I'm late for supper every night because of after-school *activities*.

Football players must get plenty of **exercise.**

**process
operation
performance
work**

Process, operation, performance, and *work* mean a series of acts or the way in which they are carried out. A *process* is the way in which you would do or make something. The *process* of cheesemaking has many different steps. The *operation* of a machine is the way it operates or acts or the way someone runs it. It takes time to learn the *operation* of a giant crane. A *performance* is the way a person or object acts or performs. The audience cheered the excellent *performance* of the rock group. The *performance* of the jet engine was perfect. The fast *work* of the crew kept the ship from sinking.

**motion
movement**

Motion and *movement* mean the action of changing place or position. Anything that is not at rest is in *motion.* The *motion* of the ship made me seasick. Some scientists study the *movement* of the planets. The *movement* of the curtain told me that someone was behind it.

exercise

Exercise means the action used to develop strength or skill. Football players must get plenty of *exercise* before a season begins.

**behavior
conduct**

Behavior and *conduct* mean action, either good or bad. The *behavior* of the crowd during the sale shocked the store manager. The *conduct* of the class improved during the school year.

See also *battle* (n).

ANTONYMS: rest (n), inactivity, stillness, idleness

25

A

active

Active is used in many ways. It means showing action, movement, or work. You are *active* when you play outdoor games, but you are inactive if you watch TV all day. Your brain is *active* when you are thinking about something, but it is idle when you're thinking about absolutely nothing. *Active* can suggest just slight action or movement, or it may mean that much energy and force are needed to accomplish something. A baby playing in its crib may be *active,* but certainly not as *active* as someone who is swimming.

lively
peppy
spirited

Lively, peppy, and *spirited* mean full of life and action. They can also mean full of, or showing, excitement. The *lively* kitten tipped over its bowl of milk. A basketball game can be *lively.* It is not slow or passive. A *peppy* person is usually full of fun. A good horse is *spirited.* There can be much excitement in a *spirited* discussion.

agile
spry

Agile and *spry* are words that describe quick actions and movements. An *agile* person moves quickly and easily. An acrobat has to be very *agile* in order to perform stunts. *Agile* can also describe a person who thinks quickly. It will take an *agile* mind to solve this puzzle. A *spry* person is one whose actions are unexpectedly lively. Quite often an old person who is unusually *agile* is called *spry.*

An acrobat has to be very **agile** in order to perform stunts.

energetic

Energetic means full of energy. An *energetic* person likes to be active. Schoolchildren are *energetic* during recess.

26

The painter applied color with **vigorous** strokes.

vigorous

You are *vigorous* if you are very active and energetic. Your physical health is so good that you do not easily become tired. Something that is done forcefully can also be called *vigorous.* The painter applied color with *vigorous* strokes.

strenuous

A *strenuous* activity requires energy and vigor. My father had a *strenuous* day at the office and was tired when he came home.

ANTONYMS: inactive, idle, slow (adj), passive

admire

Admire is one way to love and praise something or someone. You can *admire* someone's honesty. You can *admire* someone's skill in swimming. You *admire* a person if you look up to that person and respect something he or she has done. You may try to follow that person's example. You can *admire* your parents, a friend, or some of the famous people you know or have read about. Larry *admired* the courage of Harriet Tubman. You can also *admire* a beautiful object. There are many paintings to be *admired* at an art museum.

honor

If you *honor* someone, you show that you admire and appreciate that person and respect what he or she has done. On Mother's Day we *honor* mothers everywhere. We *honor* fathers on Father's Day.

respect

Respect means admire and show special care for someone. Children should *respect* their parents. When you show special care

admire continued on page 28 ▶

A

admire continued from page 27

for the rights of others, you *respect* those rights.

regard

Regard means show respect and consideration. If you *regard* a friend's opinion, you listen to what your friend says and consider it important. If you disregard the rules of a game, you pay no attention to them at all.

ANTONYMS: dishonor (v), disregard

adore

Adore is one way to love someone or something very much. If you *adore* someone, you usually show your love and admiration through praise and through doing things for that person. You may say you *adore* your baby sister. But *adore* is a very strong word. People often use *adore* when they don't really mean it. You may say you *adore* chocolate pudding, but you really mean you like it so much you could have it at every meal.

worship

Worship means show great love or devotion. Many ancient peoples *worshiped* the sea or sun. Often people made statues of the gods they *worshiped.* These statues were called idols.

idolize

Idolize means worship an idol or someone you look up to as an idol. Often *idolize* means love something or someone foolishly. A sports fan might *idolize* a famous baseball player.

exalt

Exalt is the strongest word for adore. When you praise or honor someone above all others, you *exalt* that person.

adult (adj)   *Adult* describes someone or something that is fully developed. It can describe someone who no longer does things in a childish way. A frog is an *adult* tadpole. Voting is an *adult* privilege.

mature   *Mature* also describes someone or something that is fully developed. A baby is an immature person because it is not fully developed. A butterfly is a *mature* caterpillar. As a person becomes *mature,* he or she can take on responsibilities.

grown-up   *Grown-up* is an informal word used to describe an adult or mature person or thing. *Grown-up* behavior is not juvenile.

ripe   *Ripe* means fully grown or developed. It is usually used to describe fruits and vegetables that are fully grown and ready to be eaten. *Ripe* corn is ready to be harvested.

ANTONYMS: childish, immature, juvenile, green, unripe

A butterfly is a **mature** caterpillar.

A

advance (v)

Advance means move forward or cause something to move or be moved forward. Flood waters *advanced* toward the town but receded when the rain stopped. It can also mean put something forward like an idea or plan. Dentists in the community *advanced* a new plan for preventing tooth decay.

proceed

Proceed means advance or carry on an activity, perhaps after stopping. The train *proceeded* slowly out of the station and through the fog.

progress

Progress means advance steadily toward a definite end or goal. The construction of the building has *progressed* quickly.

accelerate

Accelerate means advance by speeding up or cause something to move faster. A driver *accelerates* a car by stepping on the gas pedal and slows it by stepping on the brake. You might say you *accelerate* when you change from a walk to a run.

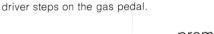

A car **accelerates** when the driver steps on the gas pedal.

promote

Promote means advance upward, or to a higher position. Jake was *promoted* to editor of the school newspaper. A cause or idea is *promoted* when someone helps it along. Ambassadors of the United States *promote* good will abroad.

further

Further means advance something by giving help. The newspaper article *furthered* the candidate's campaign.

See also *grow, help* (v).

ANTONYMS: recede, slow (v), fall back, hinder, obstruct, stay (v), stop (v)

advise	*Advise* means give a person information or suggestions that may help him or her in some way. When Tom asked me if the test was hard, I replied, "I *advise* you to study every night for a week."
counsel	*Counsel* means advise. Someone who has knowledge or experience in something may *counsel* you by telling you what to do or say. Lawyers *counsel* their clients.
caution	*Caution* means tell someone to take time to think so that he or she can avoid being hurt or getting into trouble. If I had *cautioned* Susan about the broken alarm clock, she wouldn't have overslept.
warn	*Warn* means tell a person ahead of time about some danger or problem so that it can be avoided. The weather bureau *warns* people about a tornado.
admonish	*Admonish* means remind a person of something that ought to be done, or speak to that person about something he or she has done wrong. I was *admonished* to be careful of the flowers. Then I was *admonished* for not being careful of the flowers.

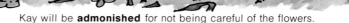

Kay will be **admonished** for not being careful of the flowers.

31

It was not hard to **admit** the other team had better players.

agree

Agree means have the same opinion or feeling about something as someone else. At first my idea differed from hers, but finally I *agreed*. If something is pleasing to you or healthful, it can be said to *agree* with you. The weather *agreed* with us.

consent
comply

Consent and *comply* mean agree to something that someone has asked or may want you to do. We asked if we could stay at Grandpa's, and Mom and Dad *consented*. When the supervisor told the workers to put down their tools, they *complied*. You *consent to* do something, but you *comply with*. Mom and Dad finally *consented to* let me go camping. The class *complied with* the committee's decision.

contract

Contract is a stronger word than agree. If you *contract* to do something, your words are usually put in writing. The builders *contracted* to begin the house next month.

admit

When you *admit* to something, you accept or agree that it is either true or false, good or bad. It was not hard to *admit* that the other team had better players.

approve

Approve can mean agree, but it also adds the meaning of having a good opinion about someone or something. Usually, *of* follows *approve*. Cindy hoped that the family would *approve of* her new wallpaper.

See also *promise* (v).

ANTONYMS: differ, disagree, disapprove, contradict, dispute (v), dissent (v), protest (v)

agreement   *Agreement* means an understanding or a promise reached between people or nations. It may or may not be written down. Alice and Marcos made an *agreement* to meet at eight o'clock. Not all the members were willing to sign the *agreement.*

• contract   A *contract* is a formal written agreement. The builders signed a *contract* promising to finish the house by the end 'of September.

• treaty   A *treaty* is an agreement between states or countries. After the countries agreed to the boundaries, they signed a *treaty.*

• pact
• compact   *Pact* and *compact* are other words for an agreement, usually between nations or groups of people. Peace was restored when the three countries signed the *pact.* The Pilgrims who came to America in 1620 signed a *compact.*

agreement continued on page 34 ◗

Peace was restored when the three countries signed the **pact.**

A

- bargain

A *bargain* is usually an agreement on the price of something. We made a *bargain* to pay more rent if the house were painted. *Bargain* can also mean something bought for less money than expected. Joan knew she had found a real *bargain* when she saw the old grandfather's clock in the junk store.

- understanding

An *understanding* can be an informal agreement. It would not be written. I reached an *understanding* with my friend in Tennessee that we would telephone each other once a month.

- approval

If you give your *approval,* you agree completely with someone or something. It is the opposite of disapproval. *Approval* also means praise. The audience showed its *approval* of the play by applauding. Peter tried to win his neighbor's *approval* by cleaning the garage and mowing the lawn.

See also *deal* (n), *pledge* (n).

ANTONYMS: disagreement, disapproval, contradiction, difference, dispute (n), dissension

alert (adj)

Alert means on the lookout for opportunities or danger.

watchful

Watchful has almost the same meaning as *alert,* but it is sometimes used with different words. You can be *alert to* traffic or you can be *watchful of* traffic. You can say someone is an *alert* driver or is *watchful* in a traffic jam. Airline pilots have to be *alert to* any dangers that might be encountered in a flight.

Airline pilots have to be **alert to** dangers.

34

awake

Awake is another word that can mean alert. Here is why. People who are asleep are not alert to what is going on around them, but those who are *awake* usually are. So you can say that people are *awake to* certain problems or *awake to* danger. Donna is a good lifeguard because she is always *awake to* the danger of someone's drowning.

vigilant

Vigilant means constantly watching for harm or danger. A forest ranger had better be *vigilant*.

ready

Ready means prepared for whatever might happen, good or bad. The goalie was *ready* to block the shot. After Yoshio had combed his hair, he was *ready* to have his picture taken.

quick

Quick means ready to act or to move fast. The fire department was *quick* to answer the alarm. A *quick* mind is the opposite of a sluggish mind.

ANTONYMS: asleep, sluggish, drowsy, dull, heedless, slow (adj)

A forest ranger had better be **vigilant.**

A

allow

Allow is the opposite of prevent. *Allow* means let something happen or be done. The sitter *allows* the children to play outside until dark. Ball playing is not *allowed* in the park.

permit

If you *permit* someone to do something, you give that person permission. Something that is not *permitted* is forbidden. The principal *permitted* the students to use the gym at night. Some people allow something even if it isn't *permitted.* The manager allowed the dog to go into the store even though the store rules didn't *permit* it.

let

Let means allow. It is often used in giving suggestions and commands. *Let's* go to the park. *Let* go! It can also mean give permission. Tony wondered if his mother would *let* him go to the circus.

admit

Admit means let in or allow to enter. Amy was *admitted* to the hospital to have her tonsils removed. These tickets will *admit* us to the movie.

- endure
- tolerate

Endure and *tolerate* are good words to use even though they are not real synonyms of *allow.* *Endure* and *tolerate* can mean put up with something, especially for a long time. You *endure* something if you do not give in to it. The child *endured* the pain of a broken leg and didn't cry. We *tolerate* the nightly hooting of our neighbor's pet owl.

ANTONYMS: prevent, forbid, deny, prohibit

amuse

Amuse means pass time in a very pleasant way. If something *amuses* you, it holds your attention and may make you laugh or smile. It does not bore you. Something that *amuses* you can also make you feel happy and perhaps even excited. That book on the history of the circus *amused* Larry. You can also *amuse* someone else. I *amused* my brother until Dad came home.

entertain

Entertain means amuse and give pleasure. Movies and books can *entertain*. You *entertain,* too, when you have someone over to your house as a guest.

delight

Delight means amuse and give joy. The magician *delighted* the audience with his magic act. *Delight* can also mean be satisfied with something. Mother was *delighted* to see that the children had cleaned the house while she was at work.

interest

If something *interests* you, it holds your attention and makes you curious. The children were *interested* in dinosaurs.

cheer

Cheer means make someone who is sad feel happy. Visitors *cheer* patients who are in the hospital. *Cheer* can also mean shout encouragement. The crowd *cheered* the team on to victory.

divert

Divert means turn someone's attention from something that is worrying him or her to something amusing or pleasing. The comic books *diverted* the child's attention.

The magician **delighted** the audience with his magic act.

ANTONYMS: bore (v), annoy, disturb, tire (v)

A

amusement

Amusement is anything that holds your attention and delights you. It usually makes you laugh and feel happy. Reading a book, playing a game, going to a movie, and working on a hobby are all forms of *amusement.*

entertainment

Entertainment means amusement usually provided by someone or something. The animals at a zoo or circus provide lots of *entertainment* for children and grown-ups.

delight
pleasure

Delight and *pleasure* are feelings of happiness and enjoyment. You can show your *delight* or *pleasure* in something by laughing or smiling. You can show your displeasure by frowning. Max's *delight* in winning the raffle was apparent to all of us. It's a *pleasure* to talk to a good friend.

fun

Fun is anything that gives amusement or makes you laugh. Sophie thinks it's *fun* to twirl a baton.

recreation

Recreation is anything you find relaxing and fun. It is not work. Skating on a pond or rink is a good form of *recreation.*

Skating on a pond or rink is a good form of **recreation.**

amusement continued

cheer

If you give *cheer* to someone, you make that person feel happy. A letter from home always brings *cheer* to a college student. *Cheers* can also mean the shouting you hear at a football or baseball game.

diversion

A *diversion* can be an amusement or simply something that catches your attention and turns you away from what you may be doing. Movies and TV programs are good *diversions.* If you want a *diversion* from your work, you can take a walk. A good magician creates a *diversion* with one hand so the audience won't see what is really happening.

interest

If you have an *interest* in something, it holds your attention and you want to know more about it. But you may or may not be amused. You can have an *interest* in a very serious subject like the operation of a computer. Collecting model cars can be an *interest.*

ANTONYMS: displeasure, work (n), boredom, sadness

anger

Anger is the strong feeling you have when something does not please you. You can feel *anger* toward yourself or someone else. You can feel *anger* at something that happens. Your *anger* would probably be directed toward yourself if you lost five dollars. If your little brother lost your five dollars, your *anger* would be directed at him. If you lost out on the chance to earn five dollars, you might also feel *anger.*

anger continued on page 40 ▶

When Carrie and Arlene lost out on a chance to earn money, they felt **anger.**

A

anger continued from page 39

irritation

Irritation is a feeling you have when you are annoyed or disturbed about something that keeps on happening. It was difficult to work with Kim because her constant whistling was an *irritation* to me.

vexation

Vexation means almost the same as irritation, but *vexation* implies a stronger feeling of anger. Grandfather says that when I am noisy, I am a *vexation*. When I am quiet, I am a pleasure.

exasperation

Exasperation is a sudden and temporary feeling of anger brought on by being repeatedly annoyed or irritated. *Exasperation* may be your feeling when you have just tried for the tenth time to phone your friend, and the line is still busy.

wrath

Wrath is a strong feeling of anger that often results in a desire to seek revenge. Roberta's *wrath* at not being invited to the slumber party caused her to make unkind remarks about her classmates.

rage

Rage is violent anger that may result in the loss of self-control. *Rage* usually suggests a boiling over of feelings. In his *rage* at striking out, Terry threw the bat to the ground.

fury

Fury is anger so violent that self-control and reason are forgotten. *Fury* is marked by such violent actions that the *fury* may seem like temporary insanity. In the movie we saw yesterday, a man's *fury* drove him to burn a barn.

ANTONYMS: pleasure, self-control, calm (n)

announce *Announce* means tell people something they don't know. Usually, *announce* means give out a public or an official statement. The mayor called a press conference to *announce* that she would retire in June. Due to the heavy snowfall, it was *announced* that there would be no school tomorrow.

The mayor called a press conference to **announce** that she would retire in June.

broadcast *Broadcast* originally meant to plant seeds by scattering them, or casting them, broadly. Now the word means make something widely known through radio, television, or a public-address system. At three o'clock we will *broadcast* the President's news conference over the public-address system. We sometimes also use the word when we mean tell something loudly or tell a lot of people over a broad area. His secret was *broadcast* all over the school by the end of the day.

herald *Herald* means call attention to something important that is about to take place. Long ago a "herald" ran or rode ahead of the king's party announcing the king's approach to people along the way. The high-school band will *herald* the senator's visit. The birth of an heir to the throne was *heralded* all over the kingdom.

publish *Publish* almost always means tell something in print. The magazine will *publish* the governor's speech. The names of all contest winners will be *published* in our next bulletin.

announce continued on page 42 ▶

Annette and Elena used walkie-talkies to **communicate** with each other.

announce continued from page 41

advertise

Advertise means call attention to something by telling people about it. Miriam *advertised* to the whole family that her birthday was coming soon. *Advertise* also means telling people about products and services so that they will want to buy them. There are many ways to *advertise*—on TV or radio, in newspapers and magazines, on billboards, or even in the sky. We can *advertise* our pet-sitting service by putting up posters in stores.

communicate

Communicate means talk with other people and listen to them. It also means share and exchange thoughts and ideas with others. The two girls used walkie-talkies to *communicate* with each other. Sometimes people *communicate* without talking. Indians in the Old West *communicated* by smoke signals.

ANTONYMS: conceal, hide (v), suppress, withhold

answer (v)

Answer means say, write, or do something as a result of what someone asks or wants or needs. You *answer* a question or a letter, a telephone or a doorbell. Usually you *answer* a question with words. But you might *answer* by shaking your head or shrugging your shoulders.

reply

Reply means answer. When you *reply* to what someone says, you tell that person something that is related to what he or she has said to you. When he told me to return my library books, I *replied* that I would

42

have to find them first. Sometimes you *reply* with action. Chuck *replied* to their angry question by calmly walking out of the room.

The mystery was **solved** when Max found the cat upstairs.

respond

Respond means react to something said or done, either with words or action. You *respond* to someone who is friendly by being friendly yourself.

retort

Retort means answer with a quick, sharp, and perhaps clever or funny reply. Should someone ask if you need a hand with your packages, you might *retort,* "No thanks, I've already got two."

solve

Solve is a good word to use when you mean explain something or find the solution to a problem. The mystery was *solved* when we found the cat upstairs.

ANTONYMS: ask, inquire, question (v), request (v)

answer (n)

An *answer* is something said or done as the result of a question or request. When you write a letter or ask a question, you expect an *answer.*

reply
response

A *reply* and a *response,* like an answer, tell you something you have asked or wondered about. If I ask you whether dogs lay eggs, I am sure your *reply* will be "No." A *response* is also an answer that tells how you feel about something. My *response* to Bob's suggestion that we go ice skating was, "I don't feel like skating today."

answer (n) continued on page 44 ▶

A

retort

solution

defense

Ed will find the **solution** to this puzzle if it takes him all day.

appropriate (adj)

suitable
fit

becoming

qualified

A *retort* is a quick, sharp reply that is clever or funny or angry. When I told my little brother to be quiet, his loud *retort* was, "I am being quiet."

A *solution* is an answer to a problem or puzzle. "The *solution* to your problem is to practice more," Paula's tuba teacher told her. I'll find the *solution* to this puzzle if it takes me all day.

A *defense* can be an answer you give when someone suggests that you have made a mistake or have done something wrong. My only *defense* after breaking the window was that the wind carried the ball too far.

ANTONYMS: question (n), query, inquiry, problem

Appropriate means right and acceptable. Rules of behavior and good manners usually measure what is *appropriate* or inappropriate. There is an *appropriate* time to work and an *appropriate* time to play. It is *appropriate* to thank someone for a gift.

Suitable and *fit* mean appropriate and ready. His clothing is *suitable* for warm weather. If a person is *fit* for a job, he or she is able to do it well. Some water must be treated before it is *fit* to drink.

If something is *becoming,* it is not only appropriate and suitable, but attractive. That new dress is very *becoming.*

Qualified is used to describe a person who meets certain requirements and standards.

COME TO OUR "BIG SAIL TODY TOODAY TODAYE"

Not everyone is **qualified** for skywriting.

A *qualified* pilot must have many hours of flight experience. Not everyone is *qualified* for skywriting.

proper
fitting

Proper and *fitting* mean appropriate and acceptable to a situation. A carpenter can work best when he or she uses the *proper* tools. Some people always know the *proper* thing to say. It is *fitting* to stand when you pledge allegiance to the flag. It is *fitting* to shake hands when you meet someone.

See also *correct* (adj).

ANTONYMS: inappropriate, unsuitable, improper, unfit

argue

Argue means give reasons for or against something. You might *argue* with people in order to convince them you are right and they are wrong. You *argue* in order to try to persuade them to accept your ideas.

disagree

You *disagree* with someone when you do not share the same opinion. You can *disagree* without having to argue. I *disagreed* with the umpire's decision but didn't say anything. The girls agreed to give their uncle a present but *disagreed* on the best gift to buy.

argue continued on page 46 ▸

A

discuss
Discuss can mean just talk something over. Persons who disagree may *discuss* their problem calmly and agree on a solution. The students *discussed* places to go on their class trip. The architects *discussed* the floor plans and decided to change them slightly to ensure the best use of space.

debate
When you *debate* with another person or group, you consider both sides of a question or problem. You defend your position and attack your opponent's point of view. There are rules to follow when you *debate* in public. You can also *debate* something with yourself. If you are lost, you might *debate* which street to take.

dispute
Dispute means argue angrily over something. It can also mean question what another person does or thinks. The contestants *disputed* the judge's decision, but they didn't withdraw from the contest.

quarrel
Quarrel means argue noisily. People usually shout when they *quarrel.* Most people don't enjoy being with someone who *quarrels* all the time.

See also *object* (v).

ANTONYMS: agree, consent (v)

The architects **discussed** floor plans.

arrangement
An *arrangement* is something made by putting things together in a certain way. Your teacher can change the *arrangement* of the desks in the classroom. A centerpiece on the table may be an *arrangement* of flowers. The *arrangement* of books on that shelf is alphabetical.

● order

Order can mean arrangement. The words in a dictionary are in alphabetical *order.* If everything has been straightened out and put in its place, it is in *order.* If your desk is in a state of disorder, you won't be able to find your papers and books easily.

● organization

An *organization* is the arrangement of parts to form a whole. A group of people working together to achieve a goal can also be called an *organization.* The United Nations is a world *organization* that is made up of representatives from many countries.

● system
● classification

A very detailed arrangement of things or ideas can be called a *system* or *classification.* The *system* by which books are grouped in a library helps you find them by title, author, or subject. In science you can study the *classification* of plants and animals.

● plan

A *plan* is the order or arrangement of steps in carrying out some activity. *Plans* to do something are first thought out and then may be written down. Having a fire drill without a *plan* would result in confusion. We haven't made *plans* for our vacation.

● preparation

Preparation can mean an arrangement made beforehand. Plans, ideas, or things are put in order or made ready for use. My parents made many *preparations* for my birthday dinner. The *preparations* for any space flight take many months.

See also *plan* (n).

ANTONYMS: disorder, confusion

A

attack (v) *Attack* means fight against or go against someone or something. Pirates used to *attack* ships and steal the cargo. A bear might *attack* a camper if it felt its cubs were in danger.

bombard *Bombard* means attack with cannon shells, bombs, or missiles. Francis Scott Key wrote "The Star-Spangled Banner" while Fort McHenry was being *bombarded.*

charge *Charge* means rush forward to attack. We *charged* our opponents' snow fort during the snowball fight. *"Charge!"* was the battle cry an officer would give to begin the attack.

ambush *Ambush* means attack suddenly from a hiding place. The outlaws *ambushed* the stagecoach.

storm *Storm* means violently attack an enemy's stronghold or fortress. A mob *stormed* and destroyed the Bastille, an old prison in Paris, on July 14, 1789.

invade *Invade* means attack, enter, and take possession of a place. When the troops *invaded* the village, they set up their headquarters in the town hall.

ANTONYMS: defend, protect, guard (v)

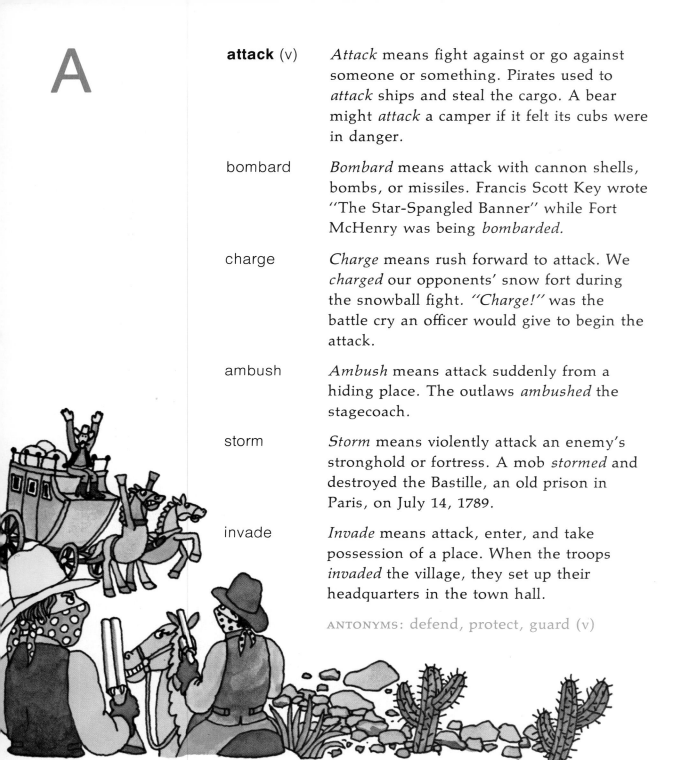

The outlaws **ambushed** the stagecoach.

attempt (v)   *Attempt* is the opposite of give up. It means make an effort to do something. The swimmer *attempted* to cross the English Channel. The pirates *attempted* to capture the ship and its cargo.

try   *Try* means attempt over and over to do something. It can also mean test or experiment with something. If at first you don't succeed, *try, try* again. I want to *try* a different recipe the next time. To "*try* one's hand at something" means attempt something new. *Try on* means see how something fits or looks on you.

undertake   *Undertake* means attempt something that you have promised to do. Our class *undertook* the job of raising money for charity projects.

endeavor   *Endeavor* is a stronger word than *attempt.* When you *endeavor* to accomplish or prove something, much effort is required. Amelia Earhart *endeavored* to fly around the world. Galileo *endeavored* to prove that the earth rotates around the sun.

strive   *Strive* is the strongest synonym for attempt. When you *strive* to do something, you have to try very hard. The firefighters *strove* to put out the fire before it spread. Sophia kept *striving* to be the best player on her basketball team.

ANTONYMS: give up, quit

B

basic

Basic describes the main part of something on which all other parts depend. The *basic* structure of a skyscraper is its steel framework. Without it, the whole building would collapse. An author develops a story from one *basic* idea.

fundamental

Fundamental can describe something like a foundation upon which other things can be built or added. One *fundamental* rule for drivers in the United States is to keep to the right side of the road. The Constitution is the *fundamental* law of the United States.

first
primary

First and *primary* mean before anything else. The *first* step in building a campfire is gathering wood, and the last step is lighting the fire. Learning to read is of *primary* importance. You develop reading skills in the *primary* grades. Red, blue, and yellow are *primary* colors. Other colors can be made from them.

necessary
essential

A part that is *necessary* or *essential* to something cannot be taken away from it. Tracks are *necessary* to a railway train. Wheels are *essential* to a car, but a clock is nonessential.

vital

Vital describes things that are basic to life or basic to staying alive. Food and water are *vital* to human beings. Breathing is a *vital* function of our bodies.

See also *important*.

ANTONYMS: last (adj), nonessential, trivial, unnecessary

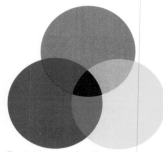

Red, blue, and yellow are **primary** colors.

battle (v)   *Battle* means fight against someone or something. People *battle* each other when they argue over something. Teams *battle* for victory. Doctors *battle* disease. The swimmer *battled* the swift current.

The jockey was **besieged** by fans seeking autographs.

struggle   *Struggle* means work very hard or make a strenuous effort to do something. The hiker *struggled* up the steep mountain path. It took me hours to *struggle* through that assignment.

combat   *Combat* means struggle and fight against something. Forest rangers *combat* forest fires. You can *combat* a cold by staying in bed.

wrestle   *Wrestle* means battle or struggle against someone or something. You can *wrestle* with a person or with a problem. If you *wrestle* with a person, you may become bruised. If you *wrestle* with a problem, you may lose a lot of sleep.

grapple   *Grapple* is very much like *wrestle.* When you *grapple* with someone, you struggle with that person to get a better hold. When you *grapple* with a problem, you struggle with it to find an answer.

besiege   *Besiege* usually means surround and attempt to capture a fort or territory. The Vikings *besieged* the town until it ran out of food and ammunition. *Besiege* also means bother with requests. The jockey was *besieged* by fans seeking autographs.

B

battle (n)

A *battle* is a meeting or a clash between enemies or people who have opposing goals. It can be between two armies, between two ships, or between two groups of aircraft. A *battle* might also be between two persons.

Battle can also be used for any kind of clash in which one person or idea struggles against another. There has always been the *battle* of man against nature. You might face a *battle* with your conscience.

action

Action can be part of a battle. Tanks went into *action* after the bombarding stopped.

combat

Combat means fighting in general. A *combat* may also mean a battle between two individuals. Soldiers must learn hand-to-hand *combat* as part of their training.

skirmish
brawl

A *skirmish* and a *brawl* are both rather small battles. Sometimes a *skirmish* is a short fight between a few troops during a battle or just before it. It doesn't last long. A *brawl* is any noisy fight or argument.

attack

An *attack* is a battle begun by one side usually taking the other side by surprise. Sentries guard an army camp against *attack.*

duel

Historically, a *duel* was a formal battle between two persons. Usually one person had insulted the other, and the one who felt offended challenged the other to a *duel.* *Duels* were fought with swords or pistols, and usually at dawn.

A **duel** was a formal battle between two persons.

52

A **contest** can be a game in which each side is struggling to win.

fight
conflict
contest

Fight, conflict, contest, are all general words for a situation in which people or animals struggle and strive to conquer, to win, or to be superior. A *fight* can be with words, with fists, teeth, claws, or with weapons. A *conflict* is any disagreement or feeling of disagreement. A *conflict* may be a world war, or it may be an argument over which TV show to turn on. A *conflict* can even be the struggle to decide between two good TV shows being shown at the same time. A *contest* can be a war or a battle, but it usually is a game in which each person or group is struggling to win over opponents.

See also *quarrel* (n).

beat (v)

Beat means strike someone or something over and over. My great-grandparents cleaned their rugs by *beating* them. That musician *beats* her drums loudly. *Beat* can also mean defeat or overcome. We *beat* the other team. I always *beat* my uncle at checkers.

beat (v) continued on page 54 ▶

B

beat (v) continued from page 53

spank

Spank means beat with an open hand. Did anyone ever *spank* you when you were little?

pummel

Pummel can mean beat with fists. Lion cubs *pummel* each other with their paws when they play.

flog

Flog means beat with a rod or whip. In the days of sailing ships, sailors who disobeyed orders were very often *flogged.*

thump

Thump can mean beat, pound, or knock. When you're very nervous or afraid, your heart may *thump.*

thrash

Thrash means beat with a stick or whip. Farmers in early times *thrashed* wheat by hand to remove the grain. *Thrash* also means toss or throw yourself around. If you're having a nightmare, you might *thrash* wildly about in your bed.

Farmers in early times **thrashed** wheat by hand.

trounce

If you *trounce* your opponents in a game or contest, you beat them by a large score.

See also *conquer, defeat* (v), *hit* (v).

beautiful

Beautiful is the opposite of ugly. Anything that you find very pleasing, attractive, or desirable can be called *beautiful.* Today *beautiful* is used to describe so many things that it may not mean much anymore.

pretty

Pretty describes those things that are pleasant and nice to look at but aren't grand enough or important enough to be called beautiful. A daisy is *pretty,* but you may not think it is the *prettiest* of all flowers. A face that isn't *pretty* might be called plain or homely.

handsome

A *handsome* person is good-looking. *Handsome* also describes those things that are very dignified, stately, and impressive. Buckingham Palace, the home of Queen Elizabeth II, is a *handsome* building.

fair

Fair can mean beautiful. The knights in the Middle Ages called young women, or maidens, *fair* instead of beautiful. We say the weather is *fair* when it is fresh and clear.

lovely

Lovely means very beautiful and delightful. It is a *lovely* day for a picnic. Horrid and hideous are very strong words to describe something that is not *lovely.*

graceful

Graceful means beautiful in form and movement. A good dancer has to be *graceful.* An elm tree looks *graceful* as it sways in the breeze.

beauteous

Beauteous means beautiful, but you would probably never hear it used today. People today speak of a beautiful evening instead of a *beauteous* evening.

gorgeous

Gorgeous means very beautiful and colorful. A *gorgeous* rainbow formed over the waterfall. The sun setting over a mountain range is a *gorgeous* sight.

exquisite

Something that is beautifully and delicately made or formed can be called *exquisite.* The spider web dotted with dew was *exquisite.*

ANTONYMS: ugly, homely, horrid, hideous, offensive

B

beginning
The *beginning* is the point at which something comes into being. It can also be the first step in an action or the first part of something. A story has a *beginning* and an end. The letter A is the *beginning* of the alphabet. A sore throat is often the *beginning* of a cold.

start
A *start* is the beginning or first part of a movement or activity. It is the opposite of a finish. We saw the race from *start* to finish. A *start* can also be a sudden, jerking movement. Juana woke with a *start* when the telephone rang.

origin
The *origin* is the beginning of something from which other things come about. Have you ever tried to trace the history of your family back to its *origin?* The legend of Paul Bunyan has its *origin* among lumber camps west of the Great Lakes.

source
A *source* is the place where something begins or from which something can be obtained. Lake Itasca in Minnesota is the *source* of the Mississippi River. Iron mines are the chief *source* of steel. A good *source* of information is an encyclopedia.

root
A *root* is the part of something from which other things have their beginnings and grow. The *roots* of plants and trees are underground. Let's get to the *root* of our problem. The *root* of the word "singer" is "sing."

ANTONYMS: end (n), finish (n), conclusion, result (n)

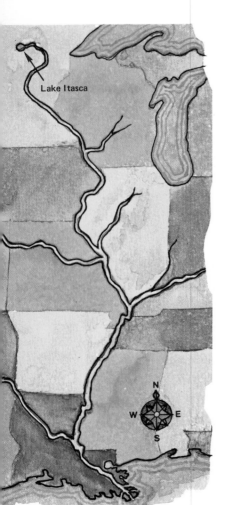

Lake Itasca

Lake Itasca is the **source** of the Mississippi River.

belief

A *belief* is a feeling that something is true and that it can be accepted without doubt. You may not be able to prove that something is completely true or that someone is worthy of your trust, but you can still have a *belief* in it or that person. A *belief* is not the same as an idea or an opinion. Some *beliefs* are shared by many people; your opinions and ideas may be yours alone. You are also not as certain of your opinions and ideas as you are of your *beliefs.* Opinions change more often than *beliefs* do. At one time most people shared the *belief* that the world was flat. Some little children share the *belief* in the tooth fairy. Modern scientists often discover facts that prove our most precious *beliefs* are not true.

faith

Faith in something or someone is a very strong belief for which there may be no proof. If you have *faith,* you believe completely in something. People have *faith* in their religion or in their friends.

conviction

A *conviction* is a very strong, firm belief. It is Al's *conviction* that truth will always win in the end. The defendant told the story with *conviction* because she was innocent.

confidence

If you have *confidence* in someone or something, you are certain that the person or thing will not fail you. If you give your parents a "vote of *confidence*," you tell them you believe in them. A mountain climber puts great *confidence* in a rope.

A mountain climber puts great **confidence** in a rope.

belief continued on page 58 ▶

B

belief continued from page 57

trust

When you place your *trust* in someone, you depend on him or her. When you gain the *trust* of a dog, it will follow you and be your friend. Children put their *trust* in their parents.

See also *idea, opinion.*

ANTONYMS: doubt (n), disbelief, mistrust (n)

big

Of all the big words in our language, one of the biggest has to be *big.* Just think of the ways people use it every day: a *big* mountain—so tall its peak is covered with snow or clouds; a *big* lake—so wide it takes a day to row across it; a *big* hole—so deep you could never climb out if you fell in. A *big* brother or sister is older than you. A *big* house has many rooms. A *big* job means there's lots of work to do. A *big* mess means things are in terrible shape. A *big* deal is something that is pretty important (or maybe not so important). A *big* hand is applause.

Come to think of it, who can tell exactly what *big* means? A *big* snowstorm? Drifts six feet deep. A *big* windstorm? Winds blowing fifty miles an hour. A *big* flash of lightning? So bright it blinds you. The whole thing is really a *big* mystery.

How *big* is *big?* Think of a *big* man and a *big* baby. Think of a *big* tree and a *big* toadstool. Think of a *big* watermelon and a *big* grape. Perhaps you can't call anything *big* unless something like it is smaller.

A *big* athlete is an expert at his or her sport. A *big* movie star is famous and beloved by the fans. A *big* official is a leader who helps run a government, an organization, or a business. A *big* figure in history or science has done something great. All these people are important. The *big* game of the season is the most important game. A *big* problem in some plan is the one that must be solved before any others can be. It is basic to the whole plan. The *big* question or the *big* issue in an argument is the basic one.

Next time you start to use *big,* look up *large* and *great* and *important* and *basic.* Try one of their synonyms on for size.

A **big** figure in history has done something great.

block (v)

Block means stop someone or something or get in the way of a motion or activity. A stalled truck *blocks* traffic. In games like football and hockey, it is important to *block* the opponent.

check

Check means keep something within certain limits. If a doctor doesn't use medicine to *check* the progress of a disease, the disease might advance quickly. Both *block* and *check* usually mean stop some activity for a while if not forever.

hinder
obstruct

Hinder and *obstruct* mean put obstacles or difficulties in the way. You *hinder* someone if you slow that person down or keep him or her from moving freely for a time. Bad weather sometimes *hinders* the construction

block (v) continued on page 60 ▶

block (v) continued from page 59

of a new highway. Use *obstruct* when a large obstacle completely halts action or progress, or blocks the sight of something. The tall building *obstructed* my view of the harbor.

delay

Delay means hold back or slow down or stop for a time. A freight train can *delay* traffic on a busy highway. We were *delayed* for an hour.

prevent

Prevent means keep something from happening. A visit to your doctor for a checkup every year may *prevent* serious illness. Visitors to national parks are asked to help *prevent* forest fires.

restrain

Restrain means hold back from action or from extremes of action. The cast on his foot *restrains* his movements. I wanted a taco for breakfast, but I *restrained* myself.

prohibit

Prohibit means refuse to allow something to be done. Signs along the highways warn that littering is *prohibited* by law.

bar

Bar means keep someone or something out of—or in—a place. Dogs are *barred* from most restaurants.

clog

Clog means slow down, and sometimes stop, certain activities or actions. Many highways are *clogged* with traffic during the summer. Do you think I *clogged* the drain when I poured grease in the sink?

See also *interfere*.

ANTONYMS: advance (v), aid (v), allow, help (v) let, permit (v), promote

The cast on his foot **restrains** his movements.

brag

Greg is **bragging** about himself.

Brag means talk with great pride about yourself or what you've done or what you own. If you *brag* a lot, you think very highly of yourself and you don't bother to conceal it. Rather than wait for someone to praise you or your efforts, you tell how great you are. If you aren't *bragging* about yourself, you may be *bragging* about something you own. There's a boy in my class who *brags* constantly about his new clothes. You would probably use *brag* and its synonyms to describe only a kind of behavior you do not like or approve of.

boast

Boast means brag and maybe even exaggerate a little. Rita *boasted* that she was the best badminton player our school has had in a hundred years. Chris *boasted* that he could fix dinner as well as an experienced chef does. *Boast* can also mean have or show proudly. Our new public library *boasts* a children's room with all the latest books.

crow

Crow means brag that you have done something better than someone else. The winning basketball team *crowed* about the uneven score—98 to 20. Suzy *crowed* about selling more tickets to the play than anyone.

gloat

Gloat, on the other hand, need not mean talk at all. You may just feel satisfied with yourself. Some actors who seem to be very modest, secretly *gloat* over their performances. People sometimes *gloat* over their accomplishments.

61

There are three main **branches** of the government.

branch (n)   A *branch* is a part of something. The *branches* of a tree extend out from its trunk. A small stream of water that flows from a river or lake can be called a *branch* of that body of water. There are three main *branches* of the United States government— judicial, legislative, and executive. Perhaps your cousin belongs to a different *branch* of your family. A main library can have a *branch,* which is a smaller library, in a different location. Your school library may be a *branch* of the public library.

• shoot   A *shoot* is a small, new branch on a plant, bush, or tree. In the spring, you can see tiny *shoots* on trees.

• bough   A *bough* is a branch, but it usually means a branch covered with flowers, leaves, or needles. The family gathered pine *boughs,* let them dry and burned them in the fireplace.

62

- limb

A *limb* is a large branch of a tree. A *limb* is also one of the parts of an animal's body that enable it to move. The wings and legs of a bird are *limbs.* Fins are the *limbs* of fish. Arms and legs are your *limbs.*

- tributary
- creek

A *tributary* and a *creek* are branches of water. They flow from or enter a main body of water, such as a river or a lake. A *creek* is often just a narrow stream of water. A *tributary* is larger than a creek. It may be a river. A *tributary* adds to the flow of the main body of water.

- wing
- addition
- extension

Wing, addition, and *extension* are good words for parts added to something that is built or organized. A *wing* of a building usually is a part that extends to one side of the main building. An *addition* can be built onto the side of a building or on top of it. Also, a city may get some land outside the city limits for an *addition* to the city. An *extension* may be added to a room or building in order to increase its space. A university often has branches in other cities. These branches are called *extensions.*

bravery

Showing *bravery* is facing or being ready to face danger whether you are afraid or not. *Bravery* is seen not only in battle; it can be seen in everyday living. *Bravery* is also facing or being ready to face terrible problems, hard work, or a difficult situation. Brenda showed *bravery* by defending Louis when everyone was against him.

bravery continued on page 64 ▶

B

Daring is shown by circus performers.

bravery continued from page 63

courage

Courage is strength of mind and will to face danger or difficulty or fear. Do you have the *courage* to say what you think? It takes *courage* to say you like something no one else likes.

gallantry

Gallantry is a showy kind of bravery. The *gallantry* of the knights of the Round Table is recorded in legends and tales of King Arthur. The knights showed their *gallantry* by willingly going into battle for their king.

boldness
daring

Boldness and *daring* mean willingness to take risks. It takes *boldness* to explore a house that is supposed to be haunted. *Daring* is shown by circus performers who don't have nets below them.

heroism
valor

Heroism and *valor* imply the greatest courage, especially against dangers that seem too hard to overcome. Boldness and daring mean willingness to take risks; *heroism* and *valor* mean willingness to take risks in order to do some good for someone. Firefighters who go into blazing buildings to rescue people show real *heroism.* Medics display *valor* on the battlefield by trying to help wounded soldiers.

ANTONYMS: cowardice, timidity

break (v)

Break means come apart suddenly or cause something to separate into parts. If you drop a glass, it may *break.* She *broke* her kite when she tried to pull it out of the tree. That dog *has broken* its leash. Maybe I can mend it with some heavy thread.

fracture	If you break a bone, you *fracture* it. She *fractured* her leg in the car accident.

shatter	*Shatter* means break suddenly into many pieces. The stone *shattered* the window. The antique dish *shattered* when it hit the floor.

Abe Lincoln **split** logs when he was a youth.

smash	*Smash* means break something forcefully. Something may be *smashed* to pieces or just dented out of shape. You can *smash* a straw hat if you sit on it. You can *smash* an egg by throwing it against a wall. My bike fender was *smashed* when I hit the pavement.

tear	*Tear* means break or separate something by pulling it apart roughly. You leave jagged or uneven edges when you *tear* something. You can *tear* a piece of paper. You *tear* a piece of cloth if you catch it on something sharp.

rip	*Rip* also means break by pulling. But when you *rip* something, you usually tear it along a line. Oscar *ripped* open the envelope. In order to mend the dress, I had to *rip* the rest of the seam.

split	*Split* means divide or separate into parts. You can *split* a candy bar with a friend. Abe Lincoln *split* logs when he was a youth.

splinter	Something *splinters* when it breaks into long, thin pieces or parts. If you drop a mirror, it will probably *splinter*.

ANTONYMS: mend, fasten, fix (v), join, repair (v), unite

65

B

break (n)

A *break* can mean the act of breaking or coming apart. A *break* or fracture of a bone would have to be set by a doctor. A *break* in a water pipe could cause a flood. A tear, a rip, and a split are *breaks.*

A *break* can also be any kind of stop or a short rest in some activity. There can be a *break* in a storm. People who take a few minutes off from their work often call that period a coffee *break.* Radio and TV programs have station *breaks.* The program is stopped just long enough for the local station to identify itself.

interruption

An *interruption* is a breaking in on some activity. The most common *interruption* to your peaceful sleep is the ringing of an alarm clock. *Interruptions* during a phone call can be annoying.

pause

A *pause* is a brief break or stop. I waited for a *pause* in the conversation before asking my question. It can also mean a short rest or even a temporary cease-fire in war. There was a *pause* in the bombing.

intermission

An *intermission* is a planned break in a play or performance. You can get something to eat and drink during an *intermission* in a movie.

recess

A *recess* is either a short or long break from business or work. A judge can call a *recess* during a trial. Your lunchtime at school is a *recess.*

lull

A *lull* is a brief period of time when some activity is stopped. It lasts until the activity

They got something to eat during an **intermission.**

66

starts up again. A *lull* in a storm is a brief period of calm, which does not last.

vacation A *vacation* is a long break in someone's routine, everyday life. It is a break (and sometimes a welcome one!) in your school year.

breakable Something that is easy to break is *breakable.* It can come apart, shatter, or be split into pieces. Glasses and dishes are *breakable.*

fragile Anything that has to be handled carefully so it won't be broken is *fragile.* Postal clerks mark *fragile* on packages that could be damaged in the mail. Our new baby seems so *fragile* that I'm afraid to pick him up.

delicate *Delicate* can mean extremely easy to break. Things that are *delicate* are usually lovely and very fine. The opposite of *delicate* is coarse. Thin crystal is *delicate* and must be treated with care. Some plane models are *delicate* to handle. An orchid is a *delicate* flower, but a dandelion is a tough flower.

brittle *Brittle* objects are hard, but they snap or shatter if they are dropped or treated roughly. It is impossible to bend a *brittle* object. Glass is *brittle,* and so is ice.

crisp *Crisp* means breakable when it describes certain foods. Crackers are *crisp* and crumble easily. Fresh lettuce is *crisp.* Toast, celery, and carrots are also *crisp.*

ANTONYMS: coarse, tough, unbreakable

B

build

Build means make something by putting materials or parts together. Carpenters *build* houses and office buildings. Birds *build* nests. Beavers *build* dams in rivers and streams. You can *build* a fire with kindling wood and dry logs. You can also *build* your hopes on something that you have counted on for a long time.

construct

Construct means build, but adds the meaning of making something according to a definite and often complicated plan. Architects, engineers, and carpenters are all needed to *construct* a skyscraper. You can *construct* a model rocket or a model ship according to directions.

manufacture
assemble

Manufacture means make or produce something using machines, usually in a factory. *Assemble* means bring or fit parts together. Each part of a car is first *manufactured,* and then all the parts are *assembled.*

fabricate

When you *fabricate* something, you make it out of many parts, according to a pattern. *Fabricate* can also mean make up a story to fool or deceive someone. She *fabricated* an excuse for being late.

develop

Develop can mean make a change, make some improvement, make available, or even grow. Exercise *develops* your muscles. A large oak tree *developed* from the young seedling. Construction plans for the shopping mall *developed* slowly.

ANTONYMS: demolish, destroy, tear down

Architects, engineers, and carpenters **construct** buildings.

C

calm (adj)

Calm means not excited or disturbed when you use it as an adjective. *Calm* people are relaxed. They don't get excited easily. How can I be *calm* when you are standing on my foot? *Calm* weather is not stormy. It is hard to stay *calm* when your team is winning.

quiet
still

Quiet and *still* can mean calm. A *quiet* person is not noisy or loud. A *quiet* street may have little or no traffic on it. *Still* adds the meaning of not moving. Sit *still*. A lake is *still* when there is no wind. An engine is *still* if it is not running.

cool

Cool people have a lot of self-control. They might be a little nervous, but no one would know it by their actions. They remain calm even in a dangerous situation. That pitcher has to keep *cool* if she wants to win the game.

peaceful
placid
tranquil
serene

Peaceful, placid, tranquil, and *serene* all describe something gentle and restful and calm. It is *peaceful* to sit by the fire after a long day of skiing. *Placid* waters are quiet and still. A *tranquil* person does not often get upset over anything. The Mona Lisa has a *serene* smile.

The Mona Lisa has a **serene** smile.

pacific

Pacific means peaceful and mild. When Magellan sailed into the South Seas on his way around the world, the waters were so calm and quiet that he called it *pacific.* Today we still call it the *Pacific* Ocean.

ANTONYMS: excited, stormy, noisy, loud, restless, nervous, disturbed

69

C

calm (v)   *Calm* means give comfort when it is used as a verb. It is the opposite of disturb or excite. You *calm* people who are afraid by talking kindly to them and making them feel less fearful. The jockey tried to *calm* the nervous horse. A person can be both *calmed* and excited by music.

quiet   *Quiet* means calm something or become still. The trainer tried to *quiet* the enraged lion. *Quiet* is often followed by *down*. Stir up would be the opposite of *quiet down*. The wind *quieted down* after the storm.

soothe   *Soothe* means calm or make less painful. You *soothe* someone's feelings when you make that person feel better. The police officer *soothed* the lost child. Cough drops can *soothe* a sore throat.

pacify   *Pacify* can mean calm someone's anger. We *pacified* the crying child by giving him a bottle of milk. The store manager tried to *pacify* the furious customer by giving back her money.

tranquilize   *Tranquilize* means calm or make someone feel less tense and nervous. A veterinarian uses medicine to *tranquilize* a frightened dog before setting its broken leg.

ANTONYMS: disturb, excite, stir up

The family **pacified** the crying child by giving him a bottle of milk.

70

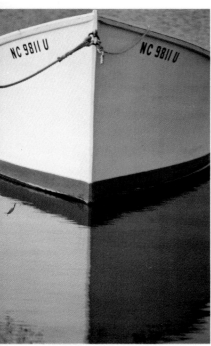

Stillness can mean calm and the absence of motion.

calm (n)

Calm, when it is used as a noun, means a condition without excitement, disturbance, or much movement. A period of *calm* followed the storm. The doctor gave me a feeling of *calm* and well-being.

quiet

Quiet is freedom from noise and confusion. The *quiet* of the country was a welcome change after the bustle of the city.

stillness

Stillness means calm and the absence of motion. The *stillness* of the air warned of a coming storm.

peace
tranquillity
serenity

Peace, tranquillity, and *serenity* all mean a gentle and restful kind of calm. Being in the wilderness filled us with *peace* and *tranquillity.* There is *serenity* in the first warm spring day.

ANTONYMS: noise, confusion

carry

Carry means hold something while you move from one place to another. You *carry* such things as books, packages, suitcases, and bags of groceries. Trains, ships, and planes *carry* objects and people.

bring

You *bring* something if you carry it with you from another place to here. But if you carry it from here to another place, you take it. For example, you *bring* the bat here, but you take the bat home. Your mother may ask you to *bring* some groceries when you come home from school. If you are at school, your teacher may ask you to *bring* a note from home.

carry continued on page 72 ▸

C

carried continued from page 71

fetch

Fetch means go and get something and bring it back. Some dogs are trained to *fetch* rabbits.

bear

Bear can mean carry or hold something very heavy. Medieval kings traveled to neighboring kingdoms *bearing* many gifts. A bridge must *bear* the weight of many cars and trucks. You may also *bear* sorrow.

transport

Transport means carry persons or goods from one place to another, usually by some vehicle or machinery. A train *transports* people and freight. Milk is *transported* from dairies by refrigerated trucks.

See also *send.*

ANTONYMS: drop (v), take

A bridge must **bear** the weight of many cars and trucks.

catch (v)

Catch is a word that has many meanings. It really means to take hold of something that is in motion or in hiding. You *catch* a ball with your hands if you don't miss it. A cat *catches* mice. You might *catch* a cold if you are *caught* in a storm. You may *catch* a glimpse of someone, or a pretty picture

Mary **caught** a lot of fish on her vacation.

catch (v) continued

may *catch* your eye. Perhaps you *caught* a lot of fish on your vacation. You *catch on* to the meaning of something and *catch up* to someone who is ahead of you.

trap
net
snare

Trap, net, and *snare* mean catch an animal with something that will hold it once it is caught. The pioneers used to *trap* wild animals for food and furs. You can also be *trapped* in a room or building if there is no way to escape or get out. You *net* fish, birds, or insects when you catch them in a net. You *snare* small animals by putting a looped rope on the ground in such a way that it will pull tight and hold an animal that steps into it.

seize
snatch

Seize and *snatch* mean take hold of or take away something suddenly. Gail *seized* my arm to keep from falling, and then, after getting her balance, she let go of it. The dog *snatched* my candy bar and ran.

arrest

Arrest usually means catch a suspect and take that person to the police station. He or she may be released later. Something can also catch or *arrest* your attention if it makes you want to look at it or listen to it and causes you to forget what you are doing.

capture

Capture means catch or take hold of something by force. Wild animals are *captured* and then sent to zoos. We tried to *capture* the runaway horse.

ANTONYMS: miss (v), let go, release (v), free (v)

C

center (n)

The *center* is a point inside a circle which is the same distance from any point on the outer edge of the circle. To draw a perfect circle you use a compass, placing the needle point on the paper and swinging the pencil point completely around it. The point where you put the needle is the *center* of the circle, no matter how large or small a circle you make. *Center* also suggests a point around which everything seems to turn, revolve, or rotate.

A shopping *center* draws shoppers from all around the area. The *center* of a hurricane is called the eye.

The point where you put the needle is the **center** of the circle.

middle

The *middle* is not an exact point, but rather an area or space around the center. You could say Wednesday is the *middle* of the week. *Middle* also suggests what is between the beginning and the end—the *middle* of a story; the *middle* of the day.

heart

We all know that the *heart* is the most important organ in our bodies. So *heart* means the innermost and most important part of something. Some people like to live in the *heart* of the city so they can walk to work. When you get to the *heart* of the matter, you get to the basic point.

hub

The *hub* is the central part of a wheel. The spokes of a wheel go out from the *hub. Hub* can also mean center of activity. Railroad tracks go out from a center, which is called the railroad *hub.* Chicago is the railroad *hub* of the United States. New York harbor is a great shipping *hub.*

core

The *core* is also the central part of something. The *core* of an apple is in the center and contains the seeds. The *core* of a paragraph is the most important sentence of the paragraph. The *core* of an argument is the main idea you are arguing about.

nucleus

Nucleus is from a Latin word meaning "kernel." Like a core, the kernel contains seeds. A *nucleus* is a center around which something gathers or collects. Downtown is the *nucleus* of a city. In science you would speak of the *nucleus* of a cell or the *nucleus* of an atom.

change (v)

Change means make different or become different. You *change* your clothes. You can also *change* your mind about something. The weather can *change* from day to day.

alter
modify

Alter and *modify* mean change only slightly. A tailor *alters* a coat when he or she makes it shorter. An adjective *modifies* a noun, but it doesn't change the meaning completely. For instance, when you write "a little dog," the word "little" *modifies,* or describes, the word "dog." You *alter* or *modify* your ideas when you make them less strong or definite. My family *modified* its rule against pets when I brought home a kitten.

vary

Vary means change slightly so that something is not always the same. The temperature *varies* with the seasons. A pilot can *vary* the speed of an airplane.

change (v) continued on page 76 ▶

change (v) continued from page 75

convert

Convert means change something for a different use. We *converted* the basement into a workshop. Petroleum is *converted* into gasoline.

shift
switch

Shift and *switch* mean change the place, position, or direction of something. A driver has to *shift* the gears in a car in order to back up. The wind *shifted* suddenly and caused the sailboat to capsize. The baggage car was *switched* to another track.

transfer

Transfer can mean change or move from one place to another. You may *transfer* a load of books from one arm to the other. You may trace a design on paper and then *transfer* it to cloth. Some students *transfer* from one school to another.

turn

Turn means change the position of something by moving. A wheel *turns*. You *turn* a key to unlock a door. You also *turn* the pages of a book. *Turn* can also mean change color. The leaves in autumn are beautiful as they *turn* red or yellow.

exchange

Exchange means substitute one thing for another. Marjorie *exchanged* the record for another one. We *exchanged* ideas on what we would grow in our garden.

transform

Transform means make a major change in the appearance or function or meaning of something. The Halloween costume *transformed* Jim into a ghost. Karen and Stan *transformed* an old box into an office.

ANTONYM: maintain

Transform means make a major change in appearance.

changeable *Changeable* means able or likely to change. The weather has been so *changeable* that I don't know whether to take sunglasses or an umbrella with me today. *Changeable* is often used to describe a person who jumps from one opinion or attitude to another. Jan is very *changeable*—one day she likes her new house and the next day she doesn't.

iridescent *Iridescent* describes something that shows changing colors. A fountain sometimes looks *iridescent* when it has the colors of the rainbow in it. A soap bubble can be described as *iridescent.*

reversible *Reversible* means able to move backward and forward or able to be turned around. A *reversible* coat has two sides that can be used as the outside.

fickle *Fickle* means often changeable without much reason. A *fickle* friend is not really a friend at all, because he or she may turn away from you at any time. He is so *fickle*—one day he's friendly and the next day he's not.

fluctuating *Fluctuating* means moving up and down. The mercury in a thermometer moves up and down during a day of *fluctuating* temperatures. Daily weather charts show *fluctuating* temperatures. Sometimes we say that a person has *fluctuating* moods. By that we mean he or she is up in the clouds one moment and down in the dumps the next.

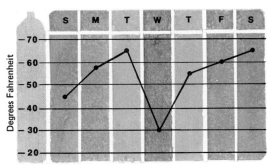

Daily weather charts show **fluctuating** temperatures.

changeable continued on page 78 ▶

C

changeable continued from page 77

unreliable

Unreliable describes persons or things that seldom do what they are expected to do. An *unreliable* paper carrier won't bother to deliver papers in bad weather. An old car may be *unreliable.*

unsteady
unstable

Unsteady and *unstable* describe someone or something that is not solid or firm. *Unsteady* describes any kind of wavering because of a lack of support. Don't climb an *unsteady* ladder. *Unstable* often describes a person who is changeable or likely to break down under stress. An *unstable* person cannot handle problems as well as a stable person can.

ANTONYMS: true, reliable, stable, unchangeable

choose

Choose means make a decision to take, accept, or do something. You usually have a reason for *choosing* something. Whatever you do not *choose,* you reject or refuse. Tom *has been chosen* to represent our class at the student council meetings next year.

select

Select means choose from many things. You *select* presents to give your family and friends. We *selected* a tie for Uncle John. Your thesaurus will help you *select* the best synonym to say exactly what you mean.

pick
prefer

Pick and *prefer* mean choose a thing because you like it better than something else. Why did you *pick* the red sweater instead of the blue one? She said she *preferred* mustard to catsup on her hamburger.

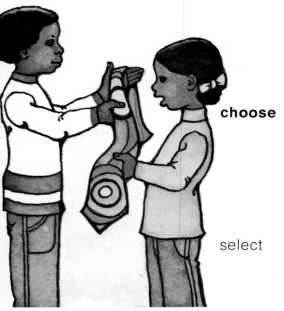

Fran and Billy **selected** a tie for Uncle John.

elect

Elect means choose a person for an office or a position. United States citizens *elect* a President every four years. You may also *elect* to do something. When my family went fishing at dawn, I *elected* to stay in bed.

decide

When you *decide* on something, or *decide* to do something, you make up your mind by choosing from many possibilities. Have you *decided* which record album you want? Annette has *decided* to become a doctor.

ANTONYMS: reject, refuse (v)

clear (adj)

Clear means bright or easily seen. It is the opposite of dim or dull. A *clear* day is not misty or hazy. You can see the sandy bottom of a *clear* stream. *Clear* can also mean easy to understand. It is the opposite of confused and obscure and vague. I had no trouble finding your house because your directions were *clear.*

plain

Plain means not only easily seen, heard, or understood, but also undecorated and simple. The point of the speech was *plain* to all. Some buildings are *plain;* others are ornate.

open

Open means plain and clear, with nothing to obstruct or hide or get in the way. It is pleasant to travel on an *open* road. Larry had an *open,* honest look.

transparent

You can see through something that is *transparent.* Window glass is *transparent.*

clear (adj) continued on page 80 ▶

C

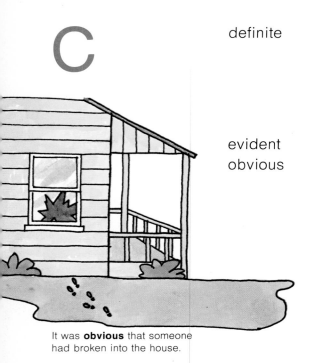

It was **obvious** that someone had broken into the house.

clear (adj) continued from page 79

definite

Definite means clear and precise. It is the opposite of vague. A *definite* statement or answer leaves no room for doubt. I want a *definite* answer by tomorrow morning at the latest.

evident
obvious

Something that is *evident* or *obvious* is immediately clear and unmistakable. Her big smile made it *evident* that she had just learned she had no cavities. It was *obvious* that someone had broken into the house while we were away.

See also *visible.*

ANTONYMS: dim (adj), dull, confused, obscure (adj), vague, ornate, doubtful, indefinite

club (n)

A *club* is one kind of gathering. A *club* is a group of people organized either for entertainment or for working together toward a goal. Usually, members of a *club* pay dues and have regular meetings. Our *club* voted to donate some money to UNICEF.

• association

Association is another word for a group of people with the same interests. Often an *association* is made up of people in the same kind of business. My dentist is attending a convention of the American Dental *Association.*

• society

A *society* is an association of people who share an interest or belief and who work actively to support a particular cause. Our neighbor is a member of the *Society* for the Prevention of Cruelty to Animals.

80

• union

A *union* is an organization in which two or more people or groups join together, or unite, to form a larger group. A labor *union,* for example, is an association of workers who have joined together to assist each other and to deal with their employer. The United States is often called the *Union,* because the states are united to form a single nation.

• alliance

An *alliance* may be an association of several nations with the same goal. Nations in an *alliance* may agree to put together their resources for the good of all, or assist each other in case of attack.

• league

A *league* can be an association of ball clubs. There are major and minor *leagues* of both baseball and football teams. Nations may also agree to combine forces in a *league.* A *league* of nations is more tightly bound than an alliance, because the nations sign a formal contract or treaty.

• federation

A *federation* is the joining of several groups or states under one central organization. Some independent labor unions joined to form the American *Federation* of Labor.

clumsy

Clumsy is used to describe someone whose actions and movements are not graceful. The *clumsy* burglar knocked over the chair. *Clumsy* can also describe something that is poorly or roughly made or is difficult to handle. It was difficult to carry the *clumsy* packages to the post office.

clumsy continued on page 82 ♦

C

clumsy continued from page 81

awkward *Awkward* can mean clumsy or embarrassing. Something is difficult to carry if it has an *awkward* shape. You would feel *awkward* if you called someone by the wrong name. Murray made an *awkward* jump for the basketball.

gawky
ungainly You are *gawky* or *ungainly* if you often are clumsy because you don't seem to have control of your arms and legs. You are not able to move quickly and easily. Someone who is *gawky* might not play tennis well. The *ungainly* boy did not make the team.

Someone who is **gawky** might not play tennis well.

bungling *Bungling* describes someone who often makes mistakes or something that is not done well. Her *bungling* efforts to pour the tea resulted in a broken cup.

ANTONYMS: graceful, dexterous, handy, skillful

come *Come* is the opposite of go and leave. It means move to or toward. If you *come* here or *come* home or *come* inside, you move from another place to where you are now, or to where the speaker is.

82

A tornado is **approaching** from the southwest.

Come is also used in other ways. Shirts *come* in many sizes. Spring *came* late this year. Have you *come* to a decision yet? My work is *coming* along nicely. My wish has just *come* true. This knot *came* untied. How did this situation *come* about? My bill *came* to three dollars.

- approach

Approach means come near or closer to something. I started to *approach* the stray dog but changed my mind when it began to bark. A tornado is *approaching* from the southwest.

- arrive

Arrive means come to, or reach, a certain place. You should *arrive* at the movie before it starts. The train will *arrive* at eleven o'clock and depart at noon.

- appear

Appear means come into sight. It is the opposite of disappear and vanish. I saw a strange face *appear* at the window. A full moon *appeared* in the sky.

- happen

Happen means take place or come about—sometimes by chance. I just *happened* to see my cousin downtown. Accidents sometimes *happen*. It *happened* to rain. What *happened* to you?

- extend

Extend means stretch out or reach to a certain point. The table *extends* to a length of twelve feet. The teacher *extended* the deadline to Friday.

See also *grow.*

ANTONYMS: go, leave (v), depart, disappear, vanish, go away, quit, withdraw

C

condition continued from page 87

week may wonder how much work you have done on it so far. He might say, "What is the *status* of your report today?"

confident

Confident means free from doubt. If you're *confident* something will happen, you firmly believe it will, and you don't worry about it. I'm *confident* the parade will still be held, but I'm doubtful about the weather.

sure

Sure is a good synonym for confident, but it is not as strong a word. When two people argue, each is *sure* that the other person is wrong. Are you *sure* you must go?

certain
positive

Certain and *positive* are strong words meaning confident. It is *certain* that the world is not flat. I am *positive* that five and five make ten.

self-reliant

A person who is *self-reliant* is confident of his or her own abilities. That person does not need help in accomplishing something. Bert is certainly *self-reliant;* he can do anything if he tries.

ANTONYMS: doubtful, uncertain, uneasy, unsure

confuse

Confuse means disturb or be disturbed. If something *confuses* you, it is hard for you to think or act clearly. Directions or questions might *confuse* you. You can be *confused* by a strange noise or an unusual sight. *Confuse* can also mean mistake one for another. I *confused* one telephone number with another and called a gas station instead of the pizza parlor.

CHIRP
CHIRP
CHIRP

Calvin was **confused** by a strange noise.

bewilder

Bewilder means confuse. Something that is very complicated, jumbled, or involved can *bewilder* you and keep you from thinking straight. The instructions for the card game have completely *bewildered* me.

dumfound

Dumfound means confuse and astonish. If something *dumfounds* you, it surprises you and may leave you speechless. Kinuko was *dumfounded* to find that she had really won the bicycle.

perplex
puzzle

If something *perplexes* or *puzzles* you, it is hard to understand or figure out. Trying to read the road map only *perplexed* her more. The instructions for assembling the model airplane *puzzled* me.

baffle

Baffle can mean confuse and amaze. The magician *baffled* the audience.

See also *disturb.*

ANTONYM: clarify

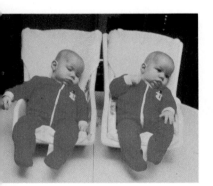

Twins create **confusion** for those who can't tell them apart.

confusion

Confusion is the state of disorder or not knowing what to do. A stalled car causes *confusion* on a highway. Twins create *confusion* for those who can't tell them apart.

bewilderment

Bewilderment is the confusion you feel when there are a number of different objects, ideas, or choices before you. Walking into a room full of laughing people might cause you *bewilderment*. Wayne's blank look showed his *bewilderment* at the auction.

confusion continued on page 90 ▶

C

confusion continued from page 89

perplexity

Perplexity is being confused, puzzled, and worried. I can't understand your *perplexity* over my simple question.

astonishment

Astonishment is what you feel when you are surprised, amazed, or shocked. The crowd looked with *astonishment* at the stunt driver's latest stunt.

ANTONYMS: calm (n), order (n)

conquer

Conquer means get the better of someone or something. Doctors *conquer* disease. Sir Edmund Hillary *conquered* Mt. Everest, the highest mountain in the world, when he reached its summit. *Conquer* and the synonyms listed here are often used by sportswriters and broadcasters to tell which team won a game. All of these words really mean win in warfare or battle with an enemy, but because they are such strong, colorful words, they are used in describing various situations.

overcome

Overcome means conquer an enemy. But you can also *overcome* a bad habit, a fear, or a fault. My little cousins soon *overcame* their fear of the dark.

overthrow

Overthrow means destroy and conquer. The rebels tried to *overthrow* their government and seize control for themselves.

rout

Rout means conquer and drive out an enemy. When you *rout* an army, you throw the troops into such confusion that they scatter and run away.

This ceremony was called a
triumph.

conquer continued

subdue

Subdue means defeat and bring an enemy or an opponent under control. The rodeo rider was able to rope and *subdue* the calf within half a minute. The wrestler *subdued* his opponent when he pinned him so that he couldn't move.

overpower
overwhelm

Overpower and *overwhelm* mean conquer something completely. But something can also *overpower* or *overwhelm* you if it is too much for you to endure. A severe headache may *overpower* you. Someone may be *overwhelmed* by sadness or despair.

See also *beat* (v), *defeat* (v).

ANTONYMS: submit, surrender (v)

conquest

A *conquest* is the winning of a struggle or a contest. A *conquest* is the opposite of a defeat. *Conquest* and its listed synonyms are also used in sports, even though they are strong words. The *conquest* of another country usually involves war. The enemy is defeated and forced to submit to the victor. Pizarro led the *conquest* of Peru. A *conquest* of nature sometimes means the successful end of some expedition or exploration. Sir Edmund Hillary achieved the *conquest* of Mt. Everest.

triumph

When the Roman armies came home from conquering new lands, they marched into the city and were received by the emperor. This ceremony was called a *triumph.* Today a *triumph* is an overwhelming and glorious conquest.

conquest continued on page 92 ▶

C

conquest continued from page 91

victory
: A *victory* is the overcoming of an enemy, some obstacle, or a certain difficulty. A defeat is the opposite of a *victory.* Shouts of *victory* could be heard all over the battlefield at Gettysburg. The daring rescue at sea was a *victory* over death.

success
: Anything that is attempted and turns out well can be called a *success.* Its opposite is a failure. Judy's experiment was a *success.*

achievement
: An *achievement* is also the good result of doing something that is very difficult. Learning to communicate with others was a great *achievement* for Helen Keller.

ANTONYMS: defeat (n), failure

consider
: *Consider* means think carefully about something. If you have an important decision to make, it is wise to *consider* every aspect of it before making up your mind. Before you buy something, you should *consider* its price. Had you really *considered* buying a flea circus? I am *considering* trying out for the track team.

weigh
: *Weigh* means balance or compare the weight, value, or importance of two or more things. You use scales to *weigh* objects, but you use your mind to *weigh* opposite or conflicting ideas. A jury has to *weigh* all the evidence given in court before reaching a verdict.

ponder
: *Ponder* means weigh or think deeply about something. Often you don't come to any decision. It is wise to *ponder* the lessons we learn from history.

Some people **contemplate** the stars for hours.

contemplate You *contemplate* something when you consider it for a long time and keep your attention on it. Some scientists *contemplate* the stars for hours. Ben *contemplated* taking a trip to Europe.

study *Study* means consider something carefully and in detail. You *study* science in order to learn and understand the subject. Mom *studied* the stock market before she invested her money.

reason *Reason* can mean consider, examine, explain, or prove something. When you *reason* with someone, it may be to make that person change his or her mind. You *reason* something out if you think about it carefully, step by step.

ANTONYMS: disregard, ignore, neglect (v)

contain *Contain* and its synonyms have many meanings. *Contain* means have or keep something within something else. The trunk *contains* old photographs. The book I'm reading *contains* stories by famous authors. *Contain* also means keep within limits. It was hard to *contain* our laughter because the joke was so funny. The pen was large enough to *contain* the hamsters.

hold *Hold* means capable of containing. This gas tank contains only three gallons right now, but it *holds,* or is capable of containing, twenty gallons of gas. *Hold* also means contain or keep. "*Hold* your tongue" means keep quiet.

contain continued on page 94 ▶

contain continued from page 93

include

Something that is *included* in something else is part of it. The trip *includes* a riverboat ride, a tour of an old plantation, and lunch at a famous restaurant. The treasurer *included* all the expenses in the report. *Include* can also mean have in addition. The first-aid kit *included* splints along with medicines and bandages.

enclose

Enclose means surround or close in or hold in. A high fence *enclosed* the garden. The baby's arms *enclosed* the teddy bear.

confine

Confine means keep within limits. Our family doesn't always *confine* its spending to things we really need. It also means take away freedom of movement. I was *confined* to bed with a sore throat and a cold.

Some families don't always **confine** their spending to things they really need.

imprison

Imprison means confine or put in a prison. People are *imprisoned* when they commit crimes and are released after they have served their sentences.

ANTONYMS: release (v), exclude

convenient

Convenient describes something that can be done or used without much effort. Would it be *convenient* for you to stop at the drugstore on your way home?

easy

Easy means convenient because something is not hard or difficult to do. Using an electric sander is an *easy* way to sand.

handy

Handy describes anything that is convenient because it is close by when you need it. An alarm clock is *handy* when you have to get up at a certain time.

An alarm clock is **handy** for getting up on time.

• comfortable

Comfortable describes someone or something that has or gives feelings of ease and restfulness. You can relax and rest on a *comfortable* couch, but you may become tense in an uncomfortable chair. You are also *comfortable* when you are with people you like.

suitable

You might use *suitable* when you want to talk about something that can be used in some situation even though it is not intended for that use. Two logs placed side by side made a *suitable* bridge across the stream.

ANTONYMS: hard, difficult, uncomfortable, inconvenient, unsuitable

conversation

A *conversation* is a talk in which two or more persons exchange opinions, ideas, or news. You have a *conversation* with someone about something.

chat

A *chat* is a very informal conversation, usually between friends. When you have a *chat* with another person, you talk about things that are interesting but not very important.

discussion

A *discussion* is usually a serious conversation. A question or problem is talked over, and some solution or conclusion is sought. A *discussion* can turn into an argument.

discourse

A *discourse* is a long, formal conversation. It can also be a long, carefully prepared

conversation continued on page 96 ▶

C

correct (adj)

Correct means right, true, and acceptable when it is used as an adjective. Something is *correct* if it is not wrong, is free from mistakes, or measures up to certain rules or standards. Marie gave the *correct* answer on the quiz show. There is a *correct* way to sit at the dinner table.

accurate

Accurate means correct because care has been taken. You take an *accurate* measurement if you place a ruler carefully and read its markings correctly.

exact
precise

Exact and *precise* mean correct or accurate in every way. They mean definite, clear, and unmistakable. If a recipe calls for an *exact* amount of flour—one cup—it means no more, no less. We yelled "Happy Birthday!" at the *precise* moment Alberta walked into the room.

appropriate

Appropriate means correct and suitable. Something is *appropriate* if it is right for the time or occasion. There is an *appropriate* way to act at a banquet, and an *appropriate* way to act at a ball game.

nice

Nice is a more formal word, meaning correct. It means exact and often fine or careful. You might raise a *nice* point in a discussion, or find a word that has a *nice* shade of meaning. *Nice* has become a tired word because many people overuse the word and misuse it to mean practically everything good or pleasant or tasty.

ANTONYMS: wrong (adj), false, inaccurate, inappropriate, incorrect, inexact

Mr. Sims **adjusts** the rear-view mirror to see what's behind him.

correct (v)   *Correct* means point out errors when it is used as a verb. It also means try to make something right. Teachers *correct* papers by marking errors. The National Park Service is trying to *correct* the impression that hand-feeding wild animals helps them survive.

punish   *Punish* means place a penalty on someone for some wrong he or she has done. Drivers usually are *punished* for speeding.

adjust   *Adjust* means correct by bringing something to a better state or condition. Dad *adjusts* the rear-view mirror so he can see what is behind him. When you look through a telescope, you may have to *adjust* it before you can see anything.

improve   *Improve* means make better or increase the value of something by correcting its faults. Cutting the lawn *improves* the appearance of a house. Some landlords try to *improve* their apartment buildings by remodeling the kitchens.

reform   *Reform* means improve by correcting or changing. Prisons usually try to *reform* people who have broken the law. To *reform* something, you change the way it has been done and show a better way to do it. Candidates for office often promise that they will *reform* the government.

remedy   *Remedy* means correct by removing the cause of trouble or harm. To *remedy* overcrowding in some schools, many more classrooms have been built.

99

C

The electric light bulb was **invented** by Thomas Edison.

create

Create means make something new. An author may *create* an interesting novel. You might *create* a new game. A sculptor may *create* a lovely figurine.

invent

Invent means create something new and useful. Often we say mechanical things are *invented;* works of art are created. The electric light bulb was *invented* by Thomas Edison.

design

Design means create a plan for something but not necessarily make or build it. Architects and engineers *design* buildings, but carpenters, steelworkers, plumbers, and other construction workers build them.

originate

Originate means begin or come into existence. Folk tales *originated* in many different countries long ago. *Originate* also means create new ideas or methods of doing things. Henry Bessemer *originated* a process of making steel from iron.

establish

Establish means create or set up some kind of organization for the first time. We speak of *establishing* laws, businesses, and colleges.

shape
form

Shape and *form* mean make something according to a definite pattern or design. Potters *shape* clay into many different figures. You can *form* dough into pretzels. You can also *shape* ideas or *form* a plan.

fashion

Fashion means make something out of something else. You can *fashion* a table out of a box or *fashion* a whistle out of a piece of wood.

100

produce

Use *produce* when you mean manufacture. Factories in Detroit *produce* more cars than factories in any other U.S. city. *Produce* can also mean give rise to something. A garden can *produce* flowers and vegetables.

See also *shape* (v).

ANTONYMS: break (v), destroy

crowd (n)

A *crowd* is a group of people gathered together in one place. Usually a *crowd* fills its space to overflowing. There was such a *crowd* in the auditorium that Myra couldn't find a place to sit.

throng

A *throng* is a large number of people moving and pushing together. A *throng* of shoppers rushed into the store as soon as the doors were opened.

mob

A *mob* is a large crowd that becomes angry and disorderly and often becomes destructive or violent. Cowboy movies sometimes show an angry *mob* standing in the main street of a town. Sometimes *mob* is used informally to mean merely a large number of people. There was a *mob* ahead of me in line at the theater.

horde

A *horde* is a crowd of people that is in a threatening or unpleasant mood. The crowd usually moves as a group. A *horde* of angry customers demanded their money back. *Horde* can also mean a swarm of insects or a pack of animals. Our picnic was ruined by a *horde* of mosquitoes.

crowd (n) continued on page 102 ▶

A **throng** of shoppers rushed into the store.

C

The cat was **curious** to see what was in the barrel.

multitude

Multitude means an extremely large number of people, animals, or things. A *multitude* of people lined the street during the Tournament of Roses Parade. Each fall birds fly south in *multitudes.* If someone at the bank asks why I need money, I can give a *multitude* of reasons.

curious

Curious means interested in finding out how and why things happen. Because the cat was so *curious* to see what was in the barrel, it fell in. A *curious* crowd gathered near the burning building to watch the firefighters. A *curious* person is one who is always eager to learn about everything. Scientists are *curious.*

inquisitive

Inquisitive describes a person who is extremely curious. Often *inquisitive* describes someone who tries to find out as much as possible about others by asking personal questions.

prying

Prying means almost the same as inquisitive, but *prying* is a stronger, meaner word. It describes people who are determined to make someone else's business their own, using any methods necessary. A *prying* person asks many personal questions and may read your mail or your diary if he or she has a chance.

nosy
snoopy

Nosy and *snoopy* are two very descriptive words that are less polite and stronger than prying and inquisitive. *Nosy* really means sticking your nose into someone else's business. *Nosy* persons are happy only when they know everything that is going on around them. *Snoopy* means prying for personal information about others. Usually *snoopy* persons are sly and sneaky about their prying.

See also *odd.*

ANTONYM: uninterested

cut (v)   *Cut* means pierce, separate, or remove with something sharp or pointed. You *cut* the grass when you mow it. My little sister likes to *cut* out pictures from magazines.

The women **clip** the wool from their sheep.

clip
prune

Clip and *prune* mean cut and trim with scissors or a similar tool. You usually *clip* hair and *prune* bushes. Farmers *clip* the wool from their sheep. A gardener *prunes* rosebushes to keep them looking neat.

cut (v) continued on page 104 ▶

cut (v) continued from page 103

Totem poles are **carved** out of wood.

slice
carve

Slice and *carve* mean cut something into thin, flat pieces. You *carve* a roast of meat and *slice* a loaf of bread. *Carve* also means cut and shape something. Totem poles are *carved* out of wood. Campers sometimes *carve* their initials on a tree, even though this may kill the tree.

chisel
engrave

Chisel and *engrave* mean cut or carve into something hard. A mason *chisels* stone with a hammer and a metal tool that has a sharp blade at one end. You can have your initials *engraved* on a ring.

slit

Slit means cut lengthwise or in long, narrow strips. You *slit* an envelope with a letter opener.

slash

You *slash* something when you recklessly make heavy, deep cuts. Irene *slashed* through the bark of the tree with her hatchet.

chop

Chop means cut with quick, hard blows. Lumberjacks *chop* down trees. A cook *chops* meat and vegetables.

See also *decrease* (v).

104

D

danger

Danger is any situation or thing that might cause serious harm or injury. There is *danger* of fire if people play with matches. A skater may be in *danger* if the ice is thin. Road signs warn drivers of *danger* ahead—curves, hills, or possible road construction.

peril

Peril means the gravest kind of danger. It is danger that is usually difficult to avoid. Columbus braved the unknown *perils* of the ocean.

hazard

A *hazard* is a great chance of injury or misfortune. *Hazards* are always present in places and actions that are dangerous and risky. Mining is an occupation that is full of *hazards.*

menace

A *menace* is a danger that seems to hang over you. No harm may really come, but you feel that it might. Floating logs can be a *menace* to someone who is paddling a canoe. Icy roads are a *menace* to traffic.

threat

A *threat,* like a menace, is a warning of danger. The clouds held a *threat* of snow.

ANTONYMS: safety, security

Floating logs can be a **menace** to someone who is paddling a canoe.

Her grandparents' **dusky** attic is filled with old photographs and antiques.

dark

Dark describes an object or place that has little or no light, or is almost black. A night sky is *dark.* Gladys tripped over a chair in the *dark* room.

dusky

Dusky means dark and shadowy. A bright, sunny day becomes *dusky* as the sun sets. My grandparents' *dusky* attic is filled with old photographs and antiques.

murky

Murky means smoke-filled or foggy. It is the opposite of clear. Driving can be very hazardous on a wet, *murky* day. Water that is very muddy is also *murky. Murky* also means dark and gloomy. My uncle's *murky* basement scares me.

dreary
gloomy

Dreary and *gloomy* mean dark, cheerless, and sad. A *dreary* room is not very bright or cheerful. A *dreary* day is cloudy and gray. *Gloomy* people are sad and unsmiling.

See also *dim* (adj).

ANTONYMS: bright, sunny, clear (adj),
cheerful, light (adj)

deal (n)

A *deal* is an agreement between two or more people. *Deal* and agreement are practically synonyms, but an agreement can be simply an opinion shared by two or more people. A *deal* is more an agreement between people to do something or exchange something that will benefit both parties—"You do this for me, and I'll do that for you." We are in agreement about my buying your football. Now let's make a *deal.* The owner of a store makes a *deal* with a customer every time a customer buys something. Customers get good *deals* if they save money or if they get their money's worth.

• transaction

A *transaction* is a business deal. When you buy a pencil and pay for it, you have made a *transaction.* When my parents sold our house, they made a *transaction.*

• purchase
• sale

A *purchase* and a *sale* are both transactions. Both mean the trading of money for something. A person who buys makes a *purchase,* while the one who sells makes a *sale.* So if you buy a cold drink on a hot day and pay a dime for it, you have made a *purchase.* The person who took your dime made a *sale.* And the whole deal was a transaction!

Sale also means a selling of goods at lower prices than usual. Most stores have special *sales* during the year. The candy store never has a clearance *sale.* You save money when you buy something on *sale.*

deal (n) continued on page 108 ▶

deal (n) continued from page 107

- exchange
- trade

An *exchange* or *trade* is a deal in which you give something and get something else in return. You may or may not be using money in this kind of deal. Stores make *exchanges* of clothing and other things with customers. The stock *exchange* is the place where stocks are bought, sold, and traded. Sometimes a baseball player moves to another team as part of a *trade* of players.

- bargain

A *bargain* is an agreement to buy, sell, or trade. It can also mean a real saving on something. Your aunt and the car dealer strike a *bargain* on a car when they finally make a deal. If your aunt doesn't have to pay as much as she expected, she gets a *bargain.*

See also *agreement.*

Aunt Joy and the car dealer struck a **bargain** on a car.

decide

Decide means make up your mind or come to a conclusion about something. Instead of staying home on a hot day, you may *decide* to go swimming. It was hard to *decide* which book to read. We tossed a penny to *decide* who would go first.

determine

Determine means decide definitely on something. The boys were *determined* to win the game, and they fought with all their might.

settle

Settle means make a final choice after you have cleared up all uncertainties and doubts. The committee finally *settled* on a day for the fair. You *settle* an argument

Paco wanted a new bike, but **settled for** his brother's.

decide continued

when you decide who is right and who is wrong. When you *settle for* something, it may not be your first choice. I wanted a new bicycle, but I *settled for* my brother's old one.

rule

Rule can mean decide what should or should not be done. The judge *ruled* that the lawyer was out of order. The referee *ruled* that the ball was out of bounds.

resolve

Resolve means decide on something once and for all. I have *resolved* to get up early every morning.

See also *choose.*

decision

A *decision* is what you decide. Every time you make up your mind, you make a *decision.* Choosing what clothes to wear is a *decision.*

settlement

A *settlement* is a decision made to settle a problem or an argument. People make a *settlement* when they come to an agreement or reach an understanding.

resolution

A *resolution* is a definite and final decision. It's what you resolve to do. Brenda made a New Year's *resolution* to make her bed every day.

ruling

A *ruling* is an official decision or statement made by someone in authority. We accepted the official's *ruling* that the other basketball team should get a free throw.

decision continued on page 110 ▶

D

decision continued from page 109

judgment
verdict

A *judgment* and a *verdict* are formal decisions. A court passes *judgment* on whether or not someone has committed a crime. The jury returned a *verdict* of "Not guilty."

See also *opinion*.

decrease (v)

Decrease means become or make less. The word can be used in many ways. An object *decreases* in value if it is damaged. A driver can either increase or *decrease* the speed of a car. Jed's fears *decreased* as the thunder and lightning stopped.

lessen

Lessen can mean decrease in number or degree. The new ceiling helped *lessen* the noise in our cafeteria. Flashing lights at railroad crossings can *lessen* the number of accidents.

diminish
dwindle

Diminish and *dwindle* mean become gradually less. Fay's fever *diminished,* and she began to feel better. *Dwindle* adds the meaning of almost disappearing. The woodpile *dwindled* as the winter wore on.

reduce

Reduce can mean decrease in amount, size, speed, or rank. If prices or taxes are lowered, they are *reduced.* Diets help people *reduce.* The pilot *reduced* the speed of the plane as she prepared for landing. The sergeant was *reduced* to the rank of private.

shorten

Shorten means make or become shorter. It is the opposite of lengthen. The days *shorten* in winter. The tailor *shortened* the sleeves of the jacket.

abbreviate

Abbreviate means shorten. We can *abbreviate* "January" to "Jan." and "continued" to "contd." The program was *abbreviated* because it was getting late.

subtract
divide

Subtract means to take away. *Divide* means to separate something into parts. You *divide* a cherry pie if you cut it into six pieces. If you eat a piece, you *subtract* one-sixth of the pie!

Sumi **divides** a pie when she cuts it into six pieces.

She **subtracts** one-sixth of the pie when she eats a piece!

cut

Cut can mean shorten. If you *cut* a speech or story, you shorten it by leaving a part of it out. If you *cut through* a neighbor's yard on your way to school, you are shortening the trip.

See also *shrink*.

ANTONYMS: increase (v), lengthen, add, accelerate, enlarge, extend, multiply

D

defeat (v)

Defeat means gain a victory or overcome an opponent. The winning team *defeats* the loser. If few people vote for a candidate, he or she is *defeated.*

win

Win means gain victory or success, sometimes over someone else. One team *wins* and the other team loses in a championship game. Alexander Graham Bell *won* fame for his invention of the telephone.

surpass

Surpass means do better or be greater than someone or something else. The winning jump *surpassed* the other by two feet. In comparing two paintings, you might think that one *surpasses* the other in beauty.

outdo

Outdo can mean surpass what has been done before or what you have done before. Geraldine *outdid* herself in preparing for the dinner party.

See also *beat* (v), *conquer.*

ANTONYM: lose

defense

Defense means both the act of defending or guarding from attack or harm, and the way of defending. It is the opposite of attack. In the Middle Ages, knights came to the *defense* of a castle. A castle itself was a *defense* against enemies. You can speak in *defense* of your school or of something you believe in. A thin coat may be your only *defense* against a cold wind. A person caught in the act of doing something wrong probably has no *defense.*

A castle was a **defense** against enemies.

shield

A *shield,* carried by a soldier in ancient times, was a defense against the arrows, spears, and swords of the enemy. Today, a *shield* is used to mean anything that keeps away something harmful or anything that covers. A *shield* is usually an object—a catcher's mask is a *shield* for the catcher's face. An umbrella is a *shield* against the sun or rain.

The lock on the door is a
protection against burglars.

protection

Protection is anything that keeps or guards from harm. A raincoat is *protection* against a storm. The lock on your door is a *protection* against burglars.

excuse

An *excuse* is a way of defending yourself if you are blamed for something. It is a reason for your actions. You may have to bring an *excuse* from home if you are absent from school.

alibi

An *alibi* is an excuse. You have an *alibi* if you were somewhere else at the very time you are said to have done something. The girl's *alibi* was that she was in school when the window was broken.

justification

A *justification* is the reason or explanation for an action. When you offer a *justification,* you do not deny you did something; instead you explain why it was right to do it. His *justification* for smashing the window was that it was the only way to rescue the dog.

See also *answer* (n), *reason* (n).

ANTONYM: attack (n)

D

delicious

Delicious describes something that is pleasant or appealing. Silence is *delicious* if you are trying to sleep. Usually *delicious* is used to describe the good taste of food. May I have more of that *delicious* chocolate cake? Food that has little taste or flavor is insipid.

luscious

Usually, *luscious* suggests that there is a special quality about something that makes it very delicious. That fruit market always has *luscious* strawberries.

delightful
delectable

Delightful and *delectable* can mean delicious. We had a *delightful* meal at Georgia's house last night. Her mother served a *delectable* banana pie.

delicate

One meaning of *delicate* is delicious. Many delicious foods, like lemon sherbet, have a *delicate* flavor.

appetizing
savory

Appetizing and *savory* can both mean agreeable or pleasant. Food that looks and smells good is *appetizing.* Sometimes *savory* is also used to describe spicy seasonings or foods. Both *appetizing* and *savory* can be used for things other than food. The critic's book review gave an *appetizing* introduction to the book. The air was filled with the *savory* smell of burning leaves.

tasty

Tasty means appetizing or pleasing to the taste. Ice cream on apple pie is *tasty.*

• palatable

Palatable is not really a synonym of delicious, but you can use *palatable* when you mean that something is fit to be eaten.

114

That wasn't the best hamburger I've ever eaten, but it was *palatable.*

• fragrant

Fragrant is not quite a synonym of delicious, but describes something that has a pleasant or sweet odor, such as food. The *fragrant* smells of home cooking help make Thanksgiving a pleasant holiday.

See also *pleasant.*

ANTONYMS: insipid, unappetizing, unpalatable, distasteful, unsavory

He's a **difficult** person to have on a canoe trip; he always wants to go his own way.

difficult

Something that is *difficult* is not easy to do or understand. *Difficult* problems must be given much thought before they can be solved. A *difficult* task requires serious thought, effort, or skill to be accomplished. A person who is hard to get along with may be called *difficult.* He's a *difficult* person to have on a canoe trip; he always wants his own way.

difficult continued on page 116 ▶

D

difficult continued from page 115

hard

Hard is the opposite of easy. It usually describes something that takes a great deal of work, strength, and maybe time. You may not have to think to do something *hard.* But you do have to think to do something difficult. It's *hard* to move a piano, but it's difficult to play it.

laborious

Something that is *laborious* takes a lot of time and effort. Shoveling snow is a *laborious* job. Building a model bridge out of toothpicks is also *laborious.*

complicated

Complicated means difficult to understand or explain because of so many parts to be remembered. *Complicated* games have many rules and regulations.

puzzling

A *puzzling* problem is a difficult one to solve. A good detective can solve a *puzzling* mystery after studying all the facts.

ANTONYMS: easy, simple, uncomplicated

A good detective can solve a **puzzling** mystery.

difficulty

Difficulty means either a condition or a situation so difficult that you can't overcome or handle it without great effort. You may have *difficulty* threading a needle in bad light.

• **hardship**

Hardship is a difficulty you might suffer for a long time. Being sick and lacking money to buy medicine is a *hardship.*

• **trouble**

Trouble may be used for difficulty. You could have *trouble* keeping a bicycle tire from going flat. *Trouble* is something disturbing or causing worry, but usually doesn't last forever.

116

• misfortune

Misfortune is the difficulty of having your luck turn bad. You could have the *misfortune* of slipping on a patch of ice and twisting an ankle.

• predicament

A *predicament* is a difficulty or situation from which there is no easy escape. When the villain in a silent movie leaves the girl tied to the railroad tracks and the train is coming, she is in a *predicament.*

• emergency

An *emergency* is a situation which occurs all of a sudden and which demands some kind of immediate action. To handle an *emergency,* a person must think and act fast. If you were cooking supper, for example, and spilled grease on the stove, you might have difficulty cleaning it up. If the grease caught fire, you'd have an *emergency.* You'd have to act fast.

• annoyance

An *annoyance* causes difficulty by getting in the way of your comfort and peace of mind, but it is not serious. Two people talking in a movie can cause *annoyance* to all the people around them.

• obstacle

An *obstacle* causes difficulty by standing in the way. You have to remove it or go around it. A tree growing in the middle of the street would be an *obstacle* to traffic.

A tree growing in the street is an **obstacle** to traffic.

• obstruction

An *obstruction* can be an obstacle or any other difficulty that holds something back or gets in the way or clogs an opening or passage. An *obstruction* in the water pipes caused a flood. Road workers cleared away all *obstructions* as they built the highway.

117

See also *command* (v).

dim (adj)   *Dim* describes something that is difficult to see, hear, or understand. A *dim* room is

disagreeable   *Disagreeable* means not to your liking. Anything that causes dislike, discomfort, or displeasure can be called *disagreeable.* You may talk about a *disagreeable* smell, *disagreeable* weather, or a *disagreeable* person. A *disagreeable* person may be unfriendly, annoying, or cross. *Disagreeable* people are hard to get along with.

unpleasant   *Unpleasant* is the opposite of pleasant or enjoyable. An *unpleasant* day might be boring, dull, or rainy. *Unpleasant* is the weakest word for disagreeable. Anything that makes you feel uncomfortable or uneasy may be described as *unpleasant.*

horrible
horrid   *Horrible* and *horrid* describe something that is very disagreeable and also frightening or shocking. *Horrible* is sometimes overused, so give it lots of rest. Getting lost in a large city can be a *horrible* experience. We saw a *horrid* accident.

offensive   *Offensive* is a strong word for disagreeable. When something is irritating or disgusting, it is *offensive.* Sometimes spoiled food has an *offensive* odor. You would draw away from an *offensive* sight. An *offensive* remark can hurt a person.

obnoxious
repulsive   *Obnoxious* and *repulsive* are the strongest words for disagreeable. You would try to avoid something that is *obnoxious* or *repulsive.* Rotten eggs have an *obnoxious* smell. This cough medicine tastes *repulsive.*

ANTONYMS: pleasant, attractive, acceptable, agreeable

This cough medicine tastes **repulsive.**

120

dishonest *Dishonest* is the opposite of honest. *Dishonest* is used to describe some people and their actions. Someone who lies, steals, or cheats is *dishonest.*

untruthful
deceitful *Untruthful* and *deceitful* mean dishonest, false, and misleading. An *untruthful* account or story doesn't report the truth. Someone who is *deceitful* gives the wrong idea of things and makes people believe things are true when they are really false.

crooked *Crooked* usually describes something, like a road or path, that has curves or bends. It is the opposite of straight. But *crooked* can also describe a person. A *crooked* person bends or twists the truth.

A **crooked** person bends or twists the truth.

untrustworthy A person who is *untrustworthy* can't be counted on to do what is right and fair. That person isn't dependable or reliable.

dishonorable *Dishonorable* means without honesty, honor, or respect. It is a very strong word. Some people have received *dishonorable* discharges from the military.

ANTONYMS: honest, straight, dependable, reliable, honorable, just, trustworthy, truthful, upright

D

disturb

Disturb means move something out of place or put something out of order. A breeze *disturbed* the quiet waters. The detective knew that someone had *disturbed* the papers on the desk. *Disturb* can also mean break in on something or someone or make a person feel uneasy and uncomfortable. Don't *disturb* me while I'm on the phone. The ghost stories we were telling last night *disturbed* me.

The detective knew that someone had **disturbed** the papers.

displace

Displace means move something out of place or put something in the place of another. After a flood, many people are *displaced* because their homes have been destroyed. Superhighways have *displaced* dirt roads between large cities.

disarrange
jumble

Disarrange and *jumble* also mean disturb by moving. You *disarrange* volumes of an encyclopedia when you change their order or arrangement on the shelf. You *jumble* clothes in a drawer when you mix or mess them up.

confuse

If something *confuses* you, it jumbles the order of your thoughts and makes it hard to think clearly. A complicated or puzzling problem may *confuse* you.

interrupt
interfere

Interrupt and *interfere* mean break into and disturb. You *interrupt* someone who is talking or thinking by breaking in with your own questions or remarks. You *interfere* when you take part in something that is none of your business or something that does not need your help or advice.

122

distract

It is hard to concentrate on what you are doing if something *distracts* you. Your attention is *distracted* by something that disturbs you. The bee buzzing around the ceiling *distracted* me while I was speaking.

The bee buzzing around the ceiling **distracted** Brenda.

rattle
fluster

Rattle and *fluster* mean disturb and confuse. If something *rattles* you, you may say or do the wrong thing. A lot of people crowding and pushing on a bus may *rattle* you. An embarrassing question can *fluster* you, and so can a lot of excitement.

upset
trouble

Upset and *trouble* can be used if something disturbs or worries you. A disappointment can *upset* you. You can *upset* your stomach if you eat too much. Bad news can *trouble* you. Eileen was *troubled* by nightmares and bad dreams.

D

dodge (v)

Dodge can mean move back and forth or from place to place or move suddenly in a new direction. In the game of *dodge* ball, players inside the circle must *dodge* balls that are thrown at them. *Dodge* can also mean keep away from something by being clever. The coach *dodged* reporters' questions by sneaking out the back door.

duck·

You *duck* your head if you lower it quickly to keep from being hit with something. You probably know that *duck* can also mean push someone's head under water. Another meaning of *duck* is get out of or dodge something. We *ducked* out of the movie before Pat saw us.

avoid
evade

Avoid and *evade* mean keep away from. But *avoid* usually means keep away from harm or danger or from something bad. If your older sister is on a diet, she *avoids* sweets. *Evade* usually means keep from doing or saying something by using a trick. You *evade* something if you don't face it directly. You may *evade* or dodge a question by asking another question or by changing the subject. You *avoid* dark caves; you wouldn't *evade* them.

When Miguel's older sister is on a diet, she **avoids** sweets.

doubt (v)   *Doubt* means feel uncertain about something. You *doubt* that you will stay downtown very long if you are uncertain about what you want to do. You could *doubt* that someone will keep a promise.

question   *Question* can mean feel a little bit uncertain. You *question* something when you wonder whether or not it is true or correct. You might *question* a friend's decision.

distrust   *Distrust* means doubt because you don't feel confident of or sure of something or someone. If someone lied to you, you might always *distrust* that person. The miser kept his money in a sock because he *distrusted* banks.

The miser kept his money in a sock because he **distrusted** banks.

suspect   *Suspect* means doubt or distrust something or someone. You can *suspect* someone of being guilty of wrongdoing even though you can't prove it. We *suspected* that birds were eating cherries from our tree.

ANTONYMS: believe, trust (v)

125

D

doubt (n)

A *doubt* is a feeling of not being sure or certain. You may have a feeling of *doubt* about someone who breaks a promise. You may suddenly have *doubts* about something you've always believed in—at some time in your life you might have had a feeling of *doubt* about the tooth fairy. When a person says "Without a *doubt*" or "There's no *doubt* about it," you know that person is sure that something is true. If you answer "I have my *doubts*," that person will know what you mean. A *doubt* can also be a feeling of not knowing what to do or what decision to make. Sometimes when you finally make a decision, you have a few *doubts* about it later.

misgiving

A *misgiving* is a doubt, especially about what will happen. You may have *misgivings* as you start to cross a creek by jumping from rock to rock.

distrust

Distrust is a feeling of doubt because you have no confidence in someone or something. The zoo keeper says he always approaches the lions with *distrust.*

skepticism

Skepticism is the feeling that you don't want to believe anything unless you have proof that it is true. Some people may show their *skepticism* when they ask you to prove something that you have just said.

suspicion

A *suspicion* is a doubt about something or someone. If you have a feeling of *suspicion* about someone, you feel that you can't trust or believe that person. As the snow began to fall, she realized that all her

Everyone in the room was placed under **suspicion.**

suspicions about a blizzard were true. Seeing a car race down the street at night without headlights on may arouse your *suspicion.* Everyone in the room at the time of the robbery was placed under *suspicion.*

ANTONYMS: confidence, belief, faith, trust (n)

dreadful   Something is *dreadful* if it fills you with dread or fear that something bad is about to happen. If you dread something, you are afraid and don't want to meet it face to face. A *dreadful* experience would be one that you could hardly bear to think of. A *dreadful* nightmare can make you shudder long after you wake up.

Most of the synonyms listed in this entry can be used wherever you mean *dreadful.* They are strong words, but many times people use them just to emphasize what they are describing. Something bad sounds even worse if you call it *dreadful.*

dreadful continued on page 128 ▶

dreadful continued from page 127

A **frightful** scream in the dark would scare the wits out of anyone.

awful

Awful describes something that is so powerful or dreadful it fills you with fear. A snowslide sweeping trees and rocks down a mountainside would be an *awful* sight.

terrible

Terrible means causing fear or filling with terror. It describes something that threatens to hurt you—a *terrible* flood, a *terrible* storm, or a *terrible* headache.

frightful

Frightful describes something that shocks or startles you. A *frightful* scream in the dark could scare the wits out of you. Seeing a *frightful* mask on a friend might shock you at first and then make you laugh.

appalling

Appalling describes something so shocking or dreadful that it leaves you speechless. An *appalling* sight could frighten you so much that you might be frozen to the spot.

dull

Dull means not bright or sharp. A *dull* day is cloudy. A *dull* person is not brilliant. A *dull* knife is not sharp enough to cut meat. *Dull* can also describe something that doesn't hold your interest. If a book is *dull,* you may never finish reading it. You might start to yawn if you have to listen to a *dull* story or a *dull* speech.

uninteresting

Uninteresting can describe anything that doesn't hold your attention. Things that are common and ordinary are often *uninteresting.* You lose interest in them right away. But something that is odd, strange, or funny is likely to be interesting because it excites your curiosity.

tiresome
tedious

Something that is *tiresome* or *tedious* is dull because it is long and tiring. Cutting the grass can be *tiresome*. Riding in a car for a long time is *tedious*. Picking weeds out of a garden can be *tedious*.

monotonous

Monotonous means dull and not varied enough to be interesting. Doing the same thing over and over is *monotonous*. Practicing a piece for a piano recital can sometimes become *monotonous*—to you and to your family.

Practicing a piece for a piano recital can sometimes become **monotonous.**

boring

Boring means dull and monotonous. A TV show may be so *boring* that you turn it off.

insipid

Insipid means dull and uninteresting. A talk or speech is *insipid* if it doesn't interest you or hold your attention.

ANTONYMS: bright, sharp, brilliant, interesting, varied, exciting

E

eager — *Eager* means interested in something and looking forward to becoming involved in it. An *eager* person is seldom indifferent to anything. If you're "ready and willing" to start a race, then you've trained faithfully and are *eager* to get on with it.

impatient
anxious — Both *impatient* and *anxious* may mean eager, but *anxious* adds the meaning of worried or afraid. The children were *impatient* for the games to start (no fear, the games would start sooner or later). Barbie and Flo were *anxious* to leave on the fishing trip before all the campsites were taken (great fear, all of the campsites had been taken before).

keen — *Keen* means sharp—a *keen* edge on a knife is sharp and cuts fast and easily. A *keen* person is sharp and alert, greatly interested in and quick to respond to whatever has captured his or her enthusiasm. *Keen* tennis players keep an eye on the ball every minute and play as hard as they can.

avid — *Avid* is a stronger word than eager. It suggests greediness. An *avid* stamp collector never has enough stamps. An *avid* baseball fan would like to see a game every day of the year.

ANTONYMS: indifferent, bored, uninterested

An **avid** stamp collector never has enough stamps.

edge (n)   An *edge* is the line or place where something ends. It can be a boundary line. The driveway marks the *edge* of our property. At the beach you may stand at the water's *edge.*

outline   An *outline* is a line that marks the edge of something. It shows the shape of an object or area. A coloring book has *outlines* of objects. Children fill in the *outlines* with colored crayons.

border   A *border* can be an edge. It can also be the area that marks the boundary of something. The Mexican *border* is a southern boundary of the United States. We planted bushes along the *border* of our yard.

frame   A *frame* can be a border that holds and supports something. A window *frame* encloses glass panes. A picture *frame* holds a picture.

margin   A *margin* is a border with a definite measurement. The *margin* of a page is the area around the edge; it has no writing on it.

curb   A *curb* is the raised edge along a sidewalk or street. It is sometimes hard to ride a bicycle over a *curb.*

rim   A *rim* is the outer edge of something curved. The *rims* of some dinner plates are decorated. When the moon is covered by a cloud, you may be able to see just its *rim.*

edge (n) continued on page 132 ▶

When people come to the **brink** of a cliff, if they take one more step, they will drop off.

brink
: A *brink* is the edge of something steep. When you come to the *brink* of a cliff, if you take one more step, you will drop off into thin air.

ANTONYM: center (n)

elastic
: *Elastic* describes something that can be stretched or bent or pulled out of shape and then be returned to its original size without any damage. A rubber band is *elastic.*

expandable
: You might say that a balloon is elastic. But you would be more accurate if you said a balloon is *expandable. Expandable* means able to be enlarged. You enlarge it when you blow air into it.

stretchable
: To understand *stretchable,* think of yourself taking a big, long stretch after you have been sitting in one place for an hour or two. When you stretch, you become taller. *Stretchable* describes something that can be pulled or made larger in one direction— length or width.

resilient
: *Resilient* is a good word to use when you mean that something easily slips back into shape when pressure on it has been

removed. A tree is *resilient* if it can remain standing through a hurricane. Something *resilient* will bend but won't break. It is not brittle. A *resilient* person is one who can undergo trouble without losing his or her good nature.

springy

Springy means both elastic and resilient. Something that is *springy* can easily withstand pressure and just as easily return to its original shape. A trampoline is *springy.* Jumping on it will make you bounce.

A trampoline is **springy.**

flexible

Flexible describes something that bends or turns without breaking. A *flexible* pipe can be bent in any direction to go around objects or corners. A *flexible* shoe bends and gives as you walk. A *flexible* person can change plans or ideas quickly if it becomes necessary.

ANTONYMS: brittle, inflexible, rigid, stiff

E

enclosed

Enclosed means closed in or held in some way. An *enclosed* porch is not an open porch but one that has walls and perhaps windows. *Enclosed* also means placed in an envelope. Father always looks at the advertisements that stores *enclose* with their monthly bills.

surrounded

If something is *surrounded,* it is enclosed or cut off on all sides. If your dog runs out of the yard, your friends might help you catch her by forming a circle around her. *Surrounded,* she couldn't get away!

blockaded

Blockaded means enclosed and cut off from everything. Ships couldn't get into the *blockaded* harbor.

fenced

Fenced is enclosed with a fence, railing, or wall. A *fenced* yard is safer for little children than an open one.

limited
restricted

Limited and *restricted* mean kept within limits or bounds. A *limited* time is usually given for a sale at a store. If you get home late from a friend's house, you may be *restricted* to your own house every evening for a week.

ANTONYMS: open (adj), unlimited, unrestricted

end (v)

End means stop doing something or come to the last part of something. It is the opposite of begin and start. This story begins and *ends* happily. When an argument starts, I always try to *end* it at once.

cease

Cease means stop or come to an end. The applause *ceased* as the curtain came down.

halt

Halt means end suddenly for a certain period of time. You *halt* if you stop when you are marching. But you might start up again. The hikers *halted* at the river.

finish
complete

Finish and *complete* mean end naturally what you started to do. You *finish* something when you have done everything that is necessary to end it. An author *finishes* a novel when he or she has written all of it. You usually *complete* a task that has been assigned to you. Have you *completed* your homework yet? I can't *complete* it until I *finish* reading the poem.

Something **terminates** when it stops and doesn't start again.

terminate

Something *terminates* when it stops and doesn't start again. You can *terminate* something that may or may not have been completed. The parade began at 169th Street and *terminated* at 180th Street. José *terminated* his subscription to the paper.

conclude

Conclude means finish something or come to a stop. It is the opposite of commence. She *concluded* her speech just as time ran out. A play commences when the curtain is raised and *concludes* when the curtain is lowered after the last act.

close

Close can mean end something by limiting the time. The swimming pool opens the first day of summer and *closes* after Labor Day.

ANTONYMS: begin, start (v), commence, open (v), originate

E

end (n)   The *end* is the last point to which something can go. Our house is at the *end* of this street. It can also mean the last part of something. *End* is the opposite of beginning. We were very tired by the *end* of our bicycle trip.

finish   The *finish* is the end of something that has been started or begun. *Finish* is usually used for the end of a race or fight. I was late for the start of the race, but I was there at the *finish.* In western movies, the sheriff and the outlaws usually fight to the *finish.*

conclusion   A *conclusion* is an end. George brought the meeting to a *conclusion.* Our teacher told us that at the *conclusion* of this book we will have a test. The detective came to the *conclusion* that the butler committed the crime.

termination   *Termination* means the end of something that has stopped but may not have been completed. A snowstorm caused the *termination* of the search.

close   A *close* is an end or a limit of time. At the *close* of day, the street lights come on.

See also *edge* (n), *limit* (n), *object* (n), *result* (n).

ANTONYMS: beginning (n), start (n), origin

endurance   *Endurance* means the power or ability to withstand hardships or difficulties. The swimmer showed great *endurance* when she swam across the English Channel.

stamina

Stamina is a good synonym for endurance. It means the strength to do something strenuous without giving up. Someone with a lot of *stamina* does not tire easily. The athletes who take part in the Olympic games need to have *stamina*.

backbone

Backbone means endurance plus strength of character. Gordon had the *backbone* to stand up for what was right even though his friends laughed at him.

fortitude

Fortitude is a very strong word. It means lasting endurance and bravery in the face of danger. Someone who possesses *fortitude* is patient, uncomplaining, and courageous. The pioneers of the American West had the *fortitude* to overcome many hardships and dangers.

See also *bravery*.

ANTONYM: weakness

The pioneers of the American West had the **fortitude** to overcome many hardships and dangers.

E

enjoy

You *enjoy* something that gives you pleasure. You can *enjoy* a good book or an exciting movie. You can also *enjoy* doing something. You might *enjoy* reading a good book or watching an exciting movie.

like

Like is a word you can use for almost anything you enjoy. If you enjoy something, you *like* it. You can *like* anything that is attractive, agreeable, or pleasing to you.

be fond of

You *are fond of* a person or thing if you like that person or object very much. You can *be fond of* your stepfather or you can *be fond of* pumpkin pie.

dote on

You *dote on* someone if you are so fond of that person that you do everything you can to please him or her. The man *dotes on* his granddaughter.

ANTONYMS: dislike (v), hate (v), detest, loathe

enlarge

Enlarge means become or make something become larger in size or capacity. When a photographer *enlarges* a picture, he or she makes it bigger. A person may *enlarge* a business by opening up new offices or hiring more salespeople.

unfold

Unfold means enlarge something by opening it up, like a blossom; spreading it out, like a blanket; or straightening it, like someone's arm. The flower petals *unfolded* in the morning sun. You may *unfold* a letter before you read it.

expand

If something *expands,* it becomes larger in size. Steel *expands* in hot weather and contracts in cold weather. Water *expands* as it freezes. You can *expand* a speech by adding more details and making it longer.

inflate

Inflate means cause something to become larger by adding air or gas. It is the opposite of deflate. If you *inflate* something, you cause it to expand. A balloon must be *inflated* with gas before it will rise. I *inflated* the flat bicycle tire.

A balloon must be **inflated** with gas before it will rise.

widen

Widen means enlarge an area or space. A new lane will *widen* a highway. Reading can help *widen* your interests.

swell

Swell can mean enlarge by puffing up. The place where a mosquito bites you usually *swells. Swell* can also mean grow or become too large. If a river *swells* from melting snow, it may overflow its banks.

magnify

Magnify means make something appear larger than it really is. Microscopes *magnify* objects. If you *magnify* a story, you exaggerate it.

amplify

Amplify usually means increase the sound or make louder. A microphone is used to *amplify* a speaker's voice. *Amplify* can also mean enlarge a statement by giving more examples or details. The reporter asked me to *amplify* my account of the accident.

See also *increase* (v).

ANTONYMS: contract (v), deflate, narrow (v), reduce, shrink

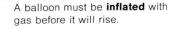

Magnify means make something appear larger than it is.

E

enter

Enter can mean merely go in or come in. We *entered* the bus at the airport. Or you can *enter* by forcing your way into something. The firefighters had to *enter* the house through a window to rescue the little boy. If someone *enters* the hospital, that person usually doesn't just go through the door, but stays awhile and is given treatment. Anyone who *enters* the shoe-repair business needs equipment to repair shoes and a store where the customers can bring and pick up their shoes. You can *enter* a conversation by joining in and taking part. You *enter* your teens on the day that you become thirteen years old.

penetrate

Penetrate means pass or see into or through something. Squirrels can *penetrate* nut shells with their teeth. My eyes could not *penetrate* the darkness in the theater. If you were deep in thought, the phone might ring three times before the sound *penetrated* your mind. Smoke *penetrated* the whole house.

Smoke **penetrated** the whole house.

pierce
: *Pierce* means enter sharply with a pointed object. You can *pierce* a piece of meat with a fork, or you can *pierce* a target with an arrow. You can also say that a shrill sound *pierces* a quiet night.

invade
: *Invade* means enter in order to conquer or to cause some harm. World War II began in Europe when Germany *invaded* Poland on September 1, 1939. In health class you learned that when germs *invade* the body, you become ill.

event
: Things are happening in the world every minute. If the things that happen are important, they are called *events. Events* such as birthdays and anniversaries are often celebrated.

incident
: An *incident* is not as important as an event. *Incidents* seldom are celebrated. Sometimes an event becomes an *incident* after many years have passed. At the time a space flight occurs it is an event. But after many years have passed and other flights have been completed, it becomes an *incident* in history.

occurrence
: An *occurrence* is an incident that is usually unexpected and has not been planned ahead of time. The bus accident was a frightening *occurrence.*

happening
: A *happening* is simply anything that takes place. Meeting a friend in that crowd was a pleasant *happening.*

event continued on page 142 ▶

episode

An *episode* is almost like an incident, but an *episode* is one of a number of related incidents. It might be one thing that happens in a story. Last night we watched the second *episode* of Flash Gordon on TV.

circumstance

A *circumstance* can be one of several incidents or events that cause other things to happen. In the sentence "The *circumstances* that made me late for my piano lesson were not my doing," *circumstances* means incidents. In the sentence "Many *circumstances* in history have helped make the problems of today," *circumstances* means events.

See also *result* (n).

examine

Examine means look at something closely and carefully. It also means find out all you can about something by asking questions. You *examine* things in order to learn more about them. A dentist *examines* your teeth to see if you have any cavities. Attorneys *examine* and cross-examine witnesses in a court trial.

investigate
inspect
scrutinize

Investigate, inspect, and *scrutinize* mean examine something thoroughly. Detectives *investigate* crimes. Meat and dairy products have to be *inspected* before they can be sold. Art critics *scrutinize* paintings.

test

Test can mean examine something to see if it measures up to a set standard. Officials of the government *test* water to see if it is safe to drink.

examine continued

explore

Explore usually means examine something new or unknown. Scientists are *exploring* outer space. A spelunker *explores* caves. If you think about doing something you have never done or that has never been done before, you might say that you are "*exploring* the possibilities" of doing it.

Some children like to **explore** caves.

example

An *example* is something that describes or explains or warns against other things which are not like it. A math book gives *examples* to show how to solve problems. My sick cousin is an *example* of what happens to people who eat green apples. An *example* can also be a person or thing to be copied. Children follow the *example* of parents or older brothers and sisters. When you "set an *example*," you do something that other people will imitate.

sample
specimen

A *sample* and a *specimen* are examples taken from something or a group of things. A salesperson shows *samples* of products to customers. You study *specimens* of insects, animals, and plants in biology.

example continued on page 144 ▶

example continued from page 143

E

illustration — An *illustration* is an example that explains or helps make something clear. Pictures, diagrams, maps, and stories can be used as *illustrations*. Your thesaurus gives you *illustrations* of how to use words and of how some words got their meanings.

original model — An *original* or a *model* is something from which other things are copied. Art students sometimes copy an *original* painted by a famous artist. They also often use a person who poses for them as a *model*. A sculptor usually makes a small *model* before she begins a huge statue.

A sculptor usually makes a small **model** before she begins a huge statue.

pattern — A *pattern* is a very detailed model showing the parts from which something is made. Mother followed a *pattern* when she cut out my costume.

ideal — An *ideal* is a perfect model or the best example to follow. John Glenn, one of the seven original astronauts, is my *ideal*.

The hikers looked **fatigued** as they stumbled into camp.

exhausted

Exhausted means used up. When you have done hard work or strenuous exercise until your strength is completely used up, you become *exhausted.* When you have used up your whole supply of something, it is *exhausted.* By the time each one in the family had taken a shower, our supply of hot water was *exhausted.*

tired

If you are *tired,* either your strength or your patience is exhausted. Lots of people and noise on a bus may make the bus driver *tired* and cross.

weary

You are *weary* if you are so tired that you can't face another minute of doing something. Riding in a car all day long may make you *weary.*

fatigued

You are *fatigued* if you have used up so much energy that you can hardly move. The hikers looked *fatigued* as they stumbled into camp. I was *fatigued* after just one game of tennis.

depleted
bankrupt

Depleted and *bankrupt* usually describe something that is exhausted because it is almost empty or because its supply has been drained away. A forest is *depleted* if so many trees have been cut down that it can hardly be called a forest any more. A *depleted* water supply may result from too little rainfall. A *bankrupt* business is unable to pay its bills. You are *bankrupt* if you have used up all your money and declare that you have no way of getting more to pay your bills.

Diane **explained** how the earth's rotation causes night and day.

explain

Explain means tell how to do something or tell the meaning of something. When you *explain* something, you make it clear, plain, and easy to understand. This pamphlet *explains* the care and feeding of a boa constrictor. Diane *explained* how the earth's rotation causes night and day.

clarify

Clarify means make something clearer than it is now. Using a word in a sentence can *clarify* its meaning. An author writes a footnote when he or she wants to *clarify* a sentence on a page.

describe
portray

Describe and *portray* mean explain in words or in pictures how something is or looks. This manual *describes* how to make a boat. A novel might *portray* the exciting adventures of an explorer.

justify

Justify means explain or give a reason for doing something you did. How can we *justify* this expensive telephone bill?

interpret

When you *interpret* something, you tell what you think it means. Different people may *interpret* the same thing in different ways. I tried to *interpret* the meaning of my dream. If you understand French and German, you can *interpret* for a Frenchman and a German who do not understand each other. You will listen to the person speaking French; then you will repeat in German to the German, what has been said in French.

solve

Solve means find an answer or explain a problem. Can you *solve* this riddle?

F

failure

A *failure* is anything that does not succeed. The *failure* of the farmers' crops was caused by a lack of rain. *Failure* also means not doing something that should be done. *Failure* to water your plants will cause them to die. My *failure* to read the road signs made me lose the way.

There are many kinds of *failure* and different words we can use for each kind.

crash

A *crash* is a violent hitting together or breaking to pieces. We speak of a *crash* or collision between two cars. But *crash* can also mean a complete failure in the whole country's business. The stock market *crash* in 1929 began the Depression.

bankruptcy

Bankruptcy is the failure of a business. A company that can't get enough money to pay its bills and goes deeply into debt may have to declare *bankruptcy*. People can also declare *bankruptcy*.

breakdown

A *breakdown* is a failure to work or function properly. The factory had to close for the day because of a *breakdown* in the machinery. A *breakdown* can also be a failure in a person's health. A person who works too long and too hard may have a *breakdown.*

collapse

A *collapse* is the falling in or giving way of something. The fire caused the *collapse* of the roof of the building.

failure continued on page 148 ▶

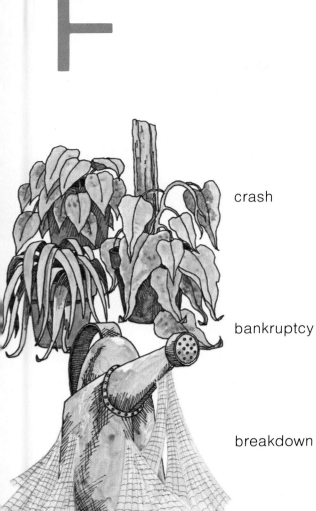

Failure to water plants will cause them to die.

The rain made the picnic a **fizzle.**

fizzle	*Fizzle* can mean the failure of something after a good start or beginning. The rain made the picnic a *fizzle.*
fiasco	*Fiasco* is a good word for a complete failure. A party is a *fiasco* if no one shows up. My bread making was a *fiasco* because I forgot to put yeast in the dough.
	ANTONYM: success
fair (adj)	*Fair* means right and honest. If something is *fair,* it is right for everyone concerned. Someone who is *fair* wants everyone to have an equal share or get the same chance as everyone else. A judge tries to be *fair* and doesn't take sides. A judge listens to everyone before making up his or her mind.
just	*Just* means right, fair, and lawful. We speak of a *just* decision, a *just* rule, a *just* punishment, or a *just* reward.

148

equal

Equal can also mean fair. In this guessing game everyone has an *equal* chance to win. When you receive an *equal* share of something, you get the same amount as everyone else.

good

Good can mean fair. We say a person is *good* if he or she does what is right, proper, and acceptable. A judge can make a *good* decision. A *good* game is one played fairly and well.

impartial
unbiased

If you are *impartial* or *unbiased*, you listen to both sides of an argument with an open mind. You don't make up your mind ahead of time. *Impartial* means without favoring or liking one thing more than another. Jury members must be *impartial* when they decide on a verdict. *Unbiased* means not letting your own personal feelings, likes, and dislikes influence your decisions. It is best to have an *unbiased* person settle an argument or quarrel.

See also *beautiful*.

ANTONYMS: unfair, biased, partial, unjust

He received an **equal** share.

They used bits of paper to make a **fake** snowstorm for a play.

fake (adj)   *Fake* means not real. Some *fake* furs look almost real. You can use bits of paper to make a *fake* snowstorm for a play.

imitation   *Imitation* means fake. Plastic material is used to make *imitation* leather.

counterfeit   *Counterfeit* money is very carefully (and dishonestly) made to look exactly like real money. A *counterfeit* painting may be an excellent copy of a famous painting, but it isn't as valuable as the original.

false   *False* is not true. A person may make a *false* statement either by mistake or on purpose to deceive you.

unreal   *Unreal* means not real or genuine. You may have a dream that seems real, but whatever happens in a dream is *unreal.*

untrue   If something is *untrue,* it is false or incorrect. You may hear a rumor about something and then find out it's *untrue.*

ANTONYMS: real, true, genuine

fall (v)

Fall means come down from a higher position or come down suddenly. It is the opposite of rise. Snow *falls*. Leaves *fall*. You may *fall* if you stumble on a rock. *Fall* can also mean become less or lower. Her voice rises when she's angry and *falls* when she's calm. A river *falls* after a flood. You also say that you *fall* asleep or that night *falls*.

descend

Descend means fall or come down slowly and gradually. An airplane *descends* for a landing. It ascends when it takes off and rises in the sky. The road *descends* into the valley.

drop

Drop means fall or let something fall suddenly or unexpectedly. Petals *drop* from flowers. Dom *dropped* the mirror when he heard the loud noise behind him.

swoop

Swoop means drop swiftly in order to seize something. The gull *swooped* down, caught a fish, and flew away.

sink

Sink means fall or become lower gradually. A boat that fills with water will *sink* to the bottom of a lake. In a silent movie we saw, a carpenter was hit with a board and *sank* to the ground. The sun *sinks* in the west.

fail

Fail can mean fall short of what is expected. You will get in trouble if you *fail* to pay your income tax. If you *fail* to get to the airport on time, you will miss your plane.

ANTONYMS: rise (v), ascend

A carpenter in a silent movie was hit and **sank** to the ground.

F

famous

Famous means widely known or honored. One act can make you *famous,* or a whole life well spent may make you *famous.* The pitcher who helps a team win a World Series is *famous* for a while. After a few months or years, that same pitcher may be forgotten and be living an obscure life. A *famous* doctor may have saved many lives.

famed

Famed is another word for famous. A *famed* restaurant is one that is well known for some special food served there. Certain parts of our country are *famed* for their mountains or weather or seashore.

noted

Noted means famous because of some accomplishment. We learned that Holland was *noted* for growing tulips.

notorious

Notorious means famous because of something bad or at least something not very good. A certain shop may be *notorious* for charging high prices. *Notorious* is almost always used when outlaws are described. Jesse James was *notorious* for robbing banks and trains.

renowned

Renowned means famous and highly honored. A *renowned* pianist may be asked to play for the President.

distinguished eminent

Distinguished and *eminent* mean noted for excellence and having a reputation above others. Who is the most *distinguished* person in the Senate? Some *eminent* doctors met to discuss the latest developments in medicine.

ANTONYMS: obscure (adj), unknown

fast (adj)

Fast is the opposite of slow. As an adjective, *fast* means moving, happening, or acting with speed. A hot rod is a *fast* car. Hockey is a *fast* game.

rapid

Rapid means fast in movement. A *rapid* river has a strong current. A sluggish person does not walk at a *rapid* pace.

speedy
swift

Speedy and *swift* mean fast moving or happening very fast. A *speedy* person hurries along and is not poky. In ancient Greece, *swift* runners delivered messages between cities. Rabbits are *swift* animals.

quick

Quick means fast in doing something. Mom had a *quick* breakfast before leaving for the office. *Quick* can also mean alert or fast in learning something. You may be *quick* in foreign languages. Or you may be *quick* to notice something new or different.

fleet

Fleet can be used to describe an animal or a person who is very fast and swift. Deer are *fleet*. The *fleet* dancers hardly touched the ground.

instant
immediate
instantaneous

Instant, immediate, and *instantaneous* can all describe something that is made or done without delay or at once. You can cook *instant* rice in a very short time. I gave an *immediate* reply to the invitation. When I stepped on the snake, its reaction was *instantaneous.*

See also *sudden.*

ANTONYMS: slow (adj), sluggish, poky

The **fleet** dancers hardly touched the ground.

F

Galley slaves were **chained** to their oars and forced to row the ancient warships across the sea.

chain	*Chain* means fasten with a chain, or series of metal links. In history we read how galley slaves were *chained* to their oars and forced to row the ancient warships across the sea.
tether	*Tether* can mean fasten something. You might *tether* a dog to a post so it can move around but can't wander away from your yard.
hitch	You *hitch* a horse to a post when you wrap the reins around the post or slip them through a ring. A stalled car is *hitched* to a tow truck with chains and hooks.

ANTONYMS: free (v), loosen, separate (v), sever, unbind, untie

fear (n)
Fear is familiar to most people. It is an unpleasant and upsetting feeling people have when they are threatened with danger. When Arnie heard a strange noise at the door, his *fear* carried him right up the stairs and into a closet. Sometimes we use *fear* to mean only a mild concern or worry about something. I have a *fear* that rain will spoil our day at the carnival.

fright
Fright is sudden fear. The sound of a siren always gives me a terrible *fright.*

alarm
Alarm also means sudden fear. You feel *alarm* when you suddenly become aware of danger nearby. *Alarm* showed on the driver's face when the bus skidded on a patch of ice.

dread
Dread is intense fear of something that may happen. It suggests fear of facing whatever is coming. The thought of returning to the empty house at night filled her with *dread.*

panic
Panic is sudden and extreme fright, which results in unreasonable and frantic activity. It was the driver's *panic* that caused him to step on the gas instead of the brake after the car went over the curb. *Panic* is often used to mean the fear felt by a group, not just one person. A shout of "Fire!" in a crowded theater can cause a *panic.*

terror
Terror is extreme and intense fright. The approaching flood spread *terror* throughout the town.

ANTONYMS: calmness, fearlessness

157

F

fierce

Fierce can be used to describe people or animals or things. It means wild or threatening or cruel. The *fierce* dog sent the letter carrier running. Walt became *fierce* when I broke his favorite toy. A *fierce* rainstorm caused the failure of our electricity.

ferocious

Ferocious means extremely fierce and wild. The most *ferocious* tiger is a hungry one. *Ferocious* usually describes actions like those of wild animals. Wendy grabbed a shovel and began a *ferocious* attack on the snowdrift.

violent

Violent means uncontrolled and destructive. Hurricanes and tornadoes are *violent.* People are sometimes *violent* when they become very angry or upset. The umpire's decision caused a *violent* reaction among the baseball fans.

raging

Raging also means violent. The *raging* fire destroyed everything in its path. "The dog chewed my new book and ruined it," roared my *raging* sister.

savage

Savage means wild or uncontrolled. The elephant herd made a *savage* attack on the village.

See also *wild.*

ANTONYMS: gentle, harmless, mild, tame (adj)

fight (v)

Fight is an everyday word. Chances are that it is even more an everyday action. You probably *fight* the idea of getting out of bed when your alarm goes off.

The **raging** fire destroyed everything in its path.

At breakfast if you drink your milk too fast, you may have to *fight* for breath. It's easier to *fight* for the last pancake than it is to *defend* the things you say in an argument with your sister. She may *attack* your excuse for forgetting to wake her. The two of you may *argue* over whose turn it is to feed the dog.

You might be trying to *fight* your way through a difficult assignment in school. During the long afternoon some people have to *combat* drowsiness or *fight* to stay awake. After school you may help your basketball team *fight* for the championship. Your team may be *battling* for first place or may be *struggling* up from the bottom.

On a rainy day you could *fight* an icy wind all the way home, then *wrestle* with homework. After you watch spacemen *invade* the earth, politicians *attack* each other in speeches, sailors *contend* with the sea, lawyers *defend* criminals, and football teams *fight* to be in a bowl game, you may feel like turning off the TV. Chances are that after such a tiring day, you won't *disagree* with anyone who suggests that it's time to go to bed.

Fight is an everyday word. You won't have to *fight* too hard to find more exciting words to use.

Argue, attack, and *battle* are other good *fight* words.

find (v)

Find means come upon something that is lost or come to know something new. Bess *found* a set of keys on the street. When you *find out* something, you come to know information about it. I finally *found out* what became of my model boat.

Abby finally **found out** what became of her model boat.

discover

Discover means find something for the first time. Whatever is *discovered* has been there before but hasn't been seen or known about. Lewis and Clark *discovered* that the Columbia River leads to the Pacific Ocean. Manufacturers have *discovered* many uses for steel.

detect

Detect means find something that is usually hidden, by carefully searching or watching for it. Johann *detected* a mistake in the violinist's performance.

learn

Learn means find out or come to know something. They are *learning* to speak French.

ascertain
determine

Ascertain and *determine* can mean find out exactly. Through investigations and experiments, scientists have *ascertained* the distances between the planets in our solar system. An eye doctor can *determine* the kind of glasses you might need by testing your eyes.

ANTONYMS: hide (v), forget, lose

160

firm (adj)   *Firm* means not easily moved out of place or out of shape when you use it as an adjective. If a player has a *firm* grip on a bat, it won't slip out of his or her hands. When mud dries in the sun, it becomes *firm*. *Firm* can also mean not easily changed. We say that someone has a *firm* belief in something or takes a *firm* stand on a subject when that person is sure that he or she is right.

hard   We say something is *hard* when it is so strong and stiff that it resists any kind of pressure or force. Maple is a *hard* wood; pine is a soft wood. *Hard* also describes something that is difficult to do. So it is *hard* to spread *hard* butter.

solid   *Solid* means hard, firm, and sturdy. A *solid* board has no holes or cracks in it. Something that is *solid* is not hollow.

stiff
rigid   *Stiff* and *rigid* mean unbending or not easily moved. They are the opposite of soft, limp, and flabby. Great-grandpa always liked *stiff* collars. Inez's arms and legs felt *stiff* after exercising for a long time. Something *rigid* cannot be bent without being broken. Ice and glass are *rigid*. We also say that rules are *rigid* when they are strictly enforced or hard to obey.

Barney's great-grandpa always liked **stiff** collars.

inflexible   *Inflexible* also means firm and not capable of being bent. A hard metal is *inflexible*, but rubber is flexible. We can also say that a person is *inflexible* or has an *inflexible*

firm (adj) continued on page 162 ▶

F

firm (adj) continued from page 161

attitude toward something if nothing can persuade that person to change his or her mind.

steady   *Steady* means firm in position or in movement. The ship remained *steady* even in the rough seas. The archer took a *steady* aim before shooting the arrow.

immovable   Something is *immovable* if it can't easily be moved out of place. The farmer used a crowbar but still couldn't loosen the *immovable* boulder.

unshaken   *Unshaken* means firm and not easily shaken or disturbed. If you cannot be bullied into doing something you don't want to do, you remain *unshaken*.

See also *tough.*

ANTONYMS: soft, hollow, limp (adj), flabby, flexible, unsteady, movable

The archer took **steady** aim before shooting the arrow.

firm (n)

A *firm* can be a business that is operated by two or more people. It could be a store or a dry-cleaning plant or a factory or even an airline. A person who finishes law school sometimes joins a *firm* of lawyers.

The Jones brothers formed a **partnership.**

• company

A *company* often is a firm that makes or sells products or services. Our washing machine was manufactured by a *company* in Michigan.

• corporation

A *corporation* is another kind of business owned by one or more persons. The owners act as one united group when dealing with other firms. Many large *corporations* have branch offices in other countries. My grandmother bought stock in a *corporation.*

• partnership

A *partnership* is a legal agreement between two or more people who are owners of a business. When the Jones brothers formed a *partnership,* they each put up ten thousand dollars.

follow

Follow means go in the same direction that something or someone else has gone. If you *follow* the ball with your eyes, you can see where it goes. You can also *follow* a trail or a park ranger through the woods.

chase

Chase means run after someone in order to overtake or catch that person. The cowhand *chased* the stray calves and drove them back to the herd. *Chase* also means cause something to leave. The mouse *chased* the cat out the door.

follow continued on page 164 ▶

F

follow continued from page 163

hunt

Hunt means go after something or someone whose whereabouts are unknown. Jenny *hunted* everywhere for her glasses and finally found them on top of her head. We had to *hunt* all morning before we found the lost dog.

pursue

Pursue means go after someone or something with determination until you are successful. The reporter *pursued* the question and finally got an answer.

track

Track means follow the path of something by watching for clues to its movements. Astronomers *track* the path of a star with a telescope. The sheriff's posse *tracked* the outlaws into the hills.

trail

Trail means follow at a distance, often by using clues such as tracks. We *trailed* the cat to the fish store.

See also *imitate.*

ANTONYMS: lead (v), precede

They **trailed** the cat to the fish store.

164

Bernie **cheated** Marie out of her piece of cake by eating it when she wasn't looking.

fool (v)   *Fool* means make someone believe that something is true or real when it actually isn't. You may *fool* someone just for fun. People *fool* each other on April Fools' Day.

cheat   *Cheat* means fool or take advantage of a person by doing something he or she doesn't notice. Bernie *cheated* me out of my piece of cake by eating it when I wasn't looking.

mislead   *Mislead* means cause to go in the wrong direction or away from the truth. If you are offered something free and later find that you have to pay for it, someone is *misleading* you. The low price of this motorcycle *misled* me into thinking that it was a real bargain.

trick   *Trick* means fool by cheating or misleading. A mind reader *tricks* the audience.

deceive hoodwink   *Deceive* and *hoodwink* mean give a false impression in order to fool and confuse someone. One person can *deceive* another person by lying or by stretching the truth. The industrial spy *hoodwinked* the other company and stole the perfume formula.

bluff   *Bluff* means fool someone by pretending that you can do something that you really won't or can't. Minnie was *bluffing* when she said she could answer all the questions.

See also *pretend.*

F

foolish

Foolish means without sense or judgment. I made a *foolish* mistake on the crossword puzzle. I was *foolish* not to wear boots on a snowy day.

funny
ridiculous

Funny and *ridiculous* describe something so foolish it makes you laugh. Something that is strange or unexpected is often called *funny.* Emmet looked very *funny* in his *ridiculous* clown costume.

silly

Silly means foolish and ridiculous because of strange ways of talking or strange behavior. The monkeys in the zoo usually do *silly* tricks in their cages.

absurd

Absurd means so foolish it doesn't make much sense. It's *absurd* never to admit your mistakes. Gina had some *absurd* dream about becoming invisible.

The **idiotic** horse refused to eat the carrots Lucy brought.

idiotic

Idiotic means very foolish and stupid. It would be *idiotic* to jump into the deep end of a pool if you can't swim. The *idiotic* horse refused to eat the carrots I brought.

nonsensical

Something that is *nonsensical* is absurd and meaningless. Gibberish is *nonsensical* talk.

ANTONYMS: reasonable, sensible, wise

166

force (v)   *Force* means use power or strength to make a person do something. You can be *forced* to do something against your will. Sally's logical argument *forced* me to change my mind. *Force* can also mean make something happen. He *forced* open the locked door. A gust of wind *forced* the sailboat to overturn.

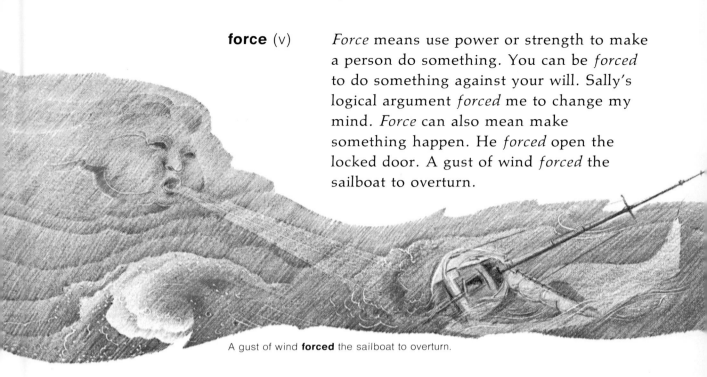

A gust of wind **forced** the sailboat to overturn.

propel   *Propel* means force to move forward or onward. Fuel *propels* jet planes and large boats. Your legs *propel* you when you swim.

require   You can be *required* to do something by law. You are *required* to pass a driver's test before you get your license.

compel   *Compel* means force a person to do something. Opal was *compelled* to clean the basement before she could invite her friends over. The heavy traffic *compelled* us to travel slowly.

coerce   *Coerce* is stronger than compel. You can be *coerced* into doing something by a punishment or a threat. The street gang *coerced* Rico into joining them.

See also *push* (v), *urge*.

167

F

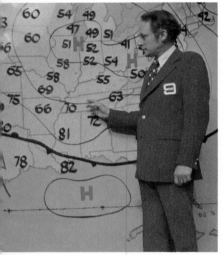

A meteorologist **forecasts** tomorrow's weather.

forecast (v)   If you *forecast* that something is going to happen, you announce that it will happen before it does. Often you can *forecast* something after you have analyzed and studied the known facts. A meteorologist, for instance, *forecasts* tomorrow's weather after studying today's weather conditions and weather maps.

predict   *Predict,* like forecast, means tell of something that will happen in the future. People can often *predict* certain things by using their knowledge and experience. Physicians can usually *predict* the course of mumps because they know how the human body reacts to this disease.

foretell   *Foretell* means tell about something before it happens. A fortune teller says that he can look at your hand and *foretell* your future. It was such a good mystery story that no one could have *foretold* the end.

prophesy   *Prophesy* means foretell future happenings. In Greek and Roman times, certain persons claimed that they were told by the gods to *prophesy.* Even today some people *prophesy* that the end of the world is coming.

anticipate   *Anticipate* means prepare ahead of time for something good or bad. If you know that your mother will be working late, you may *anticipate* a late dinner and eat a snack. *Anticipating* rain, I brought an umbrella to the picnic.

foresee

Foresee means see ahead of time that something is going to happen. No one could *foresee* that the bus would have a flat tire.

warn

Warn means tell someone of possible danger so that he or she can avoid it. You might *warn* your young sister to watch for cars when she is crossing the street.

forewarn

Forewarn means warn a person of danger well in advance. The Farm Bureau *forewarned* farmers of an early frost.

forecast (n)

A *forecast* is the announcement that something is likely to happen or take place in the future. Like the verb, a *forecast* is made after known facts have been analyzed and studied. Light rain or snow is the *forecast* for tomorrow.

prediction

A *prediction* is what has been predicted, or a telling of something in advance. A *prediction* is based on knowledge or experience. As the earliest election returns come in, computers make *predictions* about the outcome.

prophecy

A *prophecy* is a forecast of a future event. It is what you prophesy. People often make *prophecies* about what the world might be like one hundred years from now.

prognostication

A *prognostication* is a prediction. Some people make interesting *prognostications* about world affairs.

See also *warning.*

F

foreign

People who are born and reared in one country but later live in another are *foreign* to the country in which they are living. *Foreign* can also mean not belonging or out of place. *Foreign* matter in the eye may be a speck of dirt.

alien

Alien means strange or different in some way. You could say that one penguin in a flock of ducks is *alien* to the others.

outlandish

In ancient times, people traveled very little. When strangers from other countries or lands did appear, wearing their usual clothes and speaking their own languages, they were called "outlanders." So today *outlandish* means unusual or strange because it is foreign or it belongs to another country. The clothing of the people who live in the Arctic would probably seem *outlandish* to natives of a desert.

The clothing of people who live in the Arctic seems **outlandish** to natives of a desert.

extraneous

Extraneous means not forming an essential part of something, or foreign to it. Racing stripes on a car are *extraneous.* They are not needed to make the car run.

external

External means outside of something. His *external* appearance was that of a beast, but he was really an enchanted prince. An *external* force may cause you to do something you did not expect to do. Ants may be the *external* force that causes you to end a picnic suddenly.

See also *odd*.

free (v)

Free means set loose. You can *free* a butterfly from a net or *free* a clogged drain. The lumberjacks *freed* the logs that were causing a jam in the river.

release

Release also means set loose, but without the promise of lasting freedom. A manager may *release* an employee from certain duties so that person may help someone in another department.

rescue

Rescue means free something or someone from danger by quick action. I *rescued* the newspaper from a puddle by grabbing it before it got all wet.

liberate

Liberate means free or set at liberty. Prisoners in some countries are *liberated* when the king or queen pardons them.

emancipate

Emancipate means free a person from slavery or from the control or power of another. Slaves were *emancipated* during the Civil War.

ransom

Ransom means free by paying a price. The captives were *ransomed* by an agreement between the two governments.

See also *save*.

F

friendly

Friendly means acting like a friend. A *friendly* person is good-natured, pleasant, and always helpful. Someone who is *friendly* is not hostile or quarrelsome. That dog is very *friendly* when you speak to it.

kind

Kind means friendly, thoughtful, and considerate. A *kind* person is interested in other people, is willing to help them, and is never cruel.

neighborly

Neighborly really means acting like a neighbor to those who live nearby. But it can also describe anyone who is friendly and kind to others.

sociable

Someone who is *sociable* enjoys being with other people. A *sociable* person likes to entertain people and go to social gatherings.

genial

Genial means cheerful, smiling, and pleasant. A *genial* person puts people at ease and makes them feel welcome. The new student was pleased that everyone was *genial.*

amiable

An *amiable* person is friendly, agreeable, and courteous to others. He or she tries to please others and make them happy. Anita was *amiable* when I asked her to wait for me.

See also *thoughtful.*

ANTONYMS: quarrelsome, cruel, mean (adj), unfriendly, unkind

That dog is very **friendly** when you speak to it.

G

gather

Gather means bring something together into one place or group. You might *gather* leaves or *gather* wild flowers on a hike through the woods. *Gather* can also mean come together into one place or group. A group may *gather* around a campfire to toast marshmallows. A crowd often *gathers* if there has been an accident. Clouds *gather* in the sky before a storm. Another meaning of *gather* is put ideas together in your mind. From their conversation, Adam *gathered* that everyone planned to go surfing this weekend.

collect

Collect can be used to mean gather. It is often used when objects are carefully selected and gathered for a definite purpose. You might enjoy *collecting* stamps or antiques. A lawyer *collects* evidence.

harvest

Harvest means gather grain or crops. In the early days, farmers used scythes when they *harvested* their grain crop; now they use large machines.

gather continued on page 174 ▶

In the early days, farmers used scythes when they **harvested** their grain crop.

G

Things **accumulate** when they gather in a heap or pile or in one place.

gather continued from page 173

accumulate

Things *accumulate* when they gather in a heap or pile or in one place. Leaves will *accumulate* on your lawn if you do not rake them. Dust *accumulated* in the empty house. My aunt and uncle *accumulated* a fortune by saving and investing their money. Suzanne has *accumulated* a large collection of record albums.

assemble

Assemble can be used when people gather, or meet together, for a convention or a meeting. Our representatives in Congress *assemble* in Washington to make and pass laws.

congregate

Congregate is used when people come together and form a crowd. Crowds often *congregate* during a parade. When the excitement is over, the people scatter in different directions.

ANTONYMS: scatter, disperse, separate (v)

gathering

A *gathering* is a coming together or a bringing together of something. A *gathering* of corn or wheat or apples is a harvest. A *gathering* of cattle is a roundup. You can probably think of other kinds of *gatherings*. A *group* is a kind of *gathering*. Look up *group* and see the words listed there.

There are many words for *gatherings* of people. Actually, though, you'll find two kinds in this book.

A *gathering* may be people brought or called together at a certain time for some special purpose. Look up *meeting* to find words for this kind of *gathering.*

People may gather in one place at one time even though they were not actually called together. This kind of *gathering* is a *crowd.* These people may just happen to gather because they are all interested in the same thing at the same time—like swimming at the beach or pool or getting to work in the morning. Look up *crowd* (n) and the words listed in that entry.

Party sounds like a good word (and a good reason) for calling people together. But the word *party* also belongs to another kind of *gathering.* This is a group of people gathered to do something together, like a party of tourists or a political party. To see other kinds of parties or groups of people working or playing together, look at the words listed in the entry *party.*

People may form a group because they all have an interest in one special thing. These groups do not have to be gathered in a certain place, though they usually do have meetings. They may be organized with a president and vice-president and other officers. The members of groups like these may be in different parts of the world, but they are joined by this interest. Look up *club* (n) to find other groups.

Some groups of people working together are listed and explained in the entry *firm* (n).

G

gentle

Gentle means not harsh or rough or mean. A *gentle* breeze makes little ripples on a lake. A harsh wind can cause large waves. A *gentle* person is kind and considerate. He or she is not mean. A nurse is *gentle,* not rough, with patients. Leslie gave me a *gentle* pat on the shoulder. The trainer spoke to the seal in a *gentle* voice.

soft

Soft can mean gentle, not rough or loud. The child's touch was *soft,* not rough. A *soft* light is not too bright or glaring. The sun made a *soft* light in the thick forest. The air feels *soft* after a spring shower. The woman spoke to the baby in a *soft* voice. The music in the background was *soft* and quiet. Satin is a *soft* material.

tender

The **tender** buds pushed through the snow.

Tender can mean delicate and gentle. The *tender* buds pushed through the snow. She gave the sick child *tender* care.

mild

Mild means gentle and calm. A *mild* man does not often lose his temper. Clark Kent is a *mild*-mannered reporter. Winters are *mild* in the South. They are usually harsh in the North. A *mild* flavor is not bitter or sharp.

• moderate

Moderate can mean just right or about in the middle. A *moderate* climate is neither too hot nor too cold. A *moderate* price for five pounds of sugar is a price you'd be willing to pay. An excessive price might make you decide to do without sugar. A *moderate* volume on a radio is neither too loud nor too quiet.

176

soothing

Soothing means gentle, pleasing, and comforting. Quiet music is *soothing.* The vet's *soothing* touch calmed the frightened horse. Honey is *soothing* to a sore throat.

See also *calm* (adj).

ANTONYMS: harsh, rough, mean (adj), loud, bitter, sharp, excessive, hard, tough

give

Give is an interesting word. You can do many kinds of giving. You can *give* a cheer, *give* a hand, *give* a look, *give* advice. You *give* a gift. You *give* thanks. You *give* a kiss or a smile. If you think about it, though, there are really only three ways to *give.*

First, you can *present* something to someone, of your own free will and, sometimes, with your own hands. In the entry *present* (v) you will find other words for this kind of giving—whether it's something for a birthday, first prize, a Picasso, or whatever a person leaves when he or she dies.

Second, you can *allow* something. You can *give* permission or *give* the right to do something. You may *allow* something to go on or to be, just because you don't stop it or object to it. Look at the entry *allow* and see what this kind of giving includes.

Third, you can *surrender.* You can *give in, give away, give out, give up.* Look up *surrender* (v) and see.

G

grasp (v)

Grasp means get or take hold of. People *grasp* with their fingers, hands, or arms. *Grasping* the hand of another person is a sign of friendship. He *grasped* the railing to keep from falling down the stairs. A sea gull *grasps* fish with its strong beak.

grip
clasp
clutch

Grip, clasp, clutch, are other words for grasping and holding something firmly and tightly. A baseball player *grips* the bat. The boy was *clasping* a rabbit that he had found. The girl *clutched* the kitten and wouldn't let go of it.

grab
snatch

Grab and *snatch* mean grasp something quickly and suddenly. Carl *grabbed* a piece of candy before the box was passed. Denise *snatched* the picture out of my hands before I had a chance to see it.

seize

Seize means take something by force. The detective *seized* the suspect.

ANTONYMS: let go, abandon, release (v)

The detective **seized** the suspect.

The largest of the five Great Lakes is Lake **Superior.**

great

Great can mean big and large. It also means outstanding, well known, and important. People, things, and events may be *great*. A skyscraper is a *great* building, and a cottage is usually a small one. Jane Addams was a *great* American social worker. Electricity was a *great* discovery. People often say *great* when they mean wonderful or very good. The weather is *great* today.

There are a *great* number of other words you could use while *great* takes a rest.

notable

People and their accomplishments are *notable* if they are worth being noticed or are worthy of respect or admiration. Dolly Madison is a *notable* historical figure.

illustrious

Illustrious persons are well known, well liked, and greatly distinguished for their deeds or work. Theodore Roosevelt was not only President, but he was also an *illustrious* soldier, hunter, and author.

superior

Superior means higher in position or greater than something or someone else in size or importance. *Superior* is the opposite of inferior. The largest of the five Great Lakes is Lake *Superior.* A captain is *superior* in rank to a lieutenant.

supreme

Something that is *supreme* is unequaled in size, greatness, or importance. The *Supreme* Court is the highest court in the United States.

great continued on page 184 ▶

G

great continued from page 183

monumental *Monumental* describes something not only great but also massive in size or importance. A long, well-written book might be called *monumental.* Getting snow off a city's streets after a blizzard is a *monumental* task.

See also *famous, grand.*

ANTONYMS: small, inferior, petty, trivial, unknown

group (n) A number of people gathered together or having the same interests is a *group.* A band is made up of a *group* of musicians. A *group* can also be a number of objects brought together but regarded as one thing. An album is a *group* of photographs or records gathered in a book. An art collection may be a *group* of paintings gathered by one person or by a museum.

A band is made up of a **group** of musicians.

• kind
• category

Kind and *category* are words for a group of animals, objects, or ideas put together because of common interests or characteristics. An apple is a *kind* of fruit. Some *kinds* of trees do not lose their leaves in winter. These trees are not in the same *category* as those trees that do.

• class

A *class* is a group sharing the same condition. A *class* in school may be a group of pupils of approximately the same age. Some people travel in first *class* on an airplane.

There were dogs of ten different **breeds** at the dog show.

• breed

All animals of a particular *breed* have the same ancestors, and they are all similar in some way. A *breed* can be thought of as a group. There were dogs of ten different *breeds* at the dog show.

• set

A *set* is a group of things of the same kind or a group of things that have something in common. They belong together or are used together—a *set* of twins, a *set* of dishes, a *set* of encyclopedias, a *set* of numbers.

See also *party*.

G

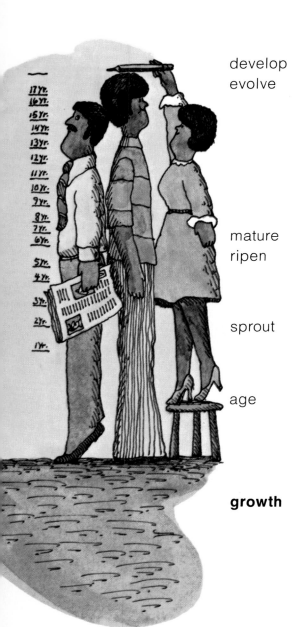

Cliff's parents have kept records of his **growth.**

grow

Grow means become bigger, larger, fuller, stronger, or better. You *grow.* Animals and plants *grow.* You can also *grow* something or make it *grow.* We also say that ideas or plans *grow* as they are carefully thought out.

develop
evolve

Develop and *evolve* mean change and grow gradually. Flowers *develop* from seeds or bulbs. Athletes *develop* their muscles by exercising. Things *evolve* over a period of time. It took a week to *evolve* the plans for the weekend retreat. Through the ages, the horse as we know it today has *evolved* from an animal that was no bigger than a dog.

mature
ripen

Mature and *ripen* mean grow and develop completely. Young children *mature* into adult men and women. When fruit *ripens,* it is ready to be picked and eaten.

sprout

Sprout means start to grow. Buds *sprout* from branches. New branches *sprout* from bushes and trees.

age

Age means become older. People *age* through the years. Some cheeses have to *age* before they can be eaten.

See also *advance* (v), *come.*

growth

Growth is the process of growing or becoming bigger. My parents started keeping records of my *growth* as soon as I could stand up against the wall. The farmer watched for signs of *growth* of his crops.

enlargement An *enlargement* is a growth in size. The *enlargement* of our tour group made the bus crowded. A photographer can make an *enlargement* of a small picture.

increase An *increase* is a growth or enlargement. Scales measure the *increase* or decrease of a person's weight. There has been a steady *increase* in the price of gasoline.

expansion We can think of an *expansion* as being an increase in size. Air causes the *expansion* of a balloon or a tire. Plans are underway for the *expansion* of the hospital.

development A *development* is a gradual growth or increase in usefulness. The *development* of that giant oak tree took many years. Scientists are working on the further *development* of using the sun as a source of energy.

maturity When something reaches *maturity,* it is fully grown. Grandpa's corn crop always reaches *maturity* in August.

ANTONYM: decrease (n)

H

habit

A *habit* is a certain way of acting or a certain way of doing something. Something you do can become a *habit* if you do it over and over again. Finally, you do it without even thinking. Some small children have the *habit* of sucking a thumb.

It is Mrs. Carr's **practice** to go jogging every morning.

custom

A *custom* can be a habit common to many people. It is the *custom* to give presents on birthdays.

practice

A *practice* is something you choose to do regularly. Reading the newspaper at night is one of Dad's *practices.* It is Mom's *practice* to go jogging every morning before breakfast.

rule

A *rule* can be something that is usually done or usually takes place. As a *rule,* I go straight home after school. But today was an exception because I stayed awhile to play basketball.

usage

Usage is a common way of using or doing or saying something. If it is done by many people, it becomes a custom. Authors follow correct English *usage* when they write. It is common *usage* to eat peas with a fork.

• system

A *system* can be an orderly way of doing a series of things. Usually a *system* has been carefully thought out and established. Then it is repeated, or followed exactly. If you have set up an alphabetical *system* for filing letters, you follow that same *system* each time you put a letter away.

ANTONYM: exception

188

happiness

Happiness is the opposite of sadness. *Happiness* is the good feeling you have when you are well and satisfied with your life. Something that gives you enjoyment can also be called *happiness.* Receiving letters from their aunt who lives in Scotland gives the family much *happiness.*

delight

Delight is a strong feeling of happiness. People often show their *delight* by getting excited, smiling, and laughing. Norman's eyes lit up with *delight* when he saw his new bicycle. Margarita took great *delight* in showing the class a letter from her friend in Africa.

joy

Joy is even stronger than delight. It is a deep and lasting feeling. *Joy* is the opposite of sorrow. You can feel *joy* when you bring happiness to others.

contentment
satisfaction

Contentment and *satisfaction* are feelings of being pleased with what you have or with what you have done. *Contentment* is a very peaceful kind of happiness. My uncle's house plants give him *contentment* all year long. Many people find *contentment* living in the country. Passing the physical-fitness test was a great *satisfaction* to Norma.

ANTONYMS: sadness, sorrow, despair (n), misery, unhappiness

Uncle Ray's house plants give him **contentment** all year long.

H

happy

Happy means feeling well and being pleased or glad about something. You are *happy* when you are having a good time. You are not sad or unhappy. Something can be called *happy* if it puts you in good spirits. *Happy* can also be used in many polite phrases. I am *happy* to meet you. I will be *happy* to help you. *Happy* New Year!

cheerful

Cheerful means merry and full of good spirits. A person who is *cheerful* is not melancholy. A *cheerful* room is sunny and pleasant and not dark and gloomy.

pleased

You are *pleased* with something if you like it and are happy with it. Hugh was *pleased* with the tremendous applause.

Hugh was **pleased** with the tremendous applause.

contented
satisfied

Contented and *satisfied* are a little stronger than pleased. They mean happy with what you have or with what you are doing—so happy that you don't wish for anything more or different. Everyone felt very full and *contented* after the Thanksgiving dinner. The scouts were well *satisfied* with their paper drive.

ANTONYMS: sad, unhappy, melancholy (adj), gloomy, downcast, frustrated, miserable

Pollution causes **harm** to lakes and beaches.

harm (n)   *Harm* is the actual pain or suffering or wrong done to someone or something. This is the noun meaning. Expecting *harm* can make you afraid of something. I meant Anna no *harm* when I said I didn't agree with her. Pollution causes *harm* to lakes and beaches.

damage   *Damage* is harm done to something. *Damage* lowers the value or usefulness of something. The tornado caused *damage* to many homes and office buildings.

injury   An *injury* is harm or wrong done to a person or a thing. Sharon didn't receive any *injuries* when she fell during the hockey game.

loss   *Loss* is harm caused by losing someone or something. A person may suffer from the *loss* of a relative. We had only two *losses* during this soccer season. His *loss* of memory was temporary.

See also *misfortune.*

ANTONYM: benefit (n), harmless

191

H

harm (v)

Harm means cause pain or suffering or loss. This is the verb meaning. You may *harm* yourself or *harm* someone or *harm* something. You can *harm* your eyes if you read in poor light. Gossip can *harm* other people. Insects can *harm* a garden.

damage

Damage means lower the value or usefulness of something or harm it. If a car has been *damaged* in an accident, it can often be repaired. The furniture was *damaged* by the fire.

hurt

Hurt means damage something or harm someone. The rain can't *hurt* this old coat. Beverly *hurt* herself when she fell from the tree.

injure

Injure means harm something or someone. Tony *injured* his leg in the skiing accident.

ANTONYMS: repair (v), benefit (v)

The rain can't **hurt** this old jacket.

harsh

Harsh means rough or unpleasant. A *harsh* surface is not smooth to touch. The weather can be very *harsh* in winter. A person who is *harsh* is unfriendly, impolite, unkind, and often cruel.

The weather can be very **harsh** in winter.

hoarse
raspy

Hoarse and *raspy* mean harsh in sound. Have you ever heard the *hoarse* croak of a bullfrog? A saw cutting metal makes a grating or *raspy* sound.

husky

A *husky* voice is low and hoarse. It is often caused by a cold or cough.

gruff

A *gruff* voice is deep and harsh and impatient. The umpire yelled "Out!" in a *gruff* voice. A stern or bad-tempered person often speaks in a *gruff* or unpleasant manner. The cashier seemed *gruff* and grouchy.

ANTONYMS: smooth, kind, gentle, mild, polite

193

H

hate (v)

The verb *hate* is a very strong word meaning you don't like something. *Hate* is the opposite of love. Many times people say they *hate* something when they really mean they don't like it. It is better to say that you don't like spinach, for instance, than to say that you *hate* it. But when you are talking about something important enough to feel strongly about, you would probably say that you *hate* it.

dislike

Dislike means disapprove of something because you don't enjoy it or don't find it interesting. It is not as strong a word as hate. Lucy *dislikes* raking leaves.

detest
despise

Detest and *despise* mean almost the same thing. *Detest* means dislike someone or something very much. I *detest* grouchy salespersons. You *despise* someone or something if you feel dislike and refuse to be bothered. I *despise* lies.

scorn

You *scorn* something if you look down on it and think it is not worth your attention. After Ryan had learned to ride his bicycle, he *scorned* the training wheels.

loathe

Loathe means detest. *Loathe* is a very strong word. If you *loathe* something, you look at it with disgust and want nothing to do with it. Glen *loathes* spiders.

ANTONYMS: like (v), love (v), enjoy, admire, appreciate

hate (n)

Hate, as a noun, is a very strong feeling against someone or something. A person may feel *hate* toward someone who is mean.

hatred

Hatred can be used in place of hate. *Hatred* is usually followed by *of.* Joy's *hatred of* water skiing grew every time she fell.

dislike
distaste

Dislike and *distaste* are not as strong as hate. Both are the feeling of not liking or enjoying something. *Dislike* can be followed by *of* or *for.* A person may show *dislike of* a movie by walking out of the theater before the movie ends. Hazel's *dislike for* cold weather caused her to move to a warmer climate. *Distaste* may be followed by *for.* People have a *distaste for* things that are unattractive, unpleasant, or disagreeable. He looked with *distaste* at the pile of dirty dishes.

After hurting her thumb, the carpenter had an **aversion** to making beds.

aversion

If you have an *aversion to* something, you don't like it and will try to avoid it. After hurting her thumb, the carpenter had an *aversion to* making beds. Some people have an *aversion to* bugs and creeping animals.

disgust

Disgust is a strong dislike and aversion to something. Something bad or sickening might fill you with *disgust.* I feel only *disgust* when I see people litter the streets.

ANTONYMS: fondness, liking (n), love (n)

195

H

heavy

Heavy is the opposite of light. Something is *heavy* if it weighs a lot. Movers lift and carry *heavy* furniture and *heavy* boxes.

Heavy can also mean more than usual. Then it is the opposite of slight or thin. The *heavy* traffic caused us to be late.

We also call something *heavy* if it is difficult or hard to bear. You can speak of a *heavy* responsibility and a *heavy* duty.

cumbersome

Cumbersome means heavy and awkward, hard to carry or move. The *cumbersome* statue was finally brought into the museum.

ponderous

Ponderous describes something that is not only heavy but very large or massive or dull. Many old pieces of furniture are *ponderous.* Books can be *ponderous.*

weighty

Weighty can mean either very heavy or very serious and important. Packages can be *weighty.* A lawyer's words may be *weighty.* The President delivered a *weighty* speech to the nation.

thick

Thick can describe something that is heavily built or something that is very dense. *Thick* is the opposite of thin. A baseball bat is *thicker* at one end than at the other. It would be hard to push your way through a *thick* crowd. The family of deer disappeared into the *thick* forest.

See also *serious.*

ANTONYMS: light (adj), slight (adj), thin, trivial

196

help (v)

Help means do something for another person. To *help* someone, you give whatever is needed, or you do whatever is useful. *Help* is the opposite of hinder. A doctor *helps* you when you are sick. He or she gives you medicine that *helps* you get well. A person in trouble may cry, "*Help* me!"

aid

Aid means help by giving relief to someone. The Red Cross *aids* people in an emergency. Our contributions will *aid* scientists in their research.

assist

Assist means work together with someone and help that person do something. We didn't *assist* the photographer much by holding the lights. The clerk *assisted* me in choosing after-shave lotion for my brother.

improve

Improve means help by making something better. Lots of practice *improved* Ida's banjo playing.

encourage

Encourage means help a person by giving that person hope. The coach discouraged me at first, but after seeing what I could do, he *encouraged* me to try out for the team.

benefit

Benefit means do good or be of use to someone. A vacation *benefits* almost everyone.

See also *advance* (v), *protect, support* (v).

ANTONYMS: hinder, discourage, obstruct

They didn't **assist** the photographer much by holding the lights.

197

H

help (n)

The *help* you give someone is what you do or give to meet his or her needs. With the *help* of two girls, the old woman was able to walk.

aid

Aid is also help—something that is needed. With the *aid* of a hammer, Pete opened the suitcase. *Aid* is often used in combination with other words—first *aid*, federal *aid*, visual *aid.*

assistance

Assistance means work done with another person to help him or her do something. Expert *assistance* from the police helped keep traffic away from the scene of the fire.

benefit

A *benefit* is something that helps or improves someone or something in some way. Having beautiful, clean parks is one of the *benefits* of putting trash in the proper containers. Good health is one of the *benefits* of proper food and exercise.

support

Support is the act of helping or upholding something or someone. A young tree may need the *support* of a stick. Her friends' loyal *support* helped Elsie win the election. *Support* can also mean the supplying to someone of whatever he or she needs to live. An elderly parent may depend on a son or daughter for *support.*

service

Service is a small help or convenience of some kind that one person provides for another. Often a *service* must be paid for. *Service* at the new restaurant was slow.

Service at the new restaurant was slow.

relief

Relief is the removal or the lightening of a burden or worry that someone is carrying. *Relief* showed on Darrel's face when he was told that his myna bird had been found. *Relief* also means aid given to needy people in the form of money or other necessities.

ANTONYMS: harm (n), hindrance

hide (v)

Hide means remove from sight. Sometimes you *hide* yourself—if you are playing a game or trying to avoid someone. In a game of hide-and-seek, you may be found after you *hide.* When you bring to light something that has been *hidden,* you reveal it.

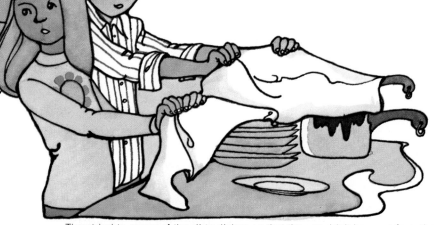

They tried to **conceal** the dirty dishes so that they couldn't be seen from the living room.

conceal

You *conceal* something if you purposely hide it or cover it up. We tried to *conceal* the dirty dishes so that they couldn't be seen from the living room. It is no fun playing rummy with you if you don't *conceal* your cards.

hide (v) continued on page 200 ▸

H

disguise

Disguise means hide a person or thing by changing its appearance so it can't be recognized. Lorna *disguised* herself so well for her part in the play that no one knew who she was.

obscure

Obscure means conceal or hide by putting something over or in front of. The big man *obscured* Wayne's view of the movie screen.

The big man **obscured** Wayne's view of the movie screen.

mask

Mask means hide the appearance or true character or feelings of something or someone. We put colorful Japanese lanterns on the lights to *mask* the ugly light bulbs. Her smile *masked* the anger she felt.

veil

Veil means cover or conceal something as if you were covering it with a *veil.* Ursula tried to *veil* her unhappiness by joking.

ANTONYMS: reveal, find (v), show (v), unmask, unveil

history

A *history* is a written account or an explanation of past events. The *history* of motion pictures, for example, begins in 1892 with Thomas Edison's invention of a device called the kinetoscope. Babe Ruth is an important name in the *history* of sports.

200

Unlike stories, which do not always tell about actual events, *histories* tell about events or situations that have actually taken place and try to explain them. There are several special kinds of *histories,* and the following words describe some of those kinds.

• record

A *record* is a history of facts or events. People keep *records* so that important information won't be forgotten.

• diary
• journal

A *diary* and a *journal* are daily records. Sometime during their lives most people keep a *diary* or *journal,* in which they write about what they are thinking and what they are doing.

• log

A *log* is a record that a ship's captain keeps during a voyage to note the ship's progress day by day.

• chronicle

A *chronicle* is a record of events written down in the order in which they happened. Usually there is no explanation of why certain events occurred as there is in a history.

• biography

A *biography* is the history of a person's life written by someone else. The historian read the ship's log before she began writing a *biography* of the captain.

• autobiography

An *autobiography* is the history of a person's life written by that person. Benjamin Franklin described his childhood in his *autobiography.*

See also *account* (n), *story, tale.*

H

hit (v)

Hit means give a blow or a whack to someone or something. You *hit* a nail with a hammer. You *hit* a tennis ball with a racket.

strike

Strike also can mean hit. You *strike* a xylophone with small wooden hammers. *Strike* is often used to mean other kinds of hitting. A grandfather clock *strikes* on the hour and half-hour. Prospectors *strike* gold when they hit, or come upon, a vein of it in the ground. If a batter in a baseball game *strikes out,* he or she didn't hit anything at all!

slap

Slap means hit with your open hand. If your cousin *slaps* you on the back, he is probably congratulating you for something.

cuff

Cuff means hit or slap, usually gently or in fun. A cat *cuffs* her kittens with her paw.

swat

Swat means hit quickly and hard. You can *swat* a fly with a fly swatter or a folded newspaper.

punch

Punch can mean hit with your fist. Pablo *punches* his pillow when he is angry.

slug

Slug means hit very hard. The heavyweight champion *slugged* the challenger with a right to the jaw.

See also *beat* (v).

A cat **cuffs** her kittens with her paw.

honesty   *Honesty* is acting and speaking truthfully. It is the opposite of deceit and dishonesty. A person shows *honesty* by not stealing, cheating, or lying. Salespersons appreciate your *honesty* if you tell them that they did not charge you enough for an item.

truthfulness   *Truthfulness* means being open with people and not trying to hide anything from them. It means always telling the truth. People are respected for *truthfulness* in their dealings with others.

sincerity   *Sincerity* also means honesty. It is saying what you really feel or doing something you really believe in. I promised in all *sincerity* to do my best.

honor   A person of *honor* is honest and fair. If someone is "held in *honor,*" that person is greatly respected. To "uphold the *honor*" of something means to defend its name and good reputation. The basketball victory upheld the *honor* of the team. You give a person your *word of honor* when you promise that you can be trusted to do something.

integrity   *Integrity* is a strong word for honesty. It means honesty and trustworthiness. A person of *integrity* can always be trusted to do what is right and just. That person would never try to deceive anyone or give someone a false impression.

ANTONYMS: deceit, dishonesty, dishonor (n), untruthfulness

H

hurry (v)

Hurry means move faster or make something go faster. *Hurry* or you'll miss the bus. *Hurry* is often followed by *up*. *Hurry up* or you'll be late for breakfast.

hasten

Hasten means be quick to go someplace or do something. Margo *hastened* her packing because it was time for her to leave.

rush

Rush means hurry or go forward very quickly. The ambulance *rushed* the sick child to the hospital. In the days of prospecting, gold miners *rushed* to California. *Rush* can also mean appear suddenly. Tears *rushed* to his eyes when he saw his wrecked model train.

The racing car **sped** around the racetrack.

speed

Speed means move fast. It is a stronger word than rush. The racing car *sped* around the race track. A police officer stopped all the drivers who were *speeding* in the school zone.

hustle

Hustle means hurry or move quickly. Father *hustled* the toddlers off to bed. *Hustle* can also mean move onward by pushing or shoving. They *hustled* through the crowd at the airport.

ANTONYMS: dawdle, delay (v), hinder, linger, loiter, slow down

I

idea

An *idea* can be the picture in your mind of something you know, think, or imagine. Some *ideas* are thought out, but, like opinions, they change and are not as firmly held as beliefs. You can have an *idea* of something without ever having seen it. Lisa's *idea* that a walrus looks like a seal is correct. An *idea* can also be a plan to do something. There are books full of *ideas* on what to do around the house on a rainy day.

notion

A *notion* is a vague idea about something. I have some *notion* about how to grow African violets from leaf cuttings. I have a *notion* to go with Jaimie on Friday, but it may be better to go on Thursday.

impression

An *impression* is an idea or feeling you receive from something. If something makes an *impression* on you, it affects you in a certain way. First *impressions* are not always correct. Cliff's *impression* of the city changed after he had been there for a while.

thought

A *thought* can be an idea about something. Books are full of new *thoughts.* What is your *thought* about having a picnic? I had a *thought* about what we might do tomorrow.

concept

A *concept* may be a general or detailed idea of what something is or ought to be like. We all have our *concepts* of happiness and of sadness.

See also *belief, opinion.*

Yumiko had a **thought** about what she might do tomorrow.

I

imaginary

Imaginary means not real or not actual or not true. The characters in most comic books are *imaginary* people.

fanciful

Fanciful describes something that is created in your mind or that does not really exist. Talking animals are *fanciful* creatures. The story about Winnie-the-Pooh is *fanciful*.

fantastic

Fantastic describes something so strange or unheard of that it can't be believed. The idea that a human being would ever walk on the moon seemed *fantastic* a hundred years ago.

unreal
fictitious

Unreal and *fictitious* describe things that are invented or supplied by the imagination. A dream is *unreal* even though it seems very real. "Fiction" means an invented story. So *fictitious* describes anything that is not real or that is not a fact. Most authors use *fictitious* names for the characters in their novels.

ANTONYMS: real, actual, true

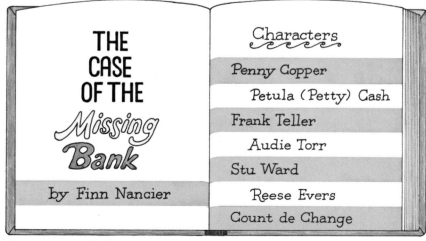

Most authors use **fictitious** names for the characters in their novels.

imagine

Imagine means see something in your mind. When you *imagine* something, you are letting your mind invent or create ideas. Can you *imagine* how you will look in ten years? *Imagine* can also mean think something is true or something will happen even though you have no proof or reason for thinking so. Since it is Saturday, I *imagine* my friend is golfing at the park. I *imagine* it's going to rain.

Molly is trying to **imagine** how she will look in ten years.

suppose

Suppose means think that something is possible. I *suppose* Andrew will make popcorn tonight.

guess

Guess means form an opinion about something when you really don't know much about it. You might *guess* how old someone is or *guess* how much that person weighs. Can you *guess* how tall that skyscraper is?

fancy

Fancy means form a picture of something in your mind. When she was young, Babe Didrikson Zaharias *fancied* herself a great athlete. Sometimes we *fancy* things that really aren't possible. He *fancied* that he was captain of a clipper ship.

realize

Realize means understand something fully and clearly. They *realized* they had made a mistake. Do you *realize* what life would be like if the car hadn't been invented?

believe

Believe means imagine and trust that something is true or real. If a person *believes* in someone or something, it is hard to change his or her mind.

209

I

A parrot can **imitate** some of the sounds it hears.

imitate   *Imitate* means try to be like something or someone else. It also means try to make or do something using a pattern or model. Small children often *imitate* the actions of their parents. A parrot can *imitate* some of the sounds it hears.

follow   *Follow* can mean imitate someone else's actions. When you *follow* another person's advice, you act as that person says he or she would act in the same situation.

trace   *Trace* means imitate or follow the lines of something. You *trace* a picture by putting a thin piece of paper over it and following the lines with a pencil or pen.

copy   *Copy* means imitate as closely as possible. A secretary may *copy* a letter for the boss by typing the same words on another piece of paper. A cook may *copy* a famous recipe by cooking a similar dish.

duplicate — *Duplicate* means imitate something exactly. You *duplicate* a key when you have another made just like it. You copy a page from a book when you write down word for word what is printed. You *duplicate* the page if you use a copying machine to make another page that shows the printed words and looks just like the page in the book.

counterfeit — *Counterfeit* means imitate in order to deceive or give a false impression. The crook was sent to jail because he had *counterfeited* one-dollar bills.

impersonate
mimic
mock — *Impersonate, mimic,* and *mock* all mean imitate. *Impersonate* is used when an actor takes the part of a character in a play or movie. Colin *impersonated* George Washington. You *mimic* when you imitate the way someone or something talks or acts. We roared with laughter as Sadie *mimicked* a frog. *Mock* is used when you imitate and make fun of a person or thing. It was mean of you to *mock* the way I fell.

important — *Important* describes something or someone of real value or meaning. An *important* decision is one that could make a big difference in what happens later. Choosing what you will eat for a snack is a trivial decision. *Important* also describes something or someone who is able to influence or change events or opinions. For example, an *important* game is one that decides the championship. A preseason game may be unimportant.

important continued on page 212 ▶

I

chief principal leading	*Chief, principal,* and *leading* all describe something or someone of greatest importance. A *chief* usher in a theater tells the other ushers where to stand and what to do. The *principal* character in a story or play is usually the hero or heroine. The *leading* industry of a city is the one for which the city is well known. Automobile manufacture is the *leading* industry of Detroit.
major	*Major* describes something more important or larger or of more interest than others. The opposite of *major* is minor. Dallas is one of the *major* cities of the United States.
main	*Main* describes the most important or most obvious part of something. The *main* library is downtown, but there is a branch library near our house. One *main* switch controls the lights all over this building. My *main* reason for going to the theater was to see the star of the show.
significant	*Significant* means important because of having some special meaning or reason. The most *significant* clue the detective found was a footprint just below the window. Whether the footprint was big or little was insignificant.
weighty	*Weighty* can mean that something is heavy because it is so important. The Senate may spend a long time in a *weighty* discussion. See also *basic, great, large, serious.* ANTONYMS: unimportant, trivial, minor, insignificant

The most **significant** clue the detective found was a footprint.

212

Theresa **added** one more leaf to her collection.

increase (v)   *Increase* means become or make larger or greater or more. *Increase* is the opposite of decrease. A crowd *increases* as more people gather, or come together. In 1959, the number of States has *increased* to fifty. A driver can *increase* the speed of a car. Your strength and weight *increase* as you grow older.

add   *Add* means increase by joining or putting one thing to another. You *add* numbers in math. Theresa *added* more leaves to her leaf collection.

• attach
• annex   *Attach* and *annex* are other good words to use for increase even though they are not real synonyms. *Attach* means join something to something else. The length of a freight train increases when a caboose is *attached*. A kite increases in weight if you *attach* a tail. *Annex* can mean increase by adding to something that is larger or more important. Hospitals *annex* buildings when more space is needed. A city may *annex* a suburb or surrounding land.

multiply   *Multiply* means increase in number. Your fears might *multiply* in a scary situation.

extend   *Extend* can mean make longer or increase in time. If you *extend* your visit with a friend, you stay longer than you had planned.

See also *enlarge*.

ANTONYMS: decrease (v), diminish, divide, subtract

I

inform

Inform means make something known to another person. You can do this by speaking or writing. You told everyone else about the meeting, but you didn't *inform* me. You *inform* someone *of* something. Magazines and newspapers *inform* us *of* recent events.

impart

Impart means share the knowledge you have of something with another person. You might *impart* a secret to a friend. An eyewitness may *impart* valuable first-hand information to a newspaper reporter.

acquaint

Acquaint means inform and familiarize someone else with the facts or details of a situation. The boss *acquainted* Judy *with* the duties and responsibilities of her new job. If you are *acquainted with* another person, you know that person quite well. Notice that you are *acquainted with* someone or you *acquaint* someone *with* something.

notify

Notify means inform, but it also adds the meaning of expecting a response of some sort. Shirley *notified* the post office of her new address and hoped her mail would be forwarded promptly. We were *notified* that the repairs on our car were completed, and that the car could be picked up.

teach
instruct

Teach and *instruct* mean give information or knowledge to another person in order that he or she may learn. You can *teach* people how to do something by simply showing them how or by offering examples, then helping them do it

Edwina **taught** her dog another trick.

themselves. *Instruct* usually means teach by guiding someone through a course of lessons or training, such as a class in school. Edwina *taught* her dog another trick. The class was *instructed* in the proper way to operate a sewing machine. *Instruct* can also mean command. Mr. Sing was *instructed* to appear for jury duty.

ANTONYMS: conceal, misinform

information   *Information* is what you learn about something by obtaining the facts. You get *information* by talking with other people or by reading books or by observing and studying something. I went to the library to get more *information* about the American Revolution.

• news   *News* is information about recent events. The *news* is reported in newspapers and on television and radio. *News* can also be something you didn't know before. Their triumphant return from the mountain climbing expedition is *news* to me.

information continued on page 216 ▶

• intelligence   *Intelligence* can be secret information. Spies and secret service agents gather *intelligence* about the plans of other countries.

• data   *Data* are facts and information from which things can be learned. The *data* of past flights are used to prepare for new space missions. The word *data* means more than one fact and should be followed by a plural verb. Are the *data* you have from one experiment enough for you to work with? However, a singular verb is often used. Here is the *data* you asked for.

• knowledge   *Knowledge* is a general word. *Knowledge* includes all that anyone knows and understands. You gain *knowledge* of things through study, education, investigation, experience, and observation.

inquire   *Inquire* means search for facts or for truth by asking questions. Some want ads tell people where to *inquire* about renting apartments. Before Mom bought her new car, she *inquired* about several kinds.

ask about   *Ask about* means inquire. You can *ask about* the price of something, or you can *ask about* someone's vacation plans. If a neighbor *asks about* your grandmother, perhaps he is inquiring about her health because he hasn't seen her for a few days.

question   You *question* someone by asking a series of questions in order to get information. During a job interview, a person may be *questioned* about his or her goals or ambitions.

investigate

Investigate means observe and inquire about something by following a specific procedure. A detective might *investigate* by first checking the scene of the crime. Then he might inquire about the people involved. He might then further *investigate* the suspects by questioning their employers, neighbors, relatives, and friends.

The lawyer for the other side is allowed to **cross-examine** that witness.

cross-examine

If the detective is very suspicious of the answers given by one suspect, he might *cross-examine* that suspect. That means the detective will ask questions which will check the answers the suspect has already given to other questions. In a courtroom after a witness has been examined, or has answered the questions of one lawyer, the lawyer for the other side is allowed to *cross-examine* that witness.

See also *examine.*

ANTONYMS: answer (v), reply (v), respond

217

I

Art's grandma received several **inquiries** about her car.

inspection

An *inspection* is made when something is looked at closely. The fire chief made an *inspection* of the old warehouse to see if the building was safe.

inquiry

An *inquiry* is a request for information. Grandma received several *inquiries* about the car she had offered for sale.

investigation

An *investigation* is a detailed inquiry into a situation in an effort to uncover facts. The *investigation* of the robbery revealed that some of the stolen jewelry had been sold.

probe

A dentist may find a cavity by poking a tooth with a pointed instrument called a *probe.* A *probe* can also be a thorough investigation—a poking into a matter to get at the truth. The Senate conducted a *probe* of the pollution of the Great Lakes. A *probe* was made to determine the cause of the accident.

scrutiny

Scrutiny is a searching study or inquiry. The *scrutiny* of the riverbank for the missing boat was put off until daylight. *Scrutiny* is also a searching look or a close watch. Before attempting a free fall, the jumpers packed their parachutes under the *scrutiny* of the instructor.

examination

An *examination* can be a formal questioning or it can be a test. It can be an inquiry by the police or what doctors do when they take your pulse and listen to your heart.

checkup

A *checkup* is any examination or close scrutiny. It is often a medical examination. It is wise to have a *checkup* once a year.

instrument   An *instrument* is something you use in order to do something. There are *instruments* for cutting and measuring, drawing and building, cooking and cleaning, farming and gardening. A compass is a very valuable *instrument* to a sailor because it shows direction. Pianos, violins, guitars, trumpets, and saxophones are musical *instruments.* There are many other kinds of *instruments* you may have used or have heard of.

• tool   A *tool* is an instrument usually operated by hand. A hammer, a saw, and a plane are only a few of the *tools* a carpenter uses.

• implement   The tools that are used in farming or gardening can be called *implements.* Rakes, hoes, and spades are all *implements.* A plow is a farm *implement* used to break the soil before seeds are planted.

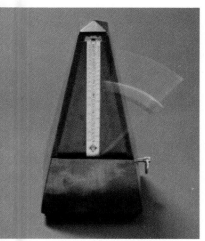

A metronome is a **device** that helps musicians keep time to music.

• device   A *device* can be an instrument or small machine that has been designed or invented for a special purpose. A car jack is an important *device* to have when a flat tire must be removed from a car. A metronome is a clocklike *device* that helps you keep time to music.

• utensil   A *utensil* is an instrument or container that is usually used in the kitchen. Pots and pans, beaters, and slicers are all *utensils.*

• appliance   An *appliance* is an instrument or device that needs some form of power to operate. A washing machine, a stove, an iron, and a vacuum cleaner are *appliances.*

I

interfere

Interfere means prevent or get in the way of someone or something. Joe's refusal to cooperate *interfered* with our plans for the open house. The storm is *interfering* with my TV reception.

meddle

Meddle means interfere in other people's concerns. Please learn to control your curiosity and stop *meddling.*

interrupt
butt in

Interrupt and *butt in* mean interfere with something by breaking in. A special news bulletin *interrupted* the television program. The telephone call *interrupted* our dinner. My little brother always *butts in* whenever I am talking to a friend. Due to the importance of the telegram, the secretary decided to *butt in* before the meeting was over.

The storm is **interfering** with the TV reception.

intercept

Intercept means interrupt the progress of something by seizing it. If a message is left for you but someone else sees it and takes it away, that person has *intercepted* it. You *intercept* a pass in football when you catch a ball that is thrown to someone else.

See also *block* (v), *disturb.*

invention

An *invention* is something new that someone has thought up or made. It may be a new tool or machine or a new way of doing something. The *invention* of the airplane has made travel easier and communication better. We can use many other words to mean something new, even though they aren't synonyms of *invention.*

• creation

A *creation* is something that has been brought into existence. Works of art can be called *creations.* We speak of a short story or a novel as being the *creation* of an author. A symphony is a musical *creation.*

Works of art can be called **creations.**

• production

A *production* is whatever is produced, caused, or manufactured. The use of an assembly line increased the *production* of automobiles. Some countries are important because of their *production* of oil. The *production* of a play depends on many people.

• fabrication

A *fabrication* is something fabricated or made up from many parts. Some modern art is a *fabrication* of nuts, bolts, and nails. We can also think of a *fabrication* as being a false story that is made up to deceive someone. We discovered that Rose's exciting adventure in the mountains was a *fabrication.*

• discovery

A *discovery* is the coming upon something that has existed before but that has never been seen or known. The *discovery* of copper in the Keweenau Peninsula in Michigan led to the rapid settlement of that area.

• finding

A *finding* is the coming upon new facts through research and experimentation and investigation. Medical magazines often tell of *findings* that result from a doctor's research. Students of chemistry experiment with chemicals, then record their *findings* in reports.

221

J

join

Join means put or bring or fasten together. You *join* a club when you become a member and take part in its activities. People may *join* each other for dinner. The Golden Gate Bridge *joins* Marin County and San Francisco. José completed an electric circuit by *joining* the wires. The caller at the square dance directed the people to *join* hands.

combine
unite

Combine and *unite* mean join things to make a new whole. A baker *combines* ingredients to make bread. The states *united* to form a new government.

connect

Connect means join or fasten things together by putting something between them. A walk may *connect* the garage to a house. Ties are used to *connect* the rails of a railroad track. The Isthmus of Panama *connects* North and South America.

link
couple

Link and *couple* also mean join or connect. The girls *linked* arms in order to steady each other as they roller-skated. A steel hook, called a coupling, is used to *couple* two railroad cars.

A steel hook, called a coupling, is used to **couple** two railroad cars.

attach

Attach means join one thing to another. Lyle *attached* the trailer to his car.

annex

Annex means join a thing to something else that is larger or more important. A country *annexes* territory.

Harry put the vase back together by **gluing** the broken pieces.

cement
glue
paste

Cement, glue, and *paste* all mean put or stick things firmly together by using something to make them stick. Your dad may *cement* flat rocks together to make a walk. Harry fixed the vase by *gluing* the broken pieces. Will you help my little cousin *paste* these paper chains together?

fit

Fit means put together parts of the right size and shape. Some people enjoy *fitting* the pieces of a jigsaw puzzle.

See also *fasten.*

ANTONYMS: detach, divide, separate (v)

K

know

Know means have knowledge of or information about something or someone. You come to *know* many things by observing what is around you, by reading books, by listening, and by studying in school. Some teen-agers *know* how to cook and sew. Some *know* a lot about sports. I *know* we will have a good time on our trip. My sister *knows* how to speak two languages. Do you *know* that girl? I *have known* her a long time. I *knew* that we could trust her with the secret.

Here are some other words you may use for *know,* even though they aren't really synonyms.

- understand
- realize

Understand and *realize* are good words to use when you know something well or have a clear idea about it. It is wise to ask a question if you don't *understand* something. Do you *understand* how to get to my house? He *realized* that he had better tell the truth about the missing piece of pie. When I tried on my new jacket, I *realized* I had sewed the zipper in upside down.

- be aware
- recognize

Be aware and *recognize* mean know and admit that something is a fact or that something is true. *Are* you *aware* that your pen is running out of ink? Carla *is aware* of the damage her dog caused when it ran through your garden. The critics *recognized* that the young singer had enough talent to become a star. *Recognize* also means know again. I *recognized* him, even though I hadn't seen him in five years.

Is she **aware** that her pen is running out of ink?

- discern
- distinguish

Discern and *distinguish* mean know the difference between things that seem to be alike, and be able to tell them apart or separate them. By the end of the inning, we *discerned* signs of weariness in the pitcher. It isn't always easy to *distinguish* between the right and the wrong thing to say.

- be sure

You can *be sure* about something that you know with certainty. *Are* you *sure* Abraham Lincoln was born in 1809? She *was sure* she had turned off the TV before leaving the house.

See also *imagine, remember.*

By the end of the inning, the batter **discerned** signs of weariness in the pitcher.

L

large

Large describes something that is bigger than usual in size or amount.

extensive
vast

Extensive and vast describe something that fills or covers a large or wide area. It is not limited to one place. The tornado caused extensive damage. My spelling was so bad that I had to make extensive corrections in my report. Antarctica is a vast, ice-covered continent. There is a vast difference between my height and yours.

immense
enormous
tremendous

Immense, enormous, and tremendous, all mean very large. Immense describes something larger than normal in size or better than usual. The boy has an immense appetite for candy. There is an immense improvement in her handwriting. Enormous and tremendous mean shockingly large. Something enormous is much larger than you would ever expect it to be. When the polar bear stood on its hind feet, it was enormous. Tremendous describes something so large it fills you with awe or terror. A tremendous crash of thunder made me jump. Niagara Falls is a tremendous sight.

huge
gigantic
mammoth

Huge, gigantic, and mammoth are good words for large. Something huge is larger than usual or ordinary in size. The huge oak tree fell across our yard, just missing our house. Something is gigantic or mammoth if it is larger than other things like it. Our rosebush has lots of buds and one gigantic blossom. Every time I tried to shoot for the basket, this mammoth guard jumped in front of me.

Every time Clay tried to shoot for the basket, this **mammoth** guard jumped in front of him.

bulky
massive

Bulky and *massive* mean large in size and often in weight. A *bulky* package may not be heavy, but it is awkward to carry. For example, if you wrapped an open umbrella, you would have a *bulky* package! Something *massive* is not only *bulky* but surprising in size and appearance. A ship is *massive.* Some mountains are *massive* piles of rock.

ANTONYMS: little, minute (adj), slight (adj), small, tiny

last (adj)

Last describes something that comes at the end or is the only one remaining. The *last* flower in the garden is the one that remains after all the others are dead. The *last* day to enter the contest is May 24. If you haven't entered the contest before then, you still have one *last* chance on that day. When the group lined up from shortest to tallest, Joe was *last.*

last (adj) continued on page 228 ▶

When the group lined up from shortest to tallest, Joe was **last.**

The **concluding** chapter of the book is very exciting.

- latest

- final

- closing
- concluding

- conclusive

- eventual

- ultimate

Last and these other words cannot always be used in place of each other, but perhaps you can see the differences as you read on.

Latest means most recent or newest. The *latest* issue of a magazine is the last one that has been printed so far. The *latest* records are played by disk jockeys.

Final means last, with no more to come, or occurring at the end of something. *Final* exams are taken at the end of the school year. Your *final* word on a subject is the last thing you say about it. His decision was *final* and he refused to discuss it.

Closing and *concluding* mean final or ending or last. In the *closing* paragraph of his letter, Raoul asked his friend to come to visit him next summer. The *concluding* chapter of the book is very exciting.

Conclusive can mean final and true beyond any questioning. *Conclusive* evidence in a trial cannot be proved false. Fingerprints are *conclusive* evidence because no two people have the same fingerprints.

Eventual means coming or happening sooner or later. We asked again if we could go to the movies because we hoped Mother's *eventual* answer would be "yes."

Ultimate means last or final or eventual. The *ultimate* goal of our swimming team is to compete in the Olympics.

ANTONYMS: basic, beginning (adj), earliest, first, primary

law
A *law* is a practice that is accepted and required in a community, state, or nation. A *law* is enforced by the police or someone else in authority. Bicycle riders must obey traffic *laws.* Taking someone else's mail from a mailbox is against the *law.*

Here are some words that are not quite synonyms of *law* but have similar meanings.

• rule
A *rule* is a guide for conduct or action. While governments make laws, other organizations have *rules.* Most schools have a *rule* forbidding pupils to run in the halls. If you don't play the game according to the *rules,* no one will want you on the team. Lola has a *rule* she follows: She always treats other people the way she'd like to be treated herself.

• regulation
A *regulation* is a rule that controls a particular group of people very strictly. According to a city *regulation,* food handlers have to pass a health examination. Our organization has so many rules and *regulations,* we can't remember them all.

One city **ordinance** forbids bicycle riding on any main streets.

• ordinance
An *ordinance* is a law passed by a local government to handle a local problem. One city *ordinance* forbids bicycle riding on any main streets.

• act
An *act* can be a law passed by a government. The Stamp *Act* was a law passed by England in 1765 to collect taxes from the American colonies.

229

L

leave (v)

Leave means go away or move away from. The train will *leave* in an hour. I didn't want to miss the TV show, so I *left* the car races as soon as I could. *Leave* can also mean go away without taking something. Where did you *leave* your book? Did Rose *leave* her sweater behind in her locker?

depart

Depart means leave one place and go to another. We will *depart* for the Smoky Mountains tomorrow morning. One plane *departed* just as another one arrived.

vacate

Vacate means go away from something, leaving no one in it. You *vacate* your chair when you get up and don't sit down again. A family *vacates* a house by moving out and not living in it any longer.

quit

Quit means leave or give up something. She *quit* her job because it no longer interested her. When you *quit* a club, you give up your membership and no longer remain a member.

abandon
desert
forsake

Abandon, desert, and *forsake* mean leave someone or something completely. If you *abandon* a place, you leave and never return. The passengers *abandoned* the sinking ship. If a watchman *deserts* his post, he leaves it unguarded. You *forsake* your friends if they're counting on your help and you let them down.

See also *surrender* (v).

ANTONYMS: stay (v), come, arrive, remain, linger

They **abandoned** the sinking ship.

lengthen

Lengthen means become or make longer. It is the opposite of shorten. A tailor *lengthens* a coat by letting down the hem. You can *lengthen* a paragraph by adding more sentences. The shadows *lengthened* as the sun dropped lower in the sky.

stretch

Stretch means make something longer, usually by pulling it rather than adding to it. You can *stretch* such things as rubber bands, pieces of cloth, material, string, and wire. You might *stretch* your arms and legs if you feel tired. If you *stretch* the truth, you pull it out of shape because you do not tell the facts correctly.

extend

Extend can mean stretch out. You *extend* your hand when you hold it out to shake hands with someone. The highway *extended* from Chicago to Cleveland. A chameleon can *extend* its tongue beyond its snout. *Extend* can also mean lengthen in time. He *extended* his vacation for another week.

A chameleon can **extend** its tongue beyond its snout.

draw out
continue
prolong

Draw out, continue, and *prolong* mean make something last a long time or keep something going on so it won't end. Storytellers can *draw out* a story by adding their own ideas. Rosa will *continue* writing her letter after dinner. Medicine *prolongs* our lives. I would have hung up sooner, but my friend kept *prolonging* the conversation.

See also *enlarge, increase* (v).

ANTONYMS: shorten, arrest (v), cut short, stop (v), terminate

L

liberty

Liberty is the state of being free to do or say what you need or want to do. The colonists fought for their *liberty* in the American Revolution. *Liberty* can also mean the state of being free from prison. The prisoner was set at *liberty* after serving his prison term.

● freedom

Freedom is liberty. *Freedom* of speech is guaranteed in the United States Constitution. People enjoy *freedom* of movement in this country; they can travel from one state to another as they wish. *Freedom* from worry means you're carefree.

● independence

Independence is the state of being free from the control of others. Some African nations have been granted *independence* from other countries which ruled them. Going to summer camp may help develop your *independence.*

● liberation
● emancipation

Liberation and *emancipation* are the acts of freeing from some control. The first act of the new governor was to arrange for the *liberation* of the innocent prisoner. President Lincoln issued the *Emancipation* Proclamation, which freed the slaves.

● license

License can be the taking of too much liberty. Liberty turns into *license* when the power of doing and saying whatever you want includes changing or destroying property and hurting other people. A play director who changes most of what the characters say is taking too much *license,* or liberty, with the author's work.

lift (v)

Lift means move something to a higher position, usually by taking it up from the ground. Tina *lifted* the book off the floor and put it on the table. A package might be too heavy to *lift. Lift* also can mean rise and go away. We speak of fog *lifting* as the sky clears.

raise

Raise means lift or cause something to rise. It is the opposite of lower. You may *raise* your hand when you know the answer to a question in school. When the flag is *raised* and then lowered halfway down the pole, it is at half-mast.

uplift
elevate

Uplift and *elevate* are good synonyms to use when your spirits are raised or lifted. Seeing a good movie can *uplift* your spirits and make you feel better. Reading a good book can *elevate* your mind.

Elevate can also mean lift or promote. She was *elevated* from vice-president to president of the company.

boost

Boost means help someone climb or move by pushing or shoving the person up from below. John *boosted* Al over the fence. Dolores tried to *boost* her big dog into the truck. It can also mean put someone in high spirits. The spirits of the losing team were *boosted* by the crowd's cheering.

heave

Heave means lift and throw something heavy. The farmer *heaved* a sack of grain into the wagon. The fisherman *heaved* the anchor into the lake.

The fisherman **heaved** the anchor into the lake.

lift (v) continued on page 234 ▶

Ginny's allowance **limits** how much she can spend each week.

lift (v) continued from page 233

hoist

Hoist means lift something, often by means of a machine. A crane is used to *hoist* cargo from a ship onto a dock. Ropes and pulleys are used to *hoist* the sails of large boats. Nancy and Celeste used a rope to *hoist* the lumber up into the tree to build their tree house.

See also *help* (v).

ANTONYM: lower (v)

limit (v)

Limit means set a boundary beyond which a person or thing cannot go or is not permitted to go. If something *limits* your view, you can't see past or beyond it. Laws *limit* the speed of traffic. This special bargain is *limited* to one per customer. My allowance *limits* how much I can spend each week.

restrict

Restrict can mean limit or put a condition on something. Zoning laws *restrict* the kinds of buildings that can be erected in an area. The students' outdoor activities are *restricted* to the school grounds.

confine

Confine means limit or restrict a person's activities. Sickness may *confine* a person to bed. I was *confined* to my room when I had the mumps. Jack McCall was *confined* to jail after shooting Wild Bill Hickok.

fence

Fence means enclose an area with a fence in order to keep something in or out. The farmer *fenced* the meadow to prevent the sheep from roaming.

See also *surround.*

234

The **end** of this game is reached when one player runs out of checkers.

limit (n)

A *limit* is the farthest point to which something or someone is allowed to go. City *limits* mark the point where the land of one city ends and the land of another begins. I had to set a *limit* on how long I talk on the phone. If a building is "off *limits,*" you may not enter it.

end

An *end* is a point where something stops. It is the opposite of a beginning or an outset. These bushes mark the *end* of our property. The *end* of this game is reached when one player runs out of checkers.

boundary
line

A *boundary* or a *line* marks the outermost limit of an area or territory. You can find the *boundary* between Canada and the United States on a map. Rivers often form *boundaries* between countries. The equator, an imaginary *line* around the middle of the earth, divides the Northern and Southern Hemispheres.

frontier

The *frontier* of a country can mean the limit or point where the settled area ends and the wilderness begins.

deadline

A *deadline* is a time limit. It is the last possible time or date that something can be done. Newspaper reporters have to meet *deadlines* when they send in their news.

restriction

A *restriction* is a limit or condition placed on something. Parents may decide to place *restrictions* on TV viewing.

See also *edge* (n).

ANTONYMS: beginning (n), outset

L

little

Little means less than something else—in amount, value, or size. I earned a *little* money by baby-sitting. *Little* is also the opposite of big and large. She is *little,* but not *little* enough to fit on a tricycle.

small
tiny
minute

Small means little, but *tiny* is even smaller. *Minute* is the smallest of all. *Small* and *tiny* describe size. That pair of shoes is too *small.* A baby's fingers are very *tiny.* *Minute* describes something so small that you can hardly see it. "You have a *minute* crack in that tooth," the dentist said.

miniature

Miniature refers to something that is scaled down or reduced from its normal size. We built a *miniature* gas station for my cousin.

• puny

Puny is not a synonym for little, but *puny* is a good word to use when you mean that something is weak and small or unimportant. I can hardly believe that this *puny* dog could frighten off a burglar.

Did this **puny** dog really frighten off a burglar?

slight
trivial
petty

Slight, trivial, and *petty,* all mean small or unimportant. Forgetting to study for your driving test was more than a *slight* mistake. How can you be angry about something as *trivial* as a broken fingernail? *Petty* arguments are a waste of time.

brief
short

Brief and *short* usually mean not lasting a long time. There was a *brief* pause in our conversation. After a *short* rest, the joggers were ready to go again.

ANTONYMS: big, large, enormous, huge, immense, important, vast

236

live (v)   *Live* is an everyday word meaning exist or make a home or spend time in a certain place. Who *lives* in the corner house? *Live* is also the opposite of die. My friend's grandmother *lived* to be one hundred.

dwell   *Dwell* and *reside* are good synonyms for
reside   live. Some desert people *dwell* in tents. Some Indians in the Southwest *dwell* in pueblos. *Reside* is a more formal word that means live permanently or officially in one place. The President *resides* in the White House while in office. Voters usually must vote in the city and state in which they *reside.*

Some Indians in the Southwest **dwell** in pueblos.

inhabit   Both people and animals *inhabit* places. *Inhabit* is used when we speak of living within a large area. Chipmunks and squirrels *inhabit* woodlands. Whales *inhabit* the sea. The hot, dry climate of many desert regions prevents people from *inhabiting* these areas.

live (v) continued on page 238 ▶

live (v) continued from page 237

The campers carried **packs** on their backs.

occupy

You *occupy* a place if you have possession of it and are actually in it. Your family *occupies* the house you live in. You *occupy* a seat in your classroom. *Occupy* can also mean fill up space or even time or attention. This farm *occupies* one hundred acres of land. We hoped Pedro would *occupy* himself with the puzzle.

ANTONYM: die

load (n)

A *load* is something that is carried or transported by a person, an animal, or a vehicle. The truck carried a *load* of stone and gravel to the building site.

cargo
freight

Cargo and *freight* can be products or merchandise that are transported from one place to another. We speak of the *cargo* of a ship or plane and the *freight* carried by a train or truck. A *cargo* of food and medical supplies was flown to the disaster area. Oranges and grapefruit are shipped as *freight* from California and Florida to many cities.

pack

A group of objects collected and tied together in a bundle for easier carrying is called a *pack.* The campers carried *packs* on their backs.

burden

A *burden* is a heavy or awkward load that is difficult to carry. Donkeys and camels are called beasts of *burden* because they are used to carrying heavy loads. A *burden* can also be something worrisome or even a problem that is difficult to solve. A person with a lot of bills has a financial *burden.*

They had a good **spot** from which to watch the parade.

weight	*Weight* is another word to use for some heavy burden that is weighing you down. If you have something that is worrying you, you are struggling under the *weight* of your problem.
location	The *location* of something is the place where it is put or where it is. A road map will show you the *location* of cities, parks, rivers, monuments, and other places of interest. The *location* of our house is far from the main road. The sheriff discovered the *location* of the stolen money.
site	A *site* is a particular location. It may be the place where something special occurred. Independence Hall was the *site* of the signing of the Declaration of Independence.
spot	A *spot* is also a particular location. We had a good *spot* from which to watch the parade.
point	A *point* is an exact and fixed location. A starting *point* is where a race begins.
locality	A *locality* is a general area that surrounds a particular place, such as a neighborhood. If you become familiar with your *locality,* you won't get lost.
position situation	The *position* or *situation* of something can be the way it is placed in relation to its surroundings. Putting the lamp in this *position* will give you the best light. The *situation* of the trees along the walk is very attractive.

L

look (v)

Look means turn your eyes toward something. It is often followed by *at.* You might *look at* some pictures in an album.

see

Look is very close in meaning to *see. See* means identify something by sight. But if you're in a very dark room, you may *look* without *seeing* anything. And you might *see* something, like daylight, without actually *looking at* it. Jessica *looked at* the sign, but I'm not really sure she *saw* it.

glance

Glance means look quickly, then look away. People often *glance* at things when they're busy or in a hurry. You *glance* at a clock to see what time it is. Roscoe *glanced* at the headline, but didn't have a chance to read the article.

peek

Peek means look quickly and slyly. We *peeked* at the construction project through the hole in the fence.

gaze

Gaze means look for a long time. You might *gaze* at something that is new or very beautiful. If you're daydreaming, you might *gaze* at the ceiling.

stare

You *stare* at something when you look at it for a long time with wide-open eyes. The children *stared* at the strange-looking animal.

peer

Peer means look closely and curiously. At the museum the students *peered* at the skeleton of a dinosaur.

glare

Glare means look angrily. If you're mad at your sister, you might *glare* at her. I *glared* at the man who bumped me.

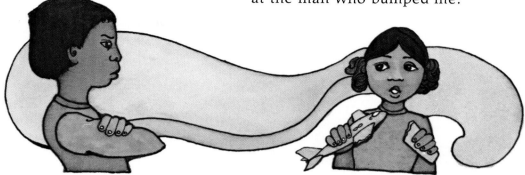

When Reuben is mad at his sister, he **glares** at her.

love (v)

Love is a wonderful word. Some people think it's the greatest word in the world. Some say love makes the world go 'round. *Love* is also a tired word. People use it too often. Why not save *love* for those persons and things most important to you, and find some other words to tell how you really feel? When you say you *love* someone or something, you really mean one of three things.

The strongest word for *love* is *adore.* In that entry you'll find words that mean *love* something more than anything else in the world.

The entry *admire* has words to use when you *love* and respect someone.

Under *enjoy* you will find words to use instead of *love* when you talk about liking food or games or something else, or just having fun.

L

loyal

A *loyal* friend is one who stands by you when you are in need. A *loyal* friend is not easily tempted to talk about you behind your back. You can trust and depend on someone who is *loyal*. A person who is *loyal* is not treacherous or traitorous. *Loyal* citizens would never betray their country or government. You are *loyal* to your team if you support it when it loses as well as when it wins.

trustworthy

Trustworthy people can be depended upon to do what they have promised or have been told to do. They are always dependable. You can expect them to be where they say they'll be when they say they'll be there.

devoted

Devoted means loyal. You can be *devoted* to another person, to a job, to a cause, or to an organization. A *devoted* person is always willing to offer help and support.

faithful
true

Persons who are *faithful* and *true* are loyal and worthy of trust and confidence. A *faithful* dog will follow its owner. A *true* friend will help you in time of need.

ANTONYMS: treacherous, traitorous, disloyal, faithless, false, fickle

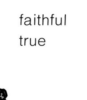

A **faithful** dog will follow its owner.

M

make

Pity the poor visitor from a foreign land who tries to understand our language the way we speak it. The word *make* is a good example. To *make* something is to bring it into being or cause it to be. But think of the strange ways in which we use *make!* We *make* a train if we catch it. We *make* tracks if we run away. We *make* money if we earn it. We *make* haste if we hurry. We *make believe* if we pretend. We *make* way if we stand back and open up a path for someone.

Look up the following entries to find good words for whatever you want to *make.*

Build contains words for *making* big things.

Start (v) has words for *making* things move.

Create has synonyms for causing things to be.

Shape (v) has words for putting form into things.

Change (v) tells how to *make* things different.

Increase (v) means *make* things more or greater.

Enlarge tells how to *make* things bigger.

Look under *lengthen* for words to *make* things longer; under *shrink,* to *make* things smaller.

Decrease (v) gives words for *making* things less.

They had an accidental
meeting.

meeting

A *meeting* is any gathering of several or many people in one place at a certain time. A *meeting* can be large or small, long or short. It is usually planned ahead of time. *Meetings* that are planned usually bring together people with the same interests. Carl and I had a *meeting* to plan our class play. At our club *meeting* we plan to talk about ways to raise money. You can, of course, have an accidental *meeting* with someone if you both just happen to be in the same place at the same time.

• assembly

An *assembly* is a planned meeting, usually attended by a large group of people for the purpose of being informed, being entertained, or making group decisions. At the school *assembly* yesterday we saw a film about fire prevention.

• conference

A *conference* is a meeting in which two or more people exchange views on a subject. Often a *conference* is a regular meeting of people who represent a group or organization. There is no school today because of the teachers' *conference.*

• convention

A *convention* is often an annual meeting to which certain members of an organization are sent to handle the group's business. A meeting of a political party is also called a *convention.*

• council

A *council* is a meeting of a small group of people chosen from a larger group to serve as advisers or consultants. The student *council* met yesterday to discuss the problem of noise in the halls.

244

misery

Misery is the state of feeling very sad or unhappy or unwell. Anything unpleasant or troublesome may cause *misery.* The severe flood brought *misery* to the villagers.

suffering

Suffering is the pain you experience when you are sick or unhappy. The medicine relieved Nick's *suffering.* You could see the *suffering* on the faces of those poor, hungry children.

distress
torment

Worry or anxiety over something can cause *distress* or *torment.* I was in *distress* after losing Grandmother's ring. Remembering the mean things I had said caused me hours of *torment.*

agony

Agony is extreme misery and suffering brought about by something that is almost impossible to endure. A toothache may cause a great deal of *agony.*

unhappiness

Unhappiness is not as strong as the other words. A slight disappointment may cause you *unhappiness,* but you'll soon get over it.

See also *sadness.*

ANTONYMS: contentment, happiness, joy, pleasure

A toothache may cause a great deal of **agony.**

misfortune

Misfortune is anything bad that happens to a person, which causes that person to be physically or mentally upset. Some people think of *misfortune* as just bad luck. Tammy overslept yesterday, and then, to add to her *misfortune,* she forgot her lunch and missed her ride.

misfortune continued on page 246 ▸

M

Eric's sister has **trouble** tying her shoes.

misfortune continued from page 245

- difficulty

A *difficulty* is a problem you find hard to solve. Don's *difficulty* is that he would rather sleep than work.

- trouble

Trouble is difficulty or misfortune. Some *troubles* are big and some are little. Since the accident last week, Dad has had *trouble* with the car. My little sister has *trouble* tying her shoes.

- distress

Distress can be a difficult or painful situation that causes suffering to someone. Ships send out an SOS whenever they are in *distress.* Usually *distress* doesn't last long and probably is not very serious. Losing that scarf caused me *distress.*

- hardship

A *hardship* is something that causes suffering and is very hard to bear. The group of backpackers who were lost in the mountains endured many *hardships* before they were finally rescued.

- ruin

Ruin is the complete collapse of someone or something. My grandpa says that failure to pay even one bill can start any family on its way to financial *ruin.* A building or an object that has been damaged or destroyed may be called a *ruin.*

- disaster

A *disaster* is a terrible misfortune that hits suddenly and often unexpectedly. The apartment fire was a *disaster* for the families who lived there.

See also *harm* (n).

ANTONYMS: blessing, happiness, help (n), pleasure, prosperity, success

mix (v)   *Mix* means put together two or more things to make something else. You *mix* flour and water to make paste. A baker makes a cake by *mixing* the ingredients together. Danny *mixed* the chocolate syrup into his milk.

combine   *Combine* means bring or join different things together. If you *combine* yellow and red, you'll get orange. Hydrogen and oxygen *combine* to make water. *Combine* can also be used when people act together. In assembling the baseball team, the coach *combined* players who were good at fielding with players who had good batting averages.

blend   *Blend* can mean mix thoroughly and smoothly. An eggbeater is used to *blend* ingredients for cooking. An artist *blends* two colors to make a third color.

fuse   *Fuse* means blend or join by melting. A soldering iron can be used to *fuse* broken wires. Brass is a metal made by *fusing* copper and zinc.

mingle
merge   *Mingle* and *merge* mean mix or come together with something or someone else. At a big party the host usually *mingles* with the guests to see that they are having a good time. Companies or business firms *merge* when they combine to make one firm. Drivers must *merge* quickly into traffic when they enter expressways. The two creeks *merged* to form a river.

ANTONYMS: scatter, separate (v), sort (v)

Left 32, right 8, left 13?

A **combination** of numbers in the right order will open the safe.

mixture

A *mixture* is a product formed by mixing or putting different things or materials together. Cement is a *mixture* of materials such as clay and limestone.

union

A *union* is the bringing together of different things to form a whole. The United States is a *union* of fifty states. A labor *union* is a group of workers who join together to improve working conditions.

combination

A *combination* can be a mixture of anything, such as persons, numbers, or chemicals. A bouquet is a *combination* of flowers. A *combination* of numbers in the right order will open the safe.

fusion

Fusion means the joining of two or more things, sometimes by melting. We speak of the *fusion* of wires in an electrical circuit.

merger

A *merger* is a combination of business firms or other organizations.

compound

A *compound* is something formed by putting different parts together. Water is a *compound* of two parts hydrogen to one part oxygen. "Blackboard" is a *compound* of two words.

blend

A *blend* is a thorough mixture. Seasonings are a *blend* of herbs. In a chorus, high and low voices form a *blend* of sounds.

assortment

An *assortment* is a collection of various kinds. An *assortment* of chocolates may include some pieces with hard centers and some with soft centers.

ANTONYM: separation

248

moist

Moist means slightly wet. Anything that is *moist* is not completely dry. Fresh bread sometimes feels *moist*. Your eyes are *moist* after you cry.

damp

Damp also means somewhat wet. I used a *damp* cloth to clean my shoes. Please check to see if the clothes on the line are still *damp*.

humid

Humid describes air that is moist or damp. A city near a river or lake may be *humid* in the summer. A jungle is hot and *humid,* but a desert is hot and arid. Today it was hot, *humid,* and sticky.

rainy

Rainy means wet with rain. It is usually quite *rainy* in a jungle. A *rainy* day may spoil your plans to go to the fair.

It is usually quite **rainy** in a jungle.

watery

Watery means containing water. *Watery* paint may be too thin to use.

juicy
succulent

Juicy and *succulent* mean full of juice or moisture. Certain fruits, vegetables, and meats are *juicy*. A cactus is a *succulent* plant. It can grow in a desert because its leaves and stem store all the water it needs.

ANTONYMS: dry (adj), arid, parched

249

M

move

Move means change position or set in motion. That is a simple definition of a simple word. But did you ever stop to think of all the ways in which things can *move* or be *moved?*

For instance, can you think of anything that can't *move* or be *moved?* Engineers who are building a highway can *move* a hill by having it blown up. Builders can *move* a house from one side of town to the other. People often *move* from city to city. Traffic *moves.* Time *moves.* A clever actor can *move* an audience to laughter or tears.

You probably can't think of many verbs that don't mean *move* or *move* something. You can *move* yourself. *Walk* (v) and *run* (v) are entries that contain several words to describe the way people and animals *move.* Look them up. Also read the entry *go.*

You can *move* something or someone. You might *lift* or *carry, take* or *send, advance* or *change* it. You may *throw* or *catch* it. You can *shake, push, pull,* or *put* many things.

Perhaps you want to *move* a person or a thing to do something. Look up *urge* and *force* (v) for synonyms. If you *move* something or someone in an unwelcome way, you *disturb.*

mystery

A *mystery* is something that has not been explained or cannot be completely understood. My disappearance was a *mystery* to them until they found my note. Scientists are gradually solving the many *mysteries* of space travel.

problem

A *problem* can be anything that you wonder what to do about. It may be a question you can't answer or a situation you are not sure how to handle. That math *problem* has me stumped. My *problem* is fitting my tape recorder into that small space.

He finds the solution to a **puzzle** by putting pieces together.

puzzle

You find the solution to a *puzzle* by putting pieces or words or information together. You are probably familiar with jigsaw *puzzles* and crossword *puzzles.* Sometimes a person is a *puzzle* if you don't understand that person's behavior.

riddle

A *riddle* is a puzzling question that usually requires hard and clever thinking to answer. The *riddle* of the disappearing hat was finally solved. Many children enjoy *riddles* and even buy books of *riddles.*

secret

A *secret* is something that one or more persons know but don't tell to anyone else. *Secrets* are a mystery to those who are left out. If you tell a *secret* to too many people, it won't be a *secret* any more.

N

neat   *Neat* means clean and in order. It can describe anything that isn't messy or sloppy. A *neat* house isn't cluttered with trash or rubbish. *Neat* clothes are not wrinkled or dirty. He has very *neat* handwriting. After she washed the car, it looked *neat* as a pin!

tidy   A *tidy* room is one in which everything is carefully arranged and in its proper place. People who are *tidy* are very careful about how they look and how they do things.

trim   *Trim* means neat, clean, and well fitting. The mail carrier looked *trim* in the new uniform.

orderly   *Orderly* means neat and tidy and in order. If I would keep my room *orderly,* I would never have any trouble finding things. Papers and books are arranged carefully in an *orderly* desk.

shipshape   Something is in *shipshape* condition if it is well cared for. When I finished sweeping the tree house, it looked *shipshape.*

ANTONYMS: messy, sloppy, disorderly, untidy

new   *New* is used in many ways. It is the opposite of old. *New* describes something or someone that has never existed before. A *new* house is one that has just been built. A *new* bud is just beginning to grow.

New also describes something that has never been used or worn before. He bought a *new* suit. My stereo is brand *new.* You may also do or think of something for the first time, and this can be called *new.* She starts her *new* job tomorrow.

current
up-to-date

Current and *up-to-date* mean new and happening right now. Newscasters report on *current* events. The automobile is a *current* means of transportation. The horse and buggy are obsolete. The old-fashioned pictures in the catalog were replaced by *up-to-date* ones.

modern
contemporary

Modern and *contemporary* mean happening or existing at the present time. Many *modern* paintings seem hard to understand. The skyscraper is a *contemporary* form of architecture. *Contemporary* also means happening or existing at about the same time. The opening of the Panama Canal and the beginning of World War I were *contemporary* events.

Many **modern** paintings seem hard to understand.

recent
late

Recent and *late* mean not long past. They describe something that has just happened or has just been made. The whole family was anxious to get the pictures of our *recent* vacation. A *late* copy of a magazine is more current than a copy from last year.

young

Young describes someone or something that is not fully developed or mature. A child is *young.* The mare is guarding her *young* colts. *Young* corn is not yet ready to be picked.

ANTONYMS: old, obsolete, old-fashioned,
            antique (adj), mature (adj),
            adult (adj), ancient

N

normal

Normal means something that is expected because it fits a standard or custom or rule. For some pupils a *normal* school day begins at 8:30 A.M. and ends at 3:00 P.M. *Normal* means not far from the average. Sometimes the bus driver finishes her route in four hours; at other times it may take her five hours; but the *normal* time is about four and one-half hours.

regular

Regular means arranged or formed according to some standard or rule. A *regular* work week is Monday through Friday.

routine
typical

Routine and *typical* mean ordinary or happening regularly and always in the same way. A *routine* inspection of an automobile must be made at certain times; certain parts of the car are always checked. A *typical* day is one that is about the same as any other day—up in the morning, off to school, back home again, and then back to bed.

A **typical** day is one that is about the same as any other day—up in the morning, off to school, and then back to bed.

natural

Natural can mean normal because of the way something is or the way something acts. It is *natural* for some birds to fly south in the winter. The *natural* dwelling place for a lion is a den.

See also *ordinary.*

ANTONYMS: irregular, abnormal, unnatural

notice (v)

Notice means catch sight of or look carefully at someone or something. Did you *notice* the boy who just passed us? I *noticed* a hole in my jacket, but I tried to ignore it.

Those faces carved on the mountainside are a sight to **behold.**

behold

Behold is an old-fashioned word that means notice something or take a look at something. Those faces carved on the mountainside are a sight to *behold.*

observe

Observe can mean notice or look closely at something. You *observe* the movements of amoebas through a microscope.

note

Note can mean notice or observe with care. A salesperson demonstrating a new vacuum cleaner might say, "*Note* how easy it is to operate." The coach asked us to *note* the correct way to hold a football.

view

View means consider or notice something that is before you. A committee tries to *view* all sides of a problem. The mayor came to *view* the damage done by the storm.

See also *examine.*

ANTONYMS:-ignore, overlook, miss (v)

255

object (n)

An *object* is anything you can see or touch. Toys are *objects* to play with. Tools are the *objects* a carpenter uses. A storekeeper displays *objects* on the shelves.

An *object* can also be something toward which an action is directed. It's what someone is working toward. Her *object* in baby-sitting was to earn enough money to go to camp. The *object* of the game is to get your marker home first.

thing
article

Thing and *article* are other words for objects. It's hard to see *things* in the dark. An *article* can be any particular thing. A shirt is an *article* of clothing. The five *articles* I brought with me are missing.

COMMUNITY FUND

— 1,000,000
— 900,000
— 800,000
— 700,000
— 600,000
— 500,000
— 400,000
— 300,000
— 200,000
— 100,000

A million dollars is the **target** of the Community Fund drive this year.

target
mark
bull's eye

A *target* and a *mark* are objects to shoot at. A *bull's eye* is the center of a target. An archer gets more points if the arrow hits the *bull's eye*. When someone hits a *target* in the center or goes right to the point of something, you might say, "You've hit the *bull's eye!*" Some people think it's fun to throw darts at a *target*. *Target* and *mark* are often used to mean an object, or goal, you are trying to reach. A million dollars is the *target* of the Community Fund drive this year. Last year's drive set a high *mark* for us to aim for this year.

purpose
end
goal

Purpose, end, and *goal* are all objects to be reached or achieved. Her *purpose* in calling was to invite me to the party. Umberto's dream was to be a violinist, and he was working toward that *end.* Dale's *goal* is to become a civil engineer.

256

intent
aim
objective

Intent, aim, and *objective* are other words you can use to mean what you have in mind to do. My *intent* was to warn her, not frighten her. Finding the North Pole was the *aim* of Admiral Peary's expedition. Our *objective* is to save enough money to buy a ten-speed bicycle.

object (v)

If you *object* to something, you argue against it, giving your own idea or opinion. You might *object* to something you oppose, such as stealing, or to something that seems unfair, such as having to go to bed every night at seven o'clock. I *objected* to turning down the stereo, but my neighbors insisted.

complain

Complain means tell someone that you are not satisfied with a situation. When you *complain,* you let people know that you are opposed to something, or at least that you are not happy with it. Ruby *complained* to the mechanic that the car was hard to start on cold mornings. Fred *complains* about the food but eats more than anyone.

Fred **complains** about the food but eats more than anyone.

disagree

Disagree is the opposite of agree. People *disagree* if their ideas or opinions are not the same. Often when people *disagree,* they argue about who is right or who has the better idea. We always seem to *disagree* about which TV programs to watch.

protest

Protest means object strongly to something that happens or doesn't happen. Often a group *protests* by presenting its views in an

object (v) continued on page 258 ▶

O

object (v) continued from page 257

organized manner, either in writing or speech. The citizens signed petitions *protesting* the building of an amusement park on good farm land.

See also *argue.*

ANTONYMS: agree, approve, consent (v)

objection   *Objection* is the act of objecting to something that is said or to something that happens. I have no *objection* to wearing boots, but I hate to carry an umbrella. *"Objection* overruled," declared the judge.

complaint   A *complaint* is an objection and is usually the result of a person's not being satisfied with a situation. She heard many *complaints* about the way the banquet was handled. I like Victor, but I get tired of listening to his *complaints.*

disapproval   *Disapproval* is the opposite of approval. You show *disapproval* by refusing to agree or to accept someone's action or opinion. If you cheat at a game, you can expect *disapproval* from your friends and opponents. When she walked into the room, *disapproval* showed on her face.

When she walked into the room, **disapproval** showed on her face.

protest

A *protest* is an objection to something that you disapprove of or feel is unfair. *Protests* against poor service should not be ignored by the post office. If an umpire's decision during a baseball game seems unfair to one team, that team may play the rest of the game under *protest.*

ANTONYMS: approval, agreement, endorsement

obtain

Obtain means get something, usually by putting forth some kind of effort or by paying for it. People *obtain* knowledge and information through reading and studying. After what seemed like weeks of waiting, Rita finally *obtained* her driver's license. If we can *obtain* the necessary tools, we can build a sailboat.

receive

Receive means get something that is given, offered, sent, or delivered to you. You may *receive* without putting forth any effort or paying. You *receive* cards and gifts on your birthday. You will *receive* a diploma when you graduate from school. Harold *received* a black eye in the fight.

inherit

Inherit means receive something when someone dies. The will indicated that Sara was to *inherit* her grandfather's farm. Also, you may be said to *inherit* something passed on to you from someone who gives it up. Bob *inherited* a coat his brother had outgrown. I *inherited* the job of keeping a record of the bazaar's profits.

obtain continued on page 260 ▶

Delia will **win** first prize if she correctly guesses the number of jellybeans in the jar.

obtain continued from page 259

buy
purchase

Buy and *purchase* mean obtain something by paying for it. He went to the store to *buy* some food for dinner. He *bought* hamburger and buns. *Purchase* is the more formal word. Our family *purchased* a new home. Yoshiko *purchased* a tennis racket.

win

Win means get something in a contest or competition. You may work hard to beat someone, or you may *win* by luck. You will *win* first prize if you correctly guess the number of jellybeans in the jar. Linda *won* a blue ribbon in the sack race.

earn

You *earn* something if you obtain it in return for work or for something you do. She *earns* her allowance by taking out the garbage every day. Many teen-agers baby-sit to *earn* money. Jason *earned* my respect by working hard at his job.

achieve

Achieve means get or obtain something by doing a lot of hard work. She finally *achieved* her goal of becoming a doctor.

ANTONYMS: give, send, give up, forgo, let go, lose, relinquish

odd

Odd describes something that is out of the ordinary. Something might seem *odd* to you if it is different from what you are used to or different from what you would normally expect. You might hear an *odd* noise or see an *odd* sight. It is *odd* that my friend didn't meet me as we had planned.

unusual

Unusual means not common or ordinary or usual. It would be *unusual* to hear a clock strike thirteen.

curious

Curious can also describe something unusual. I found some *curious* antiques in the junk shop. This belt has a *curious* brass buckle on it.

strange
mysterious

Strange and *mysterious* mean odd and hard to understand. He gave me a *strange* look after I bumped into him. The kitten was trying to figure out where the *strange* sound was coming from. I saw a *mysterious* light moving across the sky. Where is this *mysterious* shadow you say you've seen?

queer
funny

Queer and *funny* are often used to describe something odd or strange. Jellyfish have *queer* shapes. A Pekingese is a *funny* little dog with long hair and a pug nose.

quaint

Something *quaint* is odd and unfamiliar because it is old-fashioned. She took many pictures of the *quaint* little town. The square dancers wore *quaint* costumes.

peculiar

Something *peculiar* is odd or typical of one kind of person or thing, not shared by others. Mary has a *peculiar* way of snapping her fingers. The kangaroo is an animal *peculiar* to Australia. He has that stiff walk *peculiar* to some cowhands.

He has that stiff walk **peculiar** to some cowhands.

eccentric

An *eccentric* person acts in an odd or strange way. The *eccentric* old man wore his boots even in dry weather.

See also *foreign, rare.*

ANTONYMS: common, ordinary, usual, familiar, natural, normal, regular

O

opinion

An *opinion* is what you have decided is true about something. Your *opinions* may be based on facts, but they may still be questioned. Your *opinion* about something can change, and people have had different *opinions* about the same thing. You can form an *opinion* about almost anything—a book, the weather, the best candidate.

view

A *view* can be a very personal opinion. Your feelings and attitudes influence your *views*. An artist's *view* on a painting may differ from that of someone who knows little about art.

thought

A *thought* can be an opinion, or it may be just one of the ideas you use to form an opinion. What are Bill's *thoughts* on the editorial in last night's paper?

conviction

A *conviction* is a strong opinion. If you have a *conviction* about something, you are sure it is right, and you are not likely to change your mind. Many colonists in America shared the *conviction* that the king of England was mistreating them.

judgment

A *judgment* is usually the opinion of someone in authority. The jury passed *judgment* on the criminal. In my *judgment* we are not ready to enter the race.

conclusion

A *conclusion* can be your final opinion about something. It is usually based on some facts. After driving past the same building five times, she came to the *conclusion* that she was hopelessly lost.

See also *belief, idea.*

In the coach's **judgment** they are not ready to enter the race.

ordinary   *Ordinary* means natural or normal, not exceptional, or not different from what you know or expect. An *ordinary* TV program may not hold your attention, because you can guess what's going to happen.

everyday   *Everyday* describes something that happens or is used daily. You wear *everyday* clothes to school, but you might get dressed up for special occasions.

usual   *Usual* describes things that are ordinary and that can be expected. Something out of the ordinary is unusual. We had more than the *usual* amount of snow this winter. Nancy didn't order her *usual* vanilla malt.

familiar
commonplace   *Familiar* and *commonplace* mean well known. A car is a *familiar* sight today. You recognize a *familiar* song when you hear it. Something that is *commonplace* may not interest you. Mailboxes on corners are *commonplace* in cities.

common   Something that is *common* is ordinary. It happens often and is familiar. Dialing the wrong number is a *common* mistake.

One **popular** belief is that walking under a ladder brings bad luck.

popular   *Popular* means known or usual among many people. It is a *popular* practice to send get-well cards to someone in the hospital. One *popular* belief is that walking under a ladder brings bad luck.

See also *normal.*

ANTONYMS: exceptional, unusual, extraordinary, special, uncommon, unexpected

P

part (n)   Any object or idea can be separated or broken up into *parts.* So a *part* is always less than the whole of something. Since there are many ways of dividing something, there are many different kinds of *parts.*

If you drop a mirror, you probably sweep it up in *fragments.* If you eat a piece of cake, you'll have crumbs, or tiny *particles,* left on your plate. If you make a batch of cookies, you may drop *chunks* of dough on a cookie sheet. Look up the entry *piece* for words that mean *parts* of something broken away or taken away from the whole.

When you cut an apple pie into *parts* and give a piece to each member of the family, you are giving each person a *portion.* A *portion* is a *part* meant for a certain person or purpose. A *portion* may also be a definite size or amount. You'll find other good words for this kind of *part* in the entry *portion* (n).

When you think about the *parts* of animals, plants, and people, you probably think of arms and legs, branches, stems, roots, blossoms. Words for *parts* of bodies or systems are listed under *branch* (n).

Just about everything in the world is made up of *parts.* And we have all kinds of words to describe this division. Of course, air, water, and land are the three main *parts* of our earth. But take a look at *zone* (n). You'll see some interesting words that tell how we divide the face of the earth.

264

party

Party probably brings to your mind pictures of cake and ice cream and presents. But the word has another meaning. A *party* is one or more persons taking part in an activity. The search *party* hasn't come back yet. Which political *party* are you working for?

Other words can be used for different *parties.*

• group

A *group* is a gathering of two or more persons, usually with a common interest. Such a gathering can be either accidental or planned. The angry *group* of people waited five minutes for an elevator. We waited in line for ten hours to see our favorite rock *group.*

• gang

A *gang* is a group of people who work together toward some common goal. Work *gangs* repair railroad tracks. Often *gang* is used for a group that is doing something unlawful or violent. The Jets and the Sharks were rival *gangs* in "West Side Story." Sometimes *gang* is used in an informal way to mean friends. The *gang* is over for pizza tonight.

party continued on page 266 ▶

The **gang** is over for pizza tonight.

P

party continued from page 265

• band

A *band* is a group of people joined for a common purpose and working very closely together. The marching *band* performed all over Europe and the United States. Have you ever seen a *band* of gypsies?

• team

A *team* is a group of people playing or working together to reach a particular goal. A *team* of doctors worked day and night to save her life. Our golf *team* finally won the championship.

• troupe
• troop

Troupe and *troop* are both groups of people. A *troupe* is a group of performers which presents entertainment in a circus or on the stage. A *troop* is a group of members in an organization, such as the Boy Scouts or the Girl Scouts.

perfect (adj)

When something has no faults or defects or errors, you might say it is *perfect*. Homework that is free from any mistakes is *perfect*. But you also use *perfect* to describe anything that is very good or the best of its kind. The swimmer made a *perfect* dive. Today is a *perfect* day. I found the *perfect* gift for you.

The swimmer made a **perfect** dive.

There are many other words that you can use to tell just how *perfect* something is.

flawless

Flawless means free from any faults or defects. A table top is *flawless* if there are no marks or scratches on it. The diamond was valuable because it was *flawless*. The skater's performance was *flawless*, according to the judges.

perfect (adj) continued

pure
absolute

Pure and *absolute* mean perfect and not mixed with anything else. *Pure* silver doesn't contain any other material. You tell the *absolute* truth about something when you tell all you know and don't leave out any details or include anything that is false.

excellent
expert

Excellent and *expert* mean very good and very fine. You might read an *excellent* book or have an *excellent* time at the zoo. He had an *excellent* idea for the title of the variety show. An *expert* mechanic is highly skilled and does only the best work. Take your watch to an *expert* watchmaker for repairs. She is an *expert* horseback rider.

Take a broken watch to an **expert** watchmaker for repairs.

ideal

Ideal is even stronger than excellent. Something that is *ideal* is absolutely the very best. It suits the purpose exactly. This is an *ideal* spot for a picnic.

ANTONYMS: defective, imperfect

P

permission

When someone tells you that you are allowed to do something or go somewhere, that person has given you *permission*. A lawyer asks the judge for *permission* to speak in court. If you want to leave your job early, you must get *permission* from your supervisor. I was given special *permission* to paint scenes on a store window at Halloween.

Jane's **consent** was necessary before her brother could sell the table tennis set.

leave

Leave is permission to do something that is usually forbidden. The knights used the phrase "By your *leave,* my lord" when talking to King Arthur. That meant "with your permission" I will do this or that.

consent

If you give your *consent* to help someone with a project, you agree with and approve of the way that person wants to do it. *Consent* is permission, too. My *consent* was necessary before my brother could sell the table tennis set; after all, I owned half of it.

license
permit

A *license* is written permission to do something. So is a *permit.* Both are issued by people who have a legal right to do so. A *license* is needed before a person can practice medicine. A *permit* is issued so that a person can learn to drive a car.

piece

A *piece* is one of the parts into which something is divided or separated. You might have a *piece* of cake or break a glass into *pieces.* A *piece* may also be one item among several like it. A chair, for instance, is called a *piece* of furniture. A platter is a *piece* of china.

particle

A *particle* is a very small part or piece of something. (When you get a *particle* of dirt in your eye, though, it does not feel tiny.) Sand is made up of *particles* of rock. Some people are allergic to the *particles* of dust in the air.

bit

A *bit* is a small piece or amount. A *bit* of food or a *bit* of rest is welcome to one who has worked hard all day. I'd go if I had a *bit* more time to get ready. I have just a *bit* of yellow yarn left. Caroline tore the letter into *bits*.

fragment

A *fragment* usually means a piece broken off of something or an unfinished part of something. *Fragments* of glass were found beneath the broken window. We found Indian arrowheads and the *fragments* of a clay cooking dish at the site. I heard only *fragments* of the conversation.

Chris found Indian arrowheads and the **fragments** of a clay cooking dish at the site.

lump
chunk
hunk

Lump, chunk, and *hunk* are words for pieces that have no certain shape or size. Though the words are synonyms, each is used with some materials but seldom or never with others. You might speak of a *lump* of sugar or a *lump* of coal. You probably wouldn't say a *chunk* or *hunk* of sugar, though. You could call a piece of wood a *chunk* or *hunk;* you would not usually say a *lump* of wood. A *chunk* of meat or candy sounds better than a *lump* of meat or candy. A *hunk* of melon or apple sounds more appetizing than a *lump*. A *lump* of gold sounds good!

P

plan (n)

A *plan* is a method of doing or showing something. It is also a group of ideas arranged in an order that will make something happen. A *plan* may be written—like a recipe—or it may be drawn—like a floor *plan*—or it may be just an idea in your head about how to get out of doing dishes.

• outline

An *outline* is a written plan that contains only the main points of something. Before writing a book, an author may make an *outline,* setting down the events, in order, from the beginning to the end of the story. It is then easy to follow the *outline* and fill in the details.

• draft

A *draft* may be a written plan, design, or drawing. A *draft* is usually not the final version. An author often writes a rough first *draft* of an article. The first step is to write down everything without paying much attention to details. Later the writer polishes the article and finally checks the spelling and corrects all mistakes.

• diagram
• sketch

A *diagram* and a *sketch* can both be plans that are drawn. They show the main points and give a rough idea of how something will be done or made. A *diagram* would probably look less like a picture than a *sketch* would. A *diagram* of the water system in your house might show lines that represent water pipes coming into the house and going to different small squares, or rooms. On a *diagram,* items are usually labeled. Otherwise you wouldn't recognize

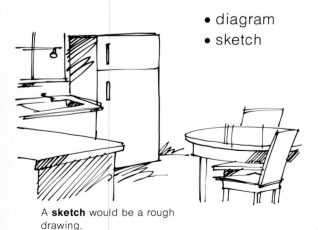
A **sketch** would be a rough drawing.

270

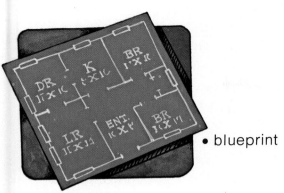

A **blueprint** is a photographic print of a precisely measured and carefully drawn plan.

what they were. A *sketch* would be a rough drawing. A *sketch* of your kitchen would be a quickly and simply drawn picture, showing doors, windows, and appliances. You wouldn't need labels to tell what the artist had drawn.

- blueprint

A *blueprint* is a photographic print of a precisely measured and carefully drawn plan, especially of a building. The lines are white on blue paper. One way to copy a plan is to make a *blueprint.*

- design

A *design* may be a sketch or plan for something that is to be made, like a *design* for a new car. It can also be a plan to accomplish something. Sometimes a *design* is a secret or evil plan. As soon as my sister finished her piece of cake, I could see she had *designs* on mine.

- scheme

A *scheme* may also be a sly or crafty plan. Often it is a plan that is poorly thought out and unsuccessful. Sometimes it is a plan to get something for nothing or by any means, fair or foul. Uncle Joe had a wild *scheme* for becoming rich overnight.

- plot

A *plot* is a carefully laid out plan to accomplish something—often bad. Police uncovered a *plot* to hijack the truck.

- project

A *project* is a long-range plan for doing something. It requires much thought and effort. During the space program's *Project* Mercury, scientists studied the effects of outer space on humans.

See also *arrangement.*

P

plan (v)

Plan means have something in mind or decide on a way to do something. You think out each step you must take to carry out your plan. You may be *planning* to go to college to study law. Or perhaps you haven't *planned* that far ahead.

intend

Intend means have in mind. If you buy a coat, you *intend* to wear it. I *intended* to wash the windows, but I got so interested in this book that I forgot to do them.

arrange

Arrange means plan or prepare and get ready for something. You may *arrange* a picnic by asking each person in your group to bring part of the lunch. Sandra *arranged* to have someone pick her up at the station.

program

Program, nowadays, can mean prepare a machine to give certain information and perform a task. For example, a large store *programs* a computer to figure out and prepare monthly bills. The name and address of each customer and the amounts of the purchases are all fed into the machine. The bill then comes out of the machine, all ready to be mailed to the customer.

Program, nowadays, can mean prepare a machine to give certain information and perform a task.

scheme
plot

Scheme and *plot* usually mean plan something secretly. Through the open window we could hear the boys *scheming* to climb the wall. Rebels are *plotting* to overthrow the dictator.

hatch

You might say someone *hatches* a scheme or plan if that person thinks it up secretly. What crazy scheme is he *hatching* now?

playful   *Playful* means full of play or fun. People who are in a *playful* mood are happy and lighthearted and not at all serious. They laugh and joke a lot. Some people become *playful* when it snows. They cannot resist throwing snowballs. The *playful* dog ran off with my shoe.

frolicsome   *Frolicsome* means playful, gay, and merry. The *frolicsome* kitten batted the ball of yarn around the room. The *frolicsome* porpoises splashed as they raced around the pool, dived through hoops, and jumped into the air.

frisky   *Frisky* means very playful, lively, and high-spirited. It is hard to saddle a *frisky* horse. The *frisky* colts galloped around the corral. The *frisky* goats tried to butt each other with their horns.

The **frisky** colts galloped around the corral.

impish   *Impish* and *mischievous* mean playful but in mischievous   a harmful or annoying way. An *impish* person plays pranks and teases other people. According to some folk tales, the *mischievous* deeds of elves caused problems for many people.

ANTONYMS: serious, businesslike, solemn

273

P

pleasant

Pleasant describes anything that pleases you or gives you a good feeling. You might spend a *pleasant* day in the city or take a *pleasant* ride through the countryside. A *pleasant* person is easy to get along with.

agreeable

Something is *agreeable* to you if you like it. Most fruits have an *agreeable* flavor or taste. The coming of spring is *agreeable* to most people. A show or movie can be *agreeable*. They spent an *agreeable* afternoon shopping at the new mall.

pleasing

Something is *pleasing* if it is agreeable and makes you feel good. Anita has a *pleasing* smile. Sitting in front of a fire can be *pleasing* on a cold, wintry day.

delightful

If something is very pleasing and enjoyable, it is *delightful*. It is *delightful* to go to a circus or watch a parade. Our tour through the candy factory was *delightful*.

Sitting in front of a fire can be **pleasing** on a cold, wintry day.

cheerful
cheery

A *cheerful* room is pleasant, sunny, and bright. Someone with a *cheery* disposition is gay and merry and fun to be with. Ernie's *cheery* letter brightened my day.

satisfying

Something is *satisfying* if it fills your need or makes you feel happy and contented. Hearing that your friends enjoyed your recital is *satisfying.* A big sandwich is *satisfying* if you're hungry.

A big sandwich is **satisfying** when they're hungry.

refreshing

Something is *refreshing* if it makes you feel rested and like new again. If you're very tired, a short nap can be *refreshing.* A glass of ice water is *refreshing* on a hot day.

charming
enchanting

Charming and *enchanting* originally meant able to cast a magic spell. Now they are used to mean very pleasant, attractive, delightful, or fascinating. Everyone feels comfortable in your home; you are a *charming* host. There are many *enchanting* stories in this old book.

See also *delicious.*

ANTONYMS: bad, displeasing, gloomy, melancholy (adj), obnoxious, repulsive, sad, unpleasant

P

An IOU is a **pledge.**

pledge (n)

A *pledge* is your statement that you will do something. You make a *pledge* to a charity when you say you will contribute some time or money to it. An IOU is a *pledge.* Sometimes you have to back up a *pledge* with something. She left a hundred dollars with the salesperson as a *pledge* that she would return and buy the car.

• promise
• word

When you make a *promise* or give your *word* to someone, that person believes and trusts that you will do what you have said you will do. I gave my *word* that I would be home in time to help her with her math. They made a *promise* never to reveal the secret formula. He did not come over, though he gave me his *word* that he would. Don't make a *promise* that you don't intend to keep.

• vow

A *vow* is a solemn, or serious, promise. When Ella and Phil got married, they made a *vow* to love each other. After spending an unhappy week at camp, she made a *vow* that she would never go again.

• agreement

People reach an *agreement* when they decide that something should or should not be done. The citizens made an *agreement* to keep the city clean. The city officials signed an *agreement* to halt construction of the new city hall.

It's fortunate that this toaster has a one-year **guarantee.**

- guarantee

A *guarantee* is a pledge that a manufacturer makes to the customers. If a product doesn't measure up to a certain standard, the manufacturer's *guarantee* pledges that the product can be returned, repaired, or replaced. It's fortunate that this toaster has a one-year *guarantee.*

- security

Security is something a person gives as a pledge to repay what was borrowed. A person who wants to get a loan from a bank might use a car as *security.* If the loan is not paid back, the bank can take the car. If you have to borrow movie money from your dad, you may give him an IOU—your written pledge to pay back the money. Or you may let him have your baseball mitt as *security.*

Charlene let her father have her baseball mitt as **security.**

polite

Polite people have good manners. They show courtesy to others. When we go to Grandma's house, Father always reminds us to be *polite.* It is impolite to interrupt when others are in the middle of a conversation. It is often difficult to be *polite* to someone who is rude.

courteous

Courteous means having good manners and being considerate of others. Henry was being *courteous* when he held the door open for the woman on crutches. *Courteous* people wait their turn in line. Rude people push ahead of others or push others out of their way. Kim was very *courteous* in letting me go ahead of her.

Henry was being **courteous** when he held the door open for the woman on crutches.

well-mannered

Well-mannered means having or showing good manners. *Well-mannered* people know how to act in different social situations. Roy is too *well-mannered* to have slammed the door in your face on purpose.

• tactful

Tactful means knowing what to do or say in order to keep from embarrassing or hurting someone. It is not really a synonym for polite, but both words mean thoughtful of other people. A *tactful* person who is allergic to chocolate might refuse a piece of cake by saying "No, thank you, but it certainly looks delicious." A tactless person might answer "No, thanks; chocolate cake makes me sick."

See also *thoughtful.*

ANTONYMS: impolite, rude, tactless

poor

Poor means having just a few things or having little or no money. Then it is the opposite of rich or wealthy. Someone who is *poor* can't afford to buy luxuries. A very *poor* person may not have enough to eat.

penniless

Penniless means without any money at all. Losing her purse left the woman *penniless*. He was *penniless* after spending the last cent of his allowance.

bankrupt

A firm or business is *bankrupt* when it hasn't enough money to pay its debts. People with no way of getting money to pay their bills may also "go *bankrupt*." You can "go *bankrupt*" or "be *bankrupt*."

A business is **bankrupt** when it hasn't enough money to pay its debts.

broke

Broke is a slang word people use to mean penniless. I'm *broke* and can't lend you a cent. As with bankrupt, you can "be *broke*" or you can "go *broke*."

needy
destitute

Needy and *destitute* mean very poor and poverty-stricken. Charities help *needy* people who haven't enough money to live on. The fire left the family *destitute*—without clothes, money, or shelter.

ANTONYMS: rich, wealthy, well-to-do

279

P

portion (n)   A *portion* is a part of something. It is usually a part that is of a certain size or amount, or it is the part that is meant for a certain person or purpose. Leon asked the waiter for a double *portion* of dessert. Each week I save a *portion* of my allowance.

share   A *share* is a portion meant for one person or contributed by one person. Did you get your *share* of the candy? I was willing to take my *share* of the blame for the accident. The girls did more than their *share* of work in cleaning the yard.

segment   A *segment* is a portion clearly marked off or separated from the whole by natural divisions. It is easy to split an orange into *segments*.

section   A *section* is a portion made by cutting or dividing a whole. The last *section* of this book is the Index. People pronounce words differently in some *sections* of the country.

unit   A *unit* is one thing or one portion of a group that makes up a whole. The parade had ten *units*. Each *unit* was made up of a band and two floats. An apartment is one *unit* of an apartment building. We just finished the third *unit* of this science book.

member   A *member* is a part of a group or a body. Our club has five *members*. Is Frank Chin a *member* of the bowling team? Your arms are *members* of your body.

element   An *element* is one of the simplest parts that are combined to make a whole. Scientists have found more than one hundred

portion (n) continued

elements in the earth. The *elements* of mathematics mean the simplest rules or principles of mathematics.

fraction

A *fraction* is a portion less than a whole, or a part that has been broken off from something. One-half and one-fourth are *fractions.* Because of the snow, just a *fraction* of the expected audience was present for the piano recital.

Water **power** makes a mill wheel turn.

power

Power is the strength and ability to do or cause something. Everyone has the *power* to think and make decisions. A flying fish has the *power* to glide through the air. An engine furnishes the *power* to move a car. Water *power* makes a mill wheel turn. A queen has the *power* to rule her people.

power continued on page 282 ▶

281

P

power continued from page 281

authority

Authority is the power to tell other people what to do in a certain situation. Parents have *authority* over their children until the children grow up. A police officer has the *authority* to arrest people who break the law.

dominion

Dominion means absolute power or supreme authority. Dictators have *dominion* over their people.

command

Command is the power to give orders and demand obedience. It can also be the order itself. A captain is in *command* of the ship. The crew had better obey these *commands!*

control

Control is the power to direct and keep someone or something in check or in order. A teacher has *control* of a class. You might lose *control* of your temper during an argument.

mastery

Mastery can mean the knowledge or skill that makes a person able to use something. Her *mastery* of spelling patterns enabled her to spell all the words correctly.

See also *strength*.

powerful

Powerful means full of power or energy to do or to cause something. A *powerful* engine has enough drive and strength to make a heavy truck move. *Powerful* speakers not only have strong, clear voices, but also speak with such confidence and authority that people listen and believe what they say. A *powerful* person may be one who can lift great weights, or one who can lead people and make them obey.

282

The cleaning fluid was so **potent** that it took all the spots off the rug.

almighty
omnipotent

Almighty and *omnipotent* mean all-powerful or having complete power over everything. Both words are usually used only when someone is speaking of a Supreme Being.

potent
mighty

Potent and *mighty* describe something or someone powerful. A *potent* drug is very strong and is able to combat disease. The cleaning fluid was so *potent* that it took all the spots off the rug. A *mighty* wind is one that is far stronger than an ordinary wind. The lumberjack chopped down the tree with one *mighty* blow of his ax.

forceful

Forceful means full of force or strength. A *forceful* person does everything with much energy and ability. This organization needs a *forceful* leader to keep all the members interested. Mia offered *forceful* arguments for disagreeing with me.

influential

Influential means powerful, or able to affect what others do or think. An *influential* senator can help get a law passed by persuading other senators to vote for it. A newspaper may be *influential* enough to defeat or elect a candidate.

effective

Effective is the weakest of these words for powerful. It means able to produce or cause some desired result. A bright poster is *effective* because it catches the eye of everyone who passes by. A scolding is *effective* if the kittens that have been scolded stop whatever they were doing.

See also *strong.*

ANTONYMS: helpless, powerless, weak

283

P

powerless

Powerless means without power or strength or force. The sultan was *powerless* after the legion stormed his palace. A person left *powerless* is unable to act. Sometimes a person becomes *powerless* out of fear or fright. Without his magic sword, the knight was *powerless* to fight the dragon.

helpless

Helpless means powerless to help yourself. A tiny baby is *helpless.* The librarian felt *helpless* without his glasses.

A dog without teeth is
defenseless.

defenseless

Defenseless means unprotected and helpless against any kind of danger, harm, or attack. When the oar was swept away, the canoeist was *defenseless* against the rushing water. A dog without teeth is *defenseless.*

weak

Weak means lacking power or strength. It is the opposite of strong. Sickness can make a person feel *weak.* The radio picked up a *weak* signal from the lost plane. *Weak* lemonade has too much water in it.

ANTONYMS: strong, healthy, powerful

practice (v)

Practice means do something over and over so that you become skilled at it. You have to *practice* if you want to be an expert cook, a safe driver, a fine musician.

drill

Drill means teach something or learn something by saying or doing it over and over until it can be done almost without thinking. Joan's sister *drilled* her on the multiplication tables. The marching band was *drilling* on the field.

exercise

Exercise means strengthen something by using it over and over. He *exercises* his muscles by running two miles every day.

- train
- develop
- repeat

Train, develop, and *repeat* are not really synonyms of practice, but they have related meanings. *Train* means prepare for something by drilling for it or being instructed. The speed skater *trained* for six months for the competition. *Develop* means make something change gradually or grow. Gretchen's cold *developed* into pneumonia. You can *develop* your muscles by exercising every day. *Repeat* means say or do something again or many times. They practiced their dance steps by *repeating* them twenty times.

The speed skaters **trained** for six months for the competition.

precious

Precious means having a high value or price. You would not want to lose something that is *precious*. A diamond is a *precious* stone. Your eyesight is *precious*. A picture of someone you love may be *precious* to you even though it is worth nothing to anyone else.

precious continued on page 286 ▶

precious continued from page 285

Some people have some old sneakers that are **dear** to them.

expensive costly	*Expensive* and *costly* mean high-priced—maybe higher than a thing is worth. An orchid is one of the most *expensive* flowers you can buy. Heating and lighting the huge mansion was very *costly.*
dear	*Dear* is sometimes used to describe things that cost a lot because they are scarce. Fresh vegetables are *dear* in winter; they may be cheap in summer. *Dear* also means well loved and valued. You may have a *dear* friend or some old sneakers that are *dear* to you. Grace is my *dearest* friend.
valuable	*Valuable* can mean important, useful, or worth a lot of money. This ring is a *valuable* piece of jewelry. A stethoscope is a *valuable* instrument to a doctor. People keep their *valuable* papers in a safe place.
priceless	*Priceless* describes something very precious and valuable because no price would be large enough to pay for it. A *priceless* object cannot be replaced. Happiness is *priceless.* The original Declaration of Independence is *priceless.*
prized cherished	Something that is *prized* or *cherished* is highly valued and cared for. The dealer would not sell us any stamps from his *prized* collection. Grandmother's most *cherished* possession is her silver teapot.

See also *rare, special.*

ANTONYMS: cheap, inexpensive

better at something than they really are. My six-year-old brother *pretends* he's old enough to drive a car. She *pretended* that she had finished her chores, even though she hadn't. He *pretended* that someone else had broken the window.

make believe
play

Make believe and *play* can mean pretend to be someone or something else. Some children may *make believe* they are the characters in a book. I taught my dog to roll over and *play* dead. An actor *plays* many different parts on stage.

act

Act means pretend. It usually refers to actors taking the parts of characters in a play or movie. My sister has *acted* in three community plays. *Act* also means pretend to feel something you don't feel. Try to *act* interested in what the speaker is saying. Jody is trying to *act* pleased about the results of the class election.

feign

Feign means give a false appearance. You might have to *feign* a look of surprise when you get a gift if you've peeked at it beforehand. I *feigned* sleep when my mother opened the door, but I had a book under my blanket.

simulate

Simulate means make something act or look like something else. For making movies, fans are used to *simulate* strong wind.

See also *fool* (v), *imitate*.

She **feigned** sleep when her mother opened the door, but she had a book under her pillow.

P

promise (v)   *Promise* means give your word to someone. I *promised* to go to the dance with Ted. The tailor has *promised* that my coat will be ready today.

agree   *Agree* means promise to go along with someone else's idea or to do what that person does. You might *agree* to play tennis with your friend even though you'd rather go swimming. They *agreed* to meet at the movie at twelve o'clock. Miriam *agreed* to wait for me if I was late.

swear   *Swear* can mean promise that something is true. When someone is put under oath, that person has to *swear* to tell the truth. When the President of the United States takes the oath of office, he *swears* he will defend the Constitution.

pledge   vow   *Pledge* and *vow* mean make a solemn, or serious, promise. You might *pledge* never to do something again. You often *pledge* your allegiance to the flag. The widow *pledged* a thousand dollars to her church. The children *vowed* to keep their meeting place a secret.

protect   *Protect* means save from harm or injury. A crystal *protects* the face of a watch from being damaged. A heavy coat or jacket *protects* you from cold weather. Welders wear goggles to *protect* their eyes.

guard   *Guard* means watch over something and protect it from danger. A watchdog *guards* its master's house. Sentries were posted to *guard* the entrances to the castle.

defend

Defend means protect against whatever danger or attack is present. He *defended* himself by using judo. A public defender is a lawyer who *defends* someone accused of a crime.

shield
screen

Shield and *screen* mean protect against something by putting up or having a barrier in between. Sunglasses *shield* your eyes from the sun. The knight wore a suit of armor to *shield* himself from attacks. The tall apartment building *screens* the sunlight from our house. The mother lion placed her cubs in the tall grass to *screen* them from the approaching hunter.

The knight wore a suit of armor to **shield** himself from attacks.

shelter
harbor

Shelter and *harbor* mean protect by offering a covering or a safe place. A tent *shelters* campers from the cold night air. An inlet *harbors* a boat. It is against the law to *harbor* someone the police are looking for.

keep

Keep means watch and take care of something. Mother *keeps* a vegetable garden. It can also mean prevent someone from having or doing something. The fence *kept* the rabbits out. Try to *keep* from catching cold.

ANTONYMS: endanger, expose

P

proud

Proud people are extremely pleased with themselves, with what they have, or with what they have done. You may be rightly *proud* of some things—*proud* of your parents or *proud* of your brother or sister. You should be *proud* of your country and your school. If you've worked hard and long to accomplish something, you certainly can be *proud* of that. But sometimes you can be too *proud,* and then there are other words to describe you.

haughty

Haughty describes people who act as if they are better than other people, either because of birth or position. Such people are often called "stuck-up." Cinderella's stepsisters were *haughty* toward her.

vain

Vain describes people who are very proud of their appearance and who want others to notice how great or beautiful they are. A *vain* boy may stop to look in every mirror (or shop window!) he passes to admire himself.

A **vain** boy may stop to look in every mirror (or shop window!) he passes to admire himself.

conceited

Conceited people have far too high an opinion of their own worth. They are so pleased with themselves that they hardly think about anyone else. We thought the new girl was *conceited* because she never spoke to anyone.

egotistical

Egotistical comes from the old Latin word "ego," which means "I." An *egotistical* person thinks and talks about himself or herself almost all the time. Practically every third word is "I" or "me."

smug

Smug people are well satisfied with themselves or with something they can do or have done. Almost anyone can be *smug* once in a while. If you are the only one in class who knows the answer to a question, you may feel *smug.* You can be *smug* one minute and humble the next. A *smug* person can be just as unpleasant as a haughty or conceited person is, but usually smugness doesn't last a lifetime, while haughtiness and conceit probably will.

ANTONYMS: humble (adj), modest

pull (v)

Pull is the opposite of push. *Pull* means move an object closer to yourself or move it in the direction you are going. Some objects are easier to *pull* than others. It would not take as much effort to *pull* an empty wagon as it would to *pull* one filled with bricks. And if you accidentally put your hand in boiling water, you would *pull* it out very quickly. Some teeth are harder to *pull* than others. If a drawer is warped, you may not be able to *pull* it open.

pluck
pick

Pluck and *pick* mean pull quickly using just your fingers. A butcher *plucks* chickens by pulling off the feathers. A guitar player *plucks* the strings on the guitar. You can *pick* apples or pears from trees.

jerk

Jerk is a good word to use when you mean pull quickly and suddenly. The rider at the rodeo *jerked* his hat down on his head as the horse started to run and buck.

pull (v) continued on page 294 ▶

P

A violinist **draws** a bow across the violin strings.

yank

Yank means pull hard and fast. You might *yank* open a drawer that is stuck. First my big sister politely asked me to move; then she *yanked* me out of her chair.

tug

Tug means make a number of short, hard pulls. If you *tug* at something very heavy or immovable, you might be able to move it only a short distance or not at all. Little children sometimes *tug* at adults' clothing to get their attention.

draw

If you *draw* something, you pull steadily and firmly. An archer *draws* a bow. A violinist *draws* a bow across the violin strings. The carriage was *drawn* by eight horses.

drag

You may *drag* an object if it is either too heavy or too clumsy to carry. You pull it along the ground—usually very slowly. A small child might *drag* a large stuffed animal across the floor. A lumberjack *drags* heavy logs. If you are extremely tired, you may *drag* your feet when you walk.

haul

Haul means pull something large or heavy for a long distance. Trucks and trains are used to *haul* many things. The truck *hauled* the oranges from Florida to Cleveland.

tow

Tow means pull something behind by using ropes, chains, or bars. You usually *tow* something that could move by itself. You wouldn't *tow* a rock or a building. The tugboats *towed* the freighter to the dock.

ANTONYMS: push (v), shove (v)

push (v)   *Push* means move an object away from yourself. It also means move or make something move forward or backward or out of the way by force. It is the opposite of pull. You may *push* open a stuck door. You *push* a button on a vending machine to obtain the kind of food you want. He *pushed* his way to the head of the line. I was sorry I *pushed* her into the pool.

nudge   *Nudge* and *poke* mean push lightly. You
poke   might *nudge* someone with your elbow to get his or her attention. The pony *nudged* my pocket with its nose, trying to find another lump of sugar. She *poked* me in the ribs. We say that busybodies *poke* their noses into other people's business.

prod   *Prod* can mean push with something sharp or pointed. The farmer *prodded* the mule with a stick. *Prod* can also mean make a person do something by urging that person over and over. Rico had to be *prodded* into joining the volleyball game.

shove   *Shove* means push roughly. People often *shove* each other when they get on and off a crowded bus. *Shove* can also mean push something along a surface. Jerry *shoved* the table across the floor.

drive   *Drive* means push onward, or make something or someone go or move or do something. Farmers *drive* their cattle across a road. A strong wind will *drive* a sailboat. A practical joke might *drive* you to tears.

push (v) continued on page 296 ▶

P

push (v) continued from page 295

thrust

Thrust means push with a lot of force. It can also mean push into something with a pointed instrument. Inga *thrust* the bushes aside and looked around for the lost ball. The baby *thrust* a finger into his oatmeal.

expel
eject

Expel and *eject* mean push out or force out or drive out. Your lungs *expel* air when you breathe out. The shouting men were *ejected* from the hall by the ushers. Anyone who disobeys certain rules may be *expelled* from the Soap Box Derby.

See also *urge*.

ANTONYM: pull (v)

put

Put usually means move something to some place or spot or position. *Put* is used in many ways. You *put* dirty dishes *in* the sink but you *put* clean ones *on* the shelf. Most people *put* their money *in* a bank. Perhaps you *put* your cat outside. If it's cold you might *put on* a sweater. Little children don't always *put away* their toys. *Put* is also used in many idioms. People *put on* airs when they pretend to be better than other people. A ship *puts out* to sea. Houses are *put up* for sale. Someone may *put in* a hard day at the office. You might *put off* doing something.

Gloria **put off** raking the leaves as long as she could.

There are other words for some of these meanings of *put*.

place
set

Place and *set* mean put in a certain position or condition. After she *had set* the table, she *placed* the flowers in the center. I *placed* my hands in my lap. To begin the exercise, *place* your feet twelve inches apart. He *set* the rock down for a moment. Grandpa *set* the baby in her highchair. The doctor *set* my broken arm.

lay

Lay means put something down in a horizontal, or lying-down, position. You *lay* a cloth on a table or *lay* a carpet on a floor. I *laid* a book on the table. If you *lay* the baby in its crib, you say the baby is lying down.

arrange

Arrange means put things in some kind of order. You *arrange* flowers in a vase. Joseph *arranged* the clothes in the drawer after he unpacked his suitcase. Please *arrange* the furniture any way you like. *Arrange* these cards alphabetically.

ANTONYMS: remove, take away

Q

quarrel (n)

A *quarrel* is a fight with words. If you have a *quarrel* with someone, you disagree over something, say harsh words, then maybe end up not speaking to each other.

argument

An *argument* can also be a fight with words. Usually each person lists reasons why his or her view about something is the right one. The umpire settled the *argument* by calling time out. We had an *argument* over whether dogs make better pets than cats.

disagreement

You have a *disagreement* with someone when you do not share the same ideas or opinions. A *disagreement* over something can end in an argument, but it doesn't have to. You may disagree with someone without letting that person know it, or you may both decide that it isn't worth it to try to change the other person's mind. There was *disagreement* among the family members over where they should go on their next vacation. We have a *disagreement* about who is the greatest tennis player in the world.

fuss

A *fuss* is an argument over something unimportant. My little brother always makes a *fuss* about going to bed. The girls made a big *fuss* over who should pay for the tickets to the circus.

dispute

A *dispute* is an argument usually carried on for a long period of time. *Disputes* between countries often have ended in wars. The neighboring farmers had a *dispute* for years over who owned the creek.

quarrel (n) continued

spat
squabble
fracas

Spat, squabble, and *fracas* are good words for short, noisy quarrels. A *spat* is very short and usually over nothing. I had a *spat* with my sister because she wouldn't close the window. Most *squabbles* are among children. There were nine *squabbles* yesterday on the playground. A *fracas* is very noisy and may include some pushing and shoving. The *fracas* ended when Jerry hit his head on the edge of the table.

See also *battle* (n).

ANTONYM: agreement

There were nine **squabbles** yesterday on the playground.

R

rare

Rare describes something that is not often found or something that seldom happens. Edelweiss is a common Alpine plant in Switzerland, but it is *rare* in the United States. Thunderstorms are *rare* in a desert. Something *rare* is usually very important and valuable. We speak of collecting *rare* books or *rare* stamps.

The penguin is an **unusual** bird.

- scarce

Scarce means not plentiful or abundant. Whatever is *scarce* is usually hard to find or get. Food and fuel may become *scarce* in a town cut off by a blizzard.

- infrequent

Infrequent means not happening or occurring very often. Mail deliveries are *infrequent* in remote mountain areas.

- unique

Something *unique* is rare because it is the only one of its kind. The Statue of Liberty is a *unique* monument.

- unusual
- uncommon

Unusual and *uncommon* mean different from the ordinary or commonplace, and often very remarkable. The penguin is an *unusual* bird. It can't fly. It is *unusual* to see snow in Florida. A horse and buggy is an *uncommon* means of transportation today.

- outstanding

Outstanding means rare; important, or excellent. We speak of *outstanding* persons and of *outstanding* achievements.

See also *odd, precious, special.*

ANTONYMS: common, plentiful, abundant, ordinary, commonplace, frequent, general, normal, usual

| **real** | *Real* means not false or artificial or made-up. *Real* pearls are found inside the shells of oysters. He was asked to give his *real* reason for arriving late. |

actual   Something is *actual* if it exists or happens. The things you dream about are not *actual* experiences. The woman thought she could repair my bike for five dollars, but the *actual* cost was ten dollars. Something is also *actual* if it has existed or has happened in the past. The San Francisco earthquake and fire was an *actual* event.

true   *True* means real and actual and not false. It is *true* that the world is round and not flat. She says that *true* adventure stories are exciting to read.

genuine   Something *genuine* is the real thing—not false, artificial, or fake. His beard was not *genuine*. The rubies in this necklace are *genuine*.

authentic   An *authentic* account of something is completely true and trustworthy. An *authentic* hundred-dollar bill is not fake. If the signature on a check is not *authentic,* it is a forged one.

His beard was not **genuine.**

original   An *original* drawing or painting is not copied or imitated from another. An *original* painting by Picasso is more valuable than copies made by other artists.

ANTONYMS: false, artificial, made-up, forged, fake (adj), imaginary, unreal

R

reason (n)
A *reason* is an explanation of why a thing was done or why something happened. Your *reason* for being late might be that you overslept. A dead battery might be the *reason* your radio doesn't work. The *reason* I fell is that I slipped on the ice on the steps. The beautiful scenery is the *reason* many people visit the Grand Canyon.

cause
A *cause* is anything that makes something happen. Drivers who don't obey traffic signs are the *cause* of many serious accidents. A smashed fender was the *cause* of the argument between the two truck drivers.

motive
A *motive* is a strong feeling or desire within someone that makes that person do something. John's *motive* for working hard was to earn money for a new pair of ice skates. The detective sought a *motive* for the crime.

spur
A *spur* can be something that urges a person on or moves that person to do something. Not being able to find her favorite record album was a *spur* to make Amy clean her room. A prize was the *spur* that made everyone enter the contest.

justification
A *justification* is a good reason for doing something. Many people become angry without *justification*. Amanda's *justification* for crossing the street was that she had to help Mr. Jacobs pick up the packages he'd dropped.

See also *defense*.

remember

Remember means think of something again or keep something in mind so you don't forget it. I can still *remember* the first house we ever lived in. Can you *remember* the address? *Remember* to lock the door when you leave. I can't *remember* where I put the key. I'm trying to *remember* what he said.

recall
recollect

Recall and *recollect* can be used to mean remember something that has been forgotten. You *recall* something when you call or bring it back to mind. The witness *recalled* what happened at the scene of the accident. I can't *recall* a winter as cold as the present one. You *recollect* an incident when you gather all your thoughts together and try to remember what took place. Can you *recollect* when you last wore your missing jacket? Wendy tried to *recollect* what had caused the argument.

remind

Remind means bring to mind or cause to remember something or someone else. Things that are very similar *remind* you of each other. A person may *remind* you of someone you once knew or someone you met a long time ago. This movie *reminds* me of a book I once read. Juan called to *remind* me of the surprise party.

recognize

Recognize means be aware of something or someone you have once seen or heard or known. I *recognize* his face, but I can't remember his name. Do you *recognize* the melody she's playing?

He **recognized** the face, but couldn't remember the name.

remember continued on page 304 ▶

R

• reflect

Reflect isn't a synonym of remember, but it can be used when you think carefully about things that you remember or things which have taken place in the past. My uncle often *reflects* on his boyhood in Montana.

ANTONYM: forget

repair (v)

Repair means put in good condition again. We *repair* things that are broken, damaged, or run-down. Sheryl sent for an electrician to *repair* the light. The hole in the fence has to be *repaired.*

fix

Fix is the word used most often to mean repair. The leak in the roof has to be *fixed.* My sister helped Dad *fix* the flat tire. Can you *fix* a broken chair?

mend

Mend means put something back into shape or in working order again. You can *mend* a torn page with tape. Dave *mended* the iron pot by welding the broken pieces together. A rip in a sleeve can be *mended* with a needle and thread.

patch

Patch means put a piece of material over a hole, a tear, or a worn spot. We *patch* old clothes. The knees of Barbara's jeans need to be *patched.*

The knees of Barbara's jeans need to be **patched.**

restore

Restore means put something back in its original condition. Part of the city of Williamsburg has been *restored* to look the way it did before the Revolutionary War. Staying in bed when you are sick helps *restore* your health.

ANTONYMS: break (v), destroy, tear (v)

report (v)   *Report* means give an account. You might *report* on something you have done or seen or heard or read. A newscaster *reports* on the news and weather. The secretary *reported* that all members were present at the meeting. A serious automobile accident has to be *reported* to the police.

• relate   *Relate* can mean tell or report something. Gus *related* some of his adventures in the West.

• narrate   *Narrate* means tell a story. A person *narrated* the play as the puppets performed.

• recite   *Recite* means read something out loud or repeat something from memory. When Marvin's grandfather was in school, he had to *recite* the Gettysburg Address.

• reveal
• divulge   *Reveal* and *divulge* mean make known something that has been hidden or kept secret. The bookcase opened to *reveal* a secret passage. The outlaw in the western movie would not *reveal* where he had hidden the stolen money. The spy *divulged* very important information to the enemy. True to her promise, she never *divulged* the secret.

The bookcase opened to **reveal** a secret passage.

305

R

request (v) *Request* means ask for something or ask someone to do something. You might *request* directions or *request* help in finding your way if you are lost. We were *requested* to leave our boots in the hall when we entered the apartment. My friend *requested* a favor from me, and I didn't refuse. Grandmother *requested* a cup of tea.

beg *Beg* means ask for something over and over again. Irma *begged* for another chance to prove she was not afraid of heights. Flo *begged* her friend to go with her to the play. Dave *begged* me to let him feed my puppy.

beseech
implore
plead *Beseech, implore,* and *plead* mean beg firmly and seriously for something. I *beseech* you to listen to me. The citizens *implored* the town council to use the land for a park instead of a parking lot. I *pleaded* with my brother to let me play his records.

coax *Coax* means ask and persuade someone to do what you want. Martin *coaxed* me to go to the movies by offering to pay my way. We finally *coaxed* the frightened kitten to come out from under the couch.

demand *Demand* means ask for something and insist that you get it. The judge *demanded* order in the court. The customer *demanded* to know why the bill was so high. Our coach *demands* that we get eight hours of sleep each night.

ANTONYMS: refuse (v), decline (v)

result (n)   Something that happens because of an action may be called the *result* of that action. I fell while I was practicing gymnastics. As a *result,* I have a sprained ankle. The candidate won the election as a *result* of the hard-fought campaign. Many people were forced to leave their homes as a *result* of the flood.

outcome   An *outcome* is also the result of something —or the way it comes out. The *outcome* of this year's World Series was hard to predict. If someone goes on and on telling a very long story, you might become impatient and say, "What's the *outcome* of this story?" I was surprised by the *outcome* of the bobsled race.

end   The *end* of something can be the outcome. The *end* of a cake-baking venture could be a disaster if you don't stick to the recipe.

consequence   *Consequence* means the result of something that happens or exists. A cold room was the *consequence* of leaving the window wide open all day. If you do something bad, you must take the *consequences.* This means that, because of what you've done, you must accept whatever happens. I suffered the *consequences* of having walked in the rain without an umbrella; I caught a cold.

effect   *Effect* also means result. One *effect* of a stuffy room may be a sleepy class. What *effect* does eating too much ice cream have on you? What is the *effect* of the drought on the corn crop?

One **effect** of a stuffy room may be a sleepy class.

307

R

right

"Where have you been? Everyone else has been here for an hour. We were wondering what had happened to you!" Bill said as Lisa, Karen, and Roger entered.

"We got lost," Karen announced.

"We were all *right* until we got to the square," explained Roger. "Then Mom made a *right* turn—"

"That wasn't the *right* turn to make!" Bill interrupted him with a laugh. "At the square the *right* turn to make would be left."

"Then those directions you gave us weren't *right*," Lisa put in.

"I'm really sorry," replied Bill. "But at least everything turned out all *right.* Let's get something to eat."

This little scene is not very dramatic, but it does show how a word like *right* can have several different meanings and many synonyms. When *right* means the opposite of left, it is a definite direction. You won't find any synonyms for that. But when *right* means the opposite of wrong, you'll find many shades of meaning. If you are looking for the *right* answer or the *right* time, look under *correct* (adj), the opposite of incorrect.

Many people have trouble finding the *right* thing to say or do in some situation. Some people discover (often too late) that their clothes are not *right* for a certain place or that their behavior is wrong for some occasion. Perhaps they wore shorts and dirty sneakers to a meeting when

right continued

everyone else looked clean and shining. Perhaps they giggled when they should have been serious. Synonyms for this kind of *right* are under *appropriate* (adj).

If you think some of the rules at school are *right* but some may be wrong, or if you feel that the punishment for disobeying a rule or law is *right* or wrong, you can look for those shades of meaning in the entry *fair* (adj).

Suppose someone handed you three one-dollar bills and told you that two of them were counterfeit. Suppose the person then said, "If you pick out the *right* one, you may spend it." You can find other words for the *right* dollar bill under *real*.

If you ever try to describe something that is just *right* in every way—something that couldn't be better—for those words turn to *perfect* (adj).

rise (v)

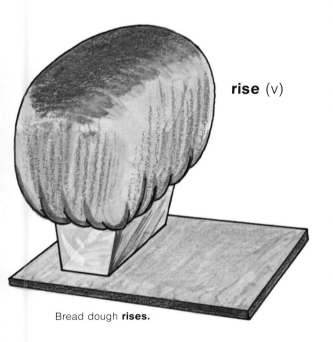

Bread dough **rises.**

Rise means go or move in an upward direction. People, animals, and things can *rise.* You *rise* when you get up from a chair. You *rise* every morning when you get out of bed. Your voice *rises* when it gets higher or louder. It falls when it gets lower or softer. And your spirits *rise* when something good or exciting happens. A kite will *rise* in the sky on a windy day. Smoke from a fire *rises.* Bread dough *rises.* Prices *rise.* A hill *rises.* The sun *rises* in the East and sets in the West.

rise (v) continued on page 310 ▶

R

rise (v) continued from page 309

Here are some other words that mean *rise* which can be used more precisely.

soar
Soar means fly at a great height or fly upward. Birds and airplanes *soar* in the sky. A ball will *soar* in the air if you hit it hard.

ascend
Ascend means gradually rise or move upward. Smoke *ascends* from a chimney. An airplane *ascends* when it takes off. It descends when it lands. A climber may *ascend* to the top of a hill or *ascend* to the peak of a mountain.

mount
Mount means go up. You *mount* the stairs or *mount* a ladder. But you also *mount* a horse when you get up on it.

ANTONYMS: fall (v), set (v), descend

rough
Rough is the opposite of smooth and of soft. It is used in many ways. We call a road *rough* when it has many ridges and bumps on it. A piece of wood that hasn't been sanded is *rough.* Coarse material like sandpaper is *rough.* When the wind makes waves on the ocean, we speak of a *rough* sea. Frank snagged his sweater on a *rough* spot on the desk. The hiker twisted an ankle on the *rough* trail.

uneven
Uneven means not smooth or straight or level. A plowed field is *uneven.* A hem on a dress is *uneven* if it is crooked and makes the dress shorter in some places than in others. The bedspread was *uneven*—longer on one side of the bed than on the other.

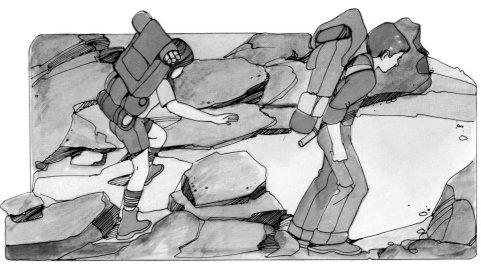

The mountain path is **rugged** and hard to walk on.

stormy

Stormy is used to describe rough weather. A *stormy* sea has huge, crashing waves. Sometimes if a person's life has been rough and unhappy, that person is said to have had a *stormy* life.

craggy
jagged

Craggy and *jagged* describe rough, uneven, hard surfaces. Rocks, cliffs, and mountain chains are *craggy* or *jagged*. A *craggy* reef can cause much damage to a ship that hits it. You might cut yourself on a *jagged* piece of glass.

rugged

A *rugged* terrain or stretch of land also has a rough surface. The mountain path was *rugged* and hard to walk on. *Rugged* periods of time, like the Great Depression of the 1930s, are harsh and difficult.

See also *rude.*

ANTONYMS: smooth, soft, even, straight, level (adj)

R

rude

Rude describes something that is unfinished or undeveloped. A *rude* hut is a small building that has little more than four walls and a roof.

Rude can also mean lacking in manners, because of carelessness or ignorance. When you are invited to a friend's house for dinner, it is *rude* to be late.

uncivilized

Uncivilized means not civilized. People living on an island that is cut off from the rest of the world may be considered *uncivilized* by certain people. People who live differently tend to think that the way they do things is better and more mannerly and correct. Therefore, *uncivilized* has come to describe actions that seem rude and wrong. I thought it was *uncivilized* of them to wear no shoes to my party.

crude

Crude means unpolished or unrefined. *Crude* oil is oil as it comes from the ground, before it has been processed in any way. Once it has been refined, it is no longer *crude* oil. People are *crude* if they are unrefined in their relationships with others. His *crude* way of inviting us to the party was "Well, you're invited, too, if you really feel you have to come."

rough

Rough means not gentle. When *rough* is applied to a person, it usually describes someone who hasn't been around people very much and doesn't know how to act with others. According to some people, cowhands who live mostly on the range may have *rough* ways of speaking.

impolite

Impolite people have bad manners. They are not careful of the way they treat others. Sara was *impolite* when she took all the candy before anyone else could get a piece.

ill-mannered
unmannerly

Ill-mannered and *unmannerly* describe people who are impolite. Sometimes it is embarrassing to eat in a restaurant with Barry because he is so *ill-mannered.* It is *unmannerly* to start eating before everyone is seated.

It is **unmannerly** to start eating before everyone is seated.

discourteous

Discourteous means not considerate of others. The librarian told the group that it was *discourteous* to be so noisy in the library.

disrespectful

Disrespectful means lacking honor for someone or something. It is *disrespectful* not to stand when "The Star-Spangled Banner" is played at a stadium.

ANTONYMS: civilized, refined, gentle, courteous, genial, mannerly, polite, respectful

R

ruin (v)

Ruin means damage something so completely that it can't be repaired or fixed. An object that has been *ruined* has lost all its value or usefulness. The floods in Italy *ruined* many priceless paintings. Moths *ruin* good woolen clothes by eating holes in them. Gwen's plans for camping will be *ruined* if it rains tomorrow.

wreck

Wreck means ruin, usually by breaking or smashing. An iceberg can *wreck* a ship. Two cars were *wrecked* in the collision on the expressway.

destroy
demolish

Destroy and *demolish* are used when something is smashed to pieces or pulled down. An earthquake and fire once *destroyed* almost an entire city. Many buildings have to be *demolished* before the new highway can be built.

Many buildings have to be **demolished** before the new highway can be built.

spoil

Spoil also means ruin something so that it can't be used. An early frost *spoiled* the farmer's crops. Milk will *spoil* if it is not kept cold.

See also *harm* (v).

ANTONYMS: repair (v), fix (v), build, construct

run (v)

Run means move fast and steadily. An animal *runs* by taking steps so long and so rapid that at one point of each step all its feet are off the ground. An engine *runs* well if all of its parts move steadily and smoothly. Water or some other liquid *runs* if it moves steadily along some route or in some direction. I poured too much milk, and it *ran* down the outside of the glass onto the table.

gallop
lope
trot

A horse can run in several different ways and at different speeds. It runs fastest when it *gallops,* using springy, leaping steps. It *lopes* when it runs with long steps in an easy, steady, fairly fast motion. It *trots* when it moves just a little faster than walking. These words are often used to describe ways a person can run.

race
sprint
jog

Race, sprint, and *jog* are three kinds of running that people often do. You *race* if you go very fast, usually to beat someone else to a goal. You can *race* to beat a time limit too. Betty *raced* me to the end of the block, but I won. You'd better *race* to the post office before it closes, or you won't get a stamp. If you run as fast as you can for just a short distance, you are *sprinting.* The bell rang as I turned the corner, so I *sprinted* the rest of the way. If you run slowly, just to be running and not to get somewhere in a hurry, you *jog.* You can get a lot of exercise if you *jog* for half an hour every morning.

run (v) continued on page 316 ▶

R

flow

Liquid *flows* when it runs steadily. Blood *flows* through veins and arteries.

operate

When an engine runs, it is *operating.* Our lawn mower *operates* on electricity. The big presses *operate* all night to print the morning newspaper. The elevator has been *operating* perfectly since it was repaired.

The big presses **operate** day and night to print magazines.

flee

You *flee* if you run away from some danger or some unpleasant situation. People *flee* from a burning house. When the burglar alarm went off, the bank robber tried to *flee* in a truck.

escape

If you get out and run away from some place where you have been shut or locked up, you *escape.* Animals sometimes *escape* from the zoo. Grandpa's canary *escaped* when he opened the door of its cage.

abscond

If you run away or leave home secretly to avoid being arrested or captured, and then hide, you are *absconding. Abscond* is often followed by *with.* The day before the bank officials came to check the books, an employee *absconded with* a million dollars.

S

sad

Sad means not feeling happy or pleased or glad about something. People feel *sad* when they lose things or when something bad happens. When my pet rabbit ran away, I felt *sad* and lonely. They were *sad* when they heard the news of the tragedy. Sue becomes very quiet when she's *sad.*

unhappy

Unhappy means sad and not cheerful. Not being included in the basketball game hurt Kay's feelings and made her *unhappy.* Al was *unhappy* when the picnic got rained out.

mournful
sorrowful

Mournful and *sorrowful* mean full of sadness and grief for something. The nation was *mournful* over the death of its leader. One kind of dove is called a "mourning dove" because of its *mournful* call. We knew something was wrong when we saw the *sorrowful* look on Tad's face.

downcast
depressed

Someone who is *downcast* or *depressed* feels sad and discouraged about something. You might feel *downcast* or *depressed* when things don't turn out the way you want them to. Jackie was *downcast* after her puppy ran away. When he didn't get the paper route, Neil was *depressed* for weeks.

gloomy
blue

Gloomy and *blue* mean low in spirits. A person can feel *blue.* And a dark, rainy day can make someone feel *gloomy.*

melancholy

Someone is in a *melancholy* mood when that person is sad and thoughtful. Some music can put you in a *melancholy* mood.

sad continued on page 318 ▸

sad continued from page 317

miserable

Miserable means very sad or unhappy. A cold can make a person feel *miserable.* *Miserable* can also describe something that makes someone feel sad or unhappy. On a *miserable* day nothing goes right.

ANTONYMS: happy, pleased, glad, cheerful, excited, gay, lively, merry

On a **miserable** day, nothing goes right.

sadness

Sadness is a feeling you have when you are sad and unhappy. There was much *sadness* at the zoo when the baby elephant hurt its leg. When they moved to another town, the children experienced *sadness* at leaving their friends.

sorrow

Sorrow is a feeling you have when you are sorrowful or grief-stricken. The people of the United States were filled with *sorrow* when President Kennedy was killed.

melancholy

Melancholy means a feeling you have when you are sad and thoughtful. Pat couldn't explain the feeling of *melancholy* that seemed to weigh him down.

gloom

Gloom is a lowness of spirits. Joyce was the picture of *gloom* as she watched her friends go off to camp.

318

woe

Woe is deep sadness or grief or suffering. The illness of his dog caused him *woe*. *Woe* is also used, at times, to mean great distress. My cousin is learning the *woes* of being a baby-sitter.

despair

Despair is a loss of hope in something or someone. People who are in *despair* have lost confidence in themselves or in others. She was in *despair* when she found it was her best friend who had made fun of her.

See also *misery*.

ANTONYMS: happiness, gladness, hope (n), expectation, hopefulness

safe (adj)

Safe is the opposite of dangerous. *Safe* means free from danger or harm or risk. You should always put your valuables in a *safe* place. Water is tested to see if it is *safe* for drinking.

secure

Secure means safe or free from fear, anxiety, or uneasiness. Dad felt *secure* after locking all the doors. If something is *secure,* it won't break, collapse, or fall. It won't be lost or stolen. Before climbing the ladder, Eve made sure it was *secure* against the building. The square knot is *secure;* it won't slip.

protected

Protected means kept safe from danger. Your basement is a *protected* place to stay during a tornado. Forest preserves, state parks, and national parks are *protected* areas where animals are safe from hunters.

safe (adj) continued on page 320 ▶

S

A **harmless** snake is not poisonous.

snug

Snug means safe and comfortable. We sometimes think of a small and cozy room as being very *snug.* The baby was *snug* and warm in the crib.

harmless

Something is *harmless* if it causes no harm or injury. Plastic scissors are *harmless* because they are not sharp or pointed. That dog barks a lot, but it is really *harmless.* A *harmless* snake is not poisonous.

ANTONYMS: dangerous, poisonous, risky, hazardous, precarious, unsafe

satisfy

If something *satisfies,* it does whatever you need or expect it to do. A bag of jellybeans *satisfied* my craving for sweets. He can't seem to *satisfy* his piano teacher, no matter how hard he tries. She couldn't join the club because she didn't *satisfy* its age requirement.

answer

Answer means satisfy or fill the needs of something. The invention of the sewing machine *answered* the need for mass production of clothes. If you can't find a screwdriver, a nail file will *answer* the purpose.

please
gratify

Please and *gratify* mean give pleasure or satisfy. A vacation in the country would *please* Mother. It always *gratifies* my grandparents to receive a letter from me. My aunt was *gratified* to hear that we had enjoyed her homemade jam.

appease

Appease means gratify completely by doing whatever is necessary to please someone.

To *appease* my brother, I promised to help him wash the car.

content

Content means satisfy to some degree, but not by meeting every wish or desire. An ice-cream cone will *content* Nelson for a while. *Content* also means limit your wishes or actions. We should try to *content* ourselves with what we have.

save

Save is the opposite of throw away and spend. *Save* means hold on to something. You might *save* a souvenir from a trip. People often *save* things that they may need later. You *save* your allowance if you don't spend it. You sometimes can *save* time by taking a shortcut.

Save also means treat something carefully. You will *save* your eyes if you always read in a good light.

Save can mean protect something or someone from harm or danger. Firefighters *save* burning buildings if they can. Doctors *save* lives.

save continued on page 322 ▶

People might **save** a souvenir from a trip.

S

save continued from page 321

keep
: *Keep* is a good synonym for save. Did you *keep* the book I gave you? The captain *kept* the ship from capsizing during a typhoon.

economize
: *Economize* means use things carefully and not waste them. We *economize* when we don't squander our money.

accumulate
: *Accumulate* can mean save gradually. You can *accumulate* a lot of money by saving regularly.

store
: *Store* means save for a later use. Our family *stored* our furniture in a warehouse until the apartment was ready.

conserve
preserve
: *Conserve* and *preserve* mean keep something safe or keep something from being used up. We speak of *conserving* forests, wildlife, and other natural resources. Scuba divers must *conserve* their oxygen supply. You *preserve* certain foods by canning them or by keeping them in a refrigerator or freezer.

rescue
: *Rescue* means save someone or something from danger or destruction. The Coast Guard *rescued* the dog that was trapped on the ice in the middle of the lake.

See also *free* (v).

ANTONYMS: throw away, spend, discard, squander, destroy, let go

A person can **accumulate** a lot of money by saving regularly.

say

Janet **professed** her belief in unidentified flying objects.

When you *say* something, you express a thought by using spoken words. What did you *say* to Uncle Howie when you saw him? It is possible for *say* to be used in other ways—What does the clock *say?* What has Aunt Marilyn *said* in her letter? The sign *says* "Danger." The look he gave me *said* more than any words he could *say.*

For finding synonyms, though, *say* is used in this book to mean speak in words.

pronounce

Pronounce means say carefully or solemnly. A judge *pronounced* sentence on the thief. The minister *pronounced* them husband and wife in the wedding ceremony.

profess

Profess means say freely and clearly that you believe something. You *profess* loyalty to your country. Janet *professed* her belief in unidentified flying objects.

swear

The word *swear* can mean say solemnly or promise something. Do you *swear* to tell the whole truth and nothing but the truth? He *swore* he'd do better next time. I could *have sworn* I knew the girl sitting across from me on the bus.

While *pronounce, profess,* and *swear* are good synonyms for *say,* you would probably never use them instead of *say* when you are writing a conversation that is set off by quotation marks. The rest of the synonyms for *say,* listed on the next page, may well be used for any kind of writing you are likely to do.

say continued on page 324 ▶

S

state

State means say. Mario *stated* his name and address when he ordered the tools. "I'll wait here," the woman *stated* firmly.

declare

Declare means say publicly or seriously. Donald Bloomfield *declared* his candidacy for the Senate. "I'm going to ski only on the beginners' slopes," *declared* Nate.

mention

Mention means say something to refer or call attention to something. Mother *mentioned* that it was getting late. I heard someone *mention* my name in the elevator. "Don't forget the pickles," Jean *mentioned* as she went out the door.

comment

Comment means state your opinion on something. Lots of people *commented* on my oil paintings. "Your shirt is dirty," *commented* Vince.

murmur
mutter

Murmur and *mutter* both mean make a low sound that is hard to hear, or say words that are hard to understand or distinguish. Mother was *murmuring* softly to the baby, hoping the child would fall asleep. Carol *murmured* something in my ear, but I only understood half of what she said. The bus driver *muttered* angrily under his breath. The boy *muttered,* "I'll get even with you." Jane walked by, *muttering* to herself.

repeat

Repeat means say again or say over and over. You can *repeat* what you have said or *repeat* what someone else has said. He had to *repeat* his name three times before I could understand it. Don't *repeat* the secret I told you.

Someone who is "**scared** stiff" might not be able to move at all.

scare (v)

Scare means fill with sudden fear. If something *scares* you, you might scream. If you're "*scared* stiff," you might not be able to move at all. Hearing strange sounds in the middle of the night *scares* me.

frighten

Frighten is another word for scare. Is Edgar *frightened* by the dark? The growling dog *frightens* everyone who walks by.

startle

Startle means scare and surprise. If something *startles* you, you might move away or jump back quickly. The sudden clap of thunder *startled* me.

alarm

Alarm can mean make afraid and worried because of some possible danger. The approaching storm *alarmed* the sailors.

intimidate
cow
bully

Intimidate, cow, and *bully* mean force a person to do something out of fear. People can *intimidate* others by threatening them. Our pile of snowballs *cowed* the enemy in the snow fort across the street. The older girls thought they could *bully* us into leaving the pool.

Bully also means pick on or tease someone younger or weaker than yourself. The kids upstairs started to *bully* the new boy.

terrify
terrorize

Terrify and *terrorize* mean cause great fear, panic, or terror. The fire in the barn *terrified* the horses. The tiger had been *terrorizing* the villagers for weeks.

ANTONYMS: calm (v), comfort (v), quiet (v), soothe

325

scatter

The crowd **scattered** when the rain began to come down.

Scatter means throw things here and there, often not caring where they land. At one time farmers *scattered* seeds by hand over a field. You might *scatter* things all over your room when you are looking for something.

Scatter also means separate or cause to go in different directions. A gust of wind will *scatter* leaves over a yard. The crowd *scattered* when it started to rain.

strew

Strew means cover an area by scattering things over it. You might *strew* your desk with books. The floor was *strewn* with the baby's toys.

spread

Spread can mean scatter or distribute. News *spreads* if it reaches many different people. An infection or disease may also *spread.*

disperse

Disperse means cause a group of people to break up and go off in different directions. The police tried to *disperse* the crowd that had gathered near the burning building. The fans *dispersed* after the game.

dispel

Dispel means scatter or drive away. The hot sun *dispelled* the rain clouds. The good news *dispelled* her worries.

squander

Squander means scatter or throw away foolishly money or something else. The inventor *squandered* his money and time on many worthless ideas.

See also *throw* (v).

ANTONYMS: gather, collect

see

Bob: My aunt can *see* with her tongue.
Bill: That's silly. What can she *see* with her tongue?
Bob: She can *see* if the soup's hot.

See means take in or receive by using your eyes. But we use the word in many more ways. You can *see* who's at the door. You can just *see* yourself leading a parade. Some folks *have seen* better days. You might suddenly *see* what someone has been trying to teach you. If you begin a project, you should *see* it through.

See and *look* or *look at* are almost synonyms. But actually when you *look,* you have to move or direct your eyes toward something. So before crossing a street, you *look* both ways. You can *see* out of the corner of your eye. You can *see* things without directly *looking at* them.

In this book you will find entries dealing with four different ways to *see.* Under *look* (v) are words for directing your eyes toward something. *Examine* and words listed there mean *look at* closely to learn, understand, or test something. *Notice* (v) has words for *seeing* and taking note of what you *see. Watch* (v) includes words for following the action of something—like a game—as well as words for carefully *seeing* that things are all right or that nothing will happen. *Look up* these entries. *Notice* the shades of difference in meaning. *Examine* your speech and writing to *see* how precise you can be. But *watch* it!

send

Send means cause something or someone to move from one place to another. It is the opposite of receive. You may have received more valentines than you *sent.* Your mother may *have sent* you on an errand. You can *send* a football flying through the air if you kick it hard.

mail

Mail means send someone a letter or a postcard or a package through the post office. After you *mail* a letter, it is transported by train or truck or plane. A letter carrier then takes it to the address of the person you sent it to.

deliver

Deliver can mean send to a destination. The pizza we ordered will be *delivered* in ten minutes. Do you know anyone who *delivers* newspapers after school?

truck
ship

Truck and *ship* mean send something aboard a truck or a ship. Farmers *truck* their produce all over the country. Some foreign nations *ship* their goods to the United States. *Ship* is also often used to mean send by any means at all. Please *ship* at once the plants and seeds we ordered. (You don't care how they are sent.)

dispatch

Dispatch means send off. A teacher might *dispatch* a student with a note for the principal.

transmit

Transmit means send a message or a signal from one place or one person to another. Telegraph operators *transmit* messages. When you talk to someone on the phone, your voice is *transmitted* over a wire.

Telegraph operators **transmit** messages.

328

drive

You *drive* someone or something when you make the person or thing go to another place. You can *drive* away some noisy birds or *drive* off a vicious dog. You *drive* a ball when you hit it hard and send it a great distance.

See also *carry.*

ANTONYMS: receive, get

serious

If something is *serious,* it is important and must not be treated lightly. A *serious* problem or decision may need a lot of thought.

Serious also describes something that is not humorous or amusing. Jenny gave a very *serious* speech about the economy.

Serious can describe people who are deeply concerned with and interested in important matters. When it comes to doing something about pollution, Bob is *serious.*

Serious also means having great importance because of some possible danger or harm. You might hear of someone being in *serious* condition in a hospital.

Other words are better to use than *serious* for some of these meanings.

sober

Sober can mean serious and thoughtful. The television announcer gave a *sober* comment on the day's news. A *sober* person is one who is sensible, levelheaded, and hard-working.

serious continued on page 330 ▶

S

A **grave** or **solemn** ceremony is very formal and impressive.

grave
solemn

Grave and *solemn* mean serious and dignified. A *grave* look on your friend's face might tell you that something is bothering your friend. A *grave* or *solemn* ceremony is very formal and impressive. The girls made a *solemn* promise never to reveal their secret meeting place.

thoughtful
earnest

Thoughtful and *earnest* describe people who think things over carefully and are serious about what they do. They don't rush into things or make hasty decisions. There was a *thoughtful* look on the man's face as he read the letter. Toshio is *earnest* about wanting to go to college.

important

Important is the opposite of trivial and frivolous. Something is *important* if it means a lot to someone and has great worth or value. We speak of making *important* decisions, meeting *important* people, and remembering *important* dates.

See also *heavy.*

ANTONYMS: flighty, trivial, frivolous, lighthearted, minor

shake (v)   *Shake* means move up and down or back and forth. You can *shake* something, or something may cause you to *shake.* You might *have shaken* a bottle of salad dressing before you poured it over your salad. Perhaps you *shook* sand out of your shoe after a day at the beach. You might *shake* your head instead of answering "no." People *shake* hands when they are introduced to each other. People or animals might *shake* if they are afraid. The whole stadium seemed to *shake* from the roar of the crowd.

The whole stadium seemed to **shake** from the roar of the crowd.

tremble
shudder
shiver

Tremble, shudder, and *shiver* mean shake without meaning to, because of fear or excitement or cold. You might *tremble* if you saw a huge grizzly bear coming toward you. People may *shudder* when they see or think of something awful or terrible. He *shuddered* at the thought of being left alone in a deserted house. People *shiver* when they are cold.

shake (v) continued on page 332 ▶

S

shake (v) continued from page 331

quiver

Quiver means shake or tremble slightly. A child's lip may *quiver* just before he or she begins to cry. Leaves on a tree *quiver* when a breeze moves them.

quake

Quake means shake violently. An explosion can make the ground *quake.* We were *quaking* with fear as we waited for the hurricane to turn inland.

sway
rock
vibrate

Sway, rock, and *vibrate* are all good words to use when something or someone moves or is caused to move back and forth or from side to side. You *sway* when you lose your balance and lean first in one direction, then in the other. Ernie *swayed* after getting off the ride at the carnival. Trees *sway* during a storm. A boat *rocks* on stormy waters. You might *rock* a baby to sleep. Something *vibrates* when it shakes rapidly. You might feel the whole house *vibrate* when a heavy truck passes.

Trees **sway** during a storm.

shape (n) Everybody and almost everything has a *shape.* The *shape* of a thing is its outward appearance, its length, width, and thickness. The *shape* of a carrot is different from the *shape* of a beet. A globe has the same *shape* as a ball. Myra's grandfather gave her a locket in the *shape* of a heart.

form The *form* of something can be the way its parts are put together or arranged. Cookies baked in the *form* of lions, tigers, and elephants are called animal crackers. In a fairy tale you may read about a prince being changed into the *form* of a frog.

figure *Figure* is another synonym for shape. Some weather vanes have the *figure* of a rooster. I saw the dim *figure* of a man in the fog.

outline An *outline* is a line that shows the outer shape of something. When children color, they sometimes begin by tracing along the *outline* before they color the picture completely.

silhouette A *silhouette* is an outline that has been filled in with a dark color. You can make a *silhouette* by cutting out a shape from black paper and placing it on a light background. That distant tree makes a lovely *silhouette* against the sky.

• profile Your *profile* is what you look like from the side. When drawing the *profile* of a face, an artist may draw only an outline or draw every feature that can be seen from just one side—one eye, one ear, and so on.

See also *plan* (n).

333

A blacksmith **forges** tools and horseshoes on a heavy iron anvil.

shape (v)   *Shape* means give a shape or form to an object or to some material. You can *shape* clay, wood, paper, metal, plastic, mud, and even snow in many ways.

mold   *Mold* can mean shape something with your hands. People *mold* clay into different figures. It can also mean shape something using a mold—a hollow frame or container. When certain liquids are poured into a mold, they take the shape of the mold as they harden. You can *mold* gelatin into many different shapes.

model   *Model* can mean shape using a plan or pattern. It often means copy something else. The boy *modeled* a horse out of clay. This building is *modeled* after an ancient temple.

forge   *Forge* means shape metals by heating and hammering them. A blacksmith *forges* tools and horseshoes on a heavy iron anvil.

bend   *Bend* is the opposite of straighten. *Bend* means shape by turning, curving, or twisting something. The plumber had to *bend* the water pipes.

fit   To *fit* something, you shape it to the right size. Jill cut the wallpaper to *fit* around the window.

form   *Form* means shape or mold something. You can *form* letters out of pipe cleaners. A gym class may *form* a circle to do exercises.

See also *create.*

shelter (n)   A *shelter* is something that covers or protects. Peggy used a box as a *shelter* for the baby chicks. Our only *shelter* against the rain was a newspaper. A *shelter* is also a place that protects. People wait in the *shelter* at the bus stop when the weather's bad.

• protection   *Protection* can refer to anything that protects or keeps from harm or injury. Vaccine is a *protection* against disease.

• shield   A *shield* is a protection against something harmful. Knights carried *shields* to protect themselves from enemy swords. Asbestos suits worn by firefighters are *shields* against the smoke and flames.

• sanctuary
• refuge   *Sanctuary* and *refuge* mean protection or shelter from danger or distress. Sometimes the United States gives *sanctuary* to people who have fled their own country. A wildlife *sanctuary* is a place where wild animals may live and not be hunted. The flood victims were given *refuge* in the school auditorium. The farmer built a bird *refuge* so that birds could stop and feed on their way south.

• dwelling   A *dwelling* is a house or a place of shelter. After a week of camping in the woods, I was glad to sleep in a comfortable *dwelling.*

• harbor   A *harbor* is a protected area of water where ships may anchor safely. Sometimes *harbor* is used to mean any safe place. The stray dog found a safe *harbor* on a farm.

S

shining

Shining describes something that gives off or reflects light. A *shining* object has a bright appearance, like the *shining* sun. Many trophies are made of *shining* silver. *Shining* can also mean very smart or outstanding. Someone is a *shining* athlete if that person performs well in sports.

radiant

Radiant means glowing or shining brightly. The sky was *radiant* as the sun rose above the hills. Someone who looks very happy can be called *radiant.* Abe had a *radiant* smile on his face when he won the state spelling bee.

lustrous

Lustrous can be used to describe a shining and glossy surface. A wood table can be kept *lustrous* by dusting and polishing. Alice's horse has a *lustrous* coat.

sparkling
twinkling

Sparkling and *twinkling* describe an unsteady light. *Sparkling* means sending out sparks or quick bursts of light. Some fireworks give off *sparkling* light. *Sparkling* snow covered the branches. A *twinkling* light seems to flash on and off. On a clear night you can see hundreds of *twinkling* stars. The *twinkling* lights of the cabin shone through the forest.

The sailboat glided across the **shimmering,** moonlit waters.

shimmering
glimmering

Shimmering and *glimmering* mean shining faintly and softly. The sailboat glided across the *shimmering,* moonlit waters. The *glimmering* wings of the airplane disappeared into the clouds.

ANTONYMS: dark, dim (adj), dull

A salesperson may clean a rug to **demonstrate** how a vacuum cleaner works.

show (v)

Show can mean cause something to be seen. You may want to *show* your new watch to a friend. By frowning, people may *show* that they are displeased with something. *Show* also means explain or make something clear. You might *show* someone how to make something.

display
exhibit

Display and *exhibit* mean show things in a way that draws the attention of other people. A store manager tries to *display* merchandise attractively so that people will want to buy it. Artists *exhibit* their work at art fairs.

demonstrate

Demonstrate means show how something is done. A salesperson may clean a rug to *demonstrate* how a vacuum cleaner works.

signify

Signify means show or make something known by a sign or a signal or a certain action. Senator Torres *signified* disapproval of the bill by voting "nay."

reveal

Reveal also means make something known. But you *reveal* things that have previously been concealed or things that should be hidden. The engineer *revealed* plans for the new shopping mall. I promised never to *reveal* the secret.

illustrate

Illustrate means make something clear by pictures or examples. The pictures in your thesaurus *illustrate* the meanings of words. Geography books are *illustrated* with maps and diagrams.

ANTONYMS: conceal, hide (v)

337

S

show (n)
A *show* is something presented for people to see or view. People who like animals would enjoy going to a horse *show* or a dog *show.* Someone who gets angry in front of others may put on quite a *show.* Josh was too sick to attend the farm *show.*

display
A *display* is something arranged to be viewed. Many stores have *displays* of merchandise in their windows. Barry set up a *display* of ancient arrowheads.

exhibit
An *exhibit* is something shown or put on view. You can see an *exhibit* of farm products or an *exhibit* of farm equipment at a county fair.

exhibition
exposition
An *exhibition* and an *exposition* are shows usually open to the public. The museum has an *exhibition* showing circus life in the 1800s. The World's Columbian *Exposition* was held in Chicago in 1893.

performance
A *performance* can be a play or some other form of entertainment. We saw the dancer's last *performance* before she retired from the stage. Lydia and Ron decided to go to the 8:00 *performance.*

spectacle
A *spectacle* is also a show. We usually think of a *spectacle* as being an unusual or exciting show. The *spectacle* of fireworks is always breathtaking.

Often *spectacle* is used to mean behavior that is not appropriate or acceptable. People who lose their tempers can "make *spectacles* of themselves."

shrink

Shrink means become or make smaller. The hot water *shrank* my wool sweater. Everyone noticed that the roast *had shrunk* while it was cooking.

contract

Contract is the opposite of expand. When something *contracts,* it becomes smaller. Pipes expand during the summer heat and *contract* in the winter cold. The pupil of your eye expands in the dark and *contracts* as light strikes it.

compress

Compress means make something smaller or make it occupy less space by pressing, squeezing, or flattening. You *compress* air when you pump it in a bicycle tire. You *compress* a handful of snow to make a snowball.

condense

Condense can mean become or make something more firmly packed. Dave *condensed* into one box the magazines that were scattered all over the floor. *Condense* can also mean write or say something in fewer words. A book reviewer *condenses* a story by leaving out details.

deflate

Deflate is the opposite of inflate. It means release the air or gas from something. If you *deflate* a balloon, it will collapse.

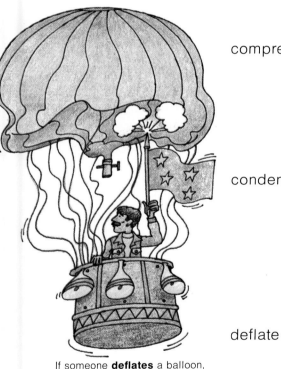

If someone **deflates** a balloon, it will collapse.

shrivel

Shrivel means shrink by drying up. Under direct sunlight grapes *shrivel* into raisins. A flower *shrivels* if it is broken from its stem and can't get water.

See also *decrease* (v).

ANTONYMS: expand, inflate, swell (v)

339

It wasn't really funny when Nick accidentally **shut** Joe **in** the closet.

shut (v)

Shut means move something into place in order to stop up an opening. *Shut* also means move something into place to stop something or somebody from coming in or going out. It is the opposite of open. You might *shut* your door if you don't want to be disturbed. You *have shut* your eyes when you go to sleep. You *shut up* when you stop talking. I lost my key and was *shut out* of the house. It wasn't really funny when Nick accidentally *shut* me *in* the closet.

close

Close means shut off an opening or a passage. You *close* a box when you put a lid on it. Karen *closed* the corral gate after exercising the horses. The street was *closed* to traffic during the parade.

suspend

Suspend means stop or shut off something for a certain time. The U.S. government *suspends* mail deliveries on national holidays. *Suspend* also means shut someone out for a period of time. A club might *suspend* a member who doesn't obey the rules.

confine

Confine means shut in. Inmates are *confined* to prisons until they have served their sentences.

exclude

Exclude means shut out. A window shade *excludes* light. You *exclude* people from an activity when you don't let them join in the fun. Anyone with mumps is confined indoors, and all visitors are *excluded.*

ANTONYMS: open (v), admit, include

340

shy

Shy means timid and uneasy in the presence of others. It also means easily frightened. *Shy* people do not have confidence in themselves. They feel uncomfortable being with and talking to other people—especially strangers. *Shy* people may have a hard time making new friends. Jeff was too *shy* to try out for the chorus. Some animals are *shy* of people.

bashful

Bashful describes a person who is shy and easily embarrassed. My little brother was too *bashful* to say hello.

modest

Modest people are not vain or conceited. *Modest* persons would rather praise other people's accomplishments than call attention to their own.

coy

A *coy* person just pretends to be shy. Some of the guests thought Alice was shy, but her friends knew she was just *coy*.

ANTONYMS: vain, conceited, confident, daring (adj)

sign (n)

A *sign* is something that stands for, represents, or points out something else. There are many kinds of *signs*. There is a stop *sign* at an intersection. A store may have a *sign* in its window. A robin may be the first *sign* of spring.

• symbol

A *symbol* is usually an object that stands for something else. The eagle is a *symbol* of the United States. The American flag is also a *symbol* of the country.

sign (n) continued on page 342 ▶

S

sign (n) continued from page 341

- signal

A *signal* can be a warning sign or a sign that alerts us to something. A flashing red light can be a *signal* that tells you to stop at a railroad crossing.

- gesture

A *gesture* is a sign made by moving some part of your body—usually your head, arms, or hands. Putting a finger to your lips is a *gesture* that says be quiet.

- symptom

A *symptom* can be a sign that a person is sick. A sore throat and a runny nose could be *symptoms* of a cold.

- token

A *token* is a sign or symbol of something. It is usually an object which substitutes for, or gives proof of, some thought, feeling, or thing. You may give someone a gift as a *token* of your friendship.

- omen

An *omen* is a sign of something that may happen in the future. People who are superstitious think that breaking a mirror is an *omen* of seven years of bad luck.

- badge

A *badge* is a small sign that someone wears. A *badge* may show that a person is a member of a certain group or organization. A *badge* may indicate that the person wearing it has done some outstanding deed or deserves special respect. Scouts work hard to earn merit *badges*. A police officer wears a *badge*.

- emblem

An *emblem* is a badge. Most organizations have *emblems*. The *emblem* of the Olympic games is five interlocking circles.

See also *warning*.

A flashing red light can be a **signal** that tells you to stop at a railroad crossing.

silent   *Silent* means without any sound or noise. A *silent* person is not talkative. You are asked to be *silent* in a library. The class was *silent* while Enrique spoke.

quiet   *Quiet* means without much noise or commotion. Mom and Dad wanted to spend a *quiet* evening at home after a busy day at their offices.

still   *Still* means silent and motionless. The air is *still* when there isn't any wind. There wasn't a ripple on the *still* pond.

noiseless   *Noiseless* means with little or no noise. Chess is a *noiseless* game, but you wouldn't call football *noiseless.*

dumb
speechless
mute   *Dumb, speechless,* and *mute,* all mean unable or unwilling to speak. Animals are *dumb.* Some people are *speechless* when something frightens, shocks, or surprises them. Millie was *speechless* when she saw the washed-out bridge ahead. Chuck remained *mute* instead of admitting his mistake. Some people who are deaf and *mute* can learn to speak.

ANTONYMS: talkative, restless, boisterous, loud, noisy

simple   *Simple* means not hard or difficult to do or understand. It doesn't take very long to solve a *simple* problem. It's *simple* to ride a bike, once you learn how. Jo's directions to her house were so *simple* that I had no trouble following them.

simple continued on page 344 ▶

S

easy
: Something is *easy* if it takes just a little work or effort to do. Some books are *easy* to read. It's *easy* to make a cake from a cake mix. It's *easy* for a stranger to get lost in a big city.

effortless
: *Effortless* means needing little strength, energy, or thought. Something can become *effortless* through practice. Riding a horse seems *effortless* for an experienced rider. Putting all the names in alphabetical order seemed *effortless* by the time Craig got to the "R"s.

Riding a horse seems **effortless** for an experienced rider.

uncomplicated
: *Uncomplicated* means simple and not at all confusing. If the instructions on a hobby kit are *uncomplicated,* they are easy to figure out.

plain
: *Plain* means clear and obvious. The moral of that fable is as *plain* as day. It is *plain* to see that Harvey has the measles.

ANTONYMS: hard, difficult, complex, complicated, intricate

skillful	*Skillful* means able to do something well. The most *skillful* students displayed their pottery in an exhibit.
able capable	*Able* and *capable* mean skillful. They often suggest that someone can do something exceptionally well and often quite easily. Because he was such an *able* pilot, he successfully landed the crippled plane on the road. Alice is *capable* of playing three instruments.
ingenious	*Ingenious* means skillful in inventing or discovering things. Thomas A. Edison was an *ingenious* scientist. The light bulb is an *ingenious* invention.
clever cunning	*Clever* and *cunning* mean skillful in a quick or crafty way. Aunt Ellen did not expect Rose to give such a *clever* answer to the riddle. The fox is a *cunning* hunter.
dexterous handy	*Dexterous* and *handy* describe people with the ability to use their hands well. A dentist has to be *dexterous*. A *dexterous* typist is constantly in demand. Mom and Dad are *handy* at fixing things around the house.

ANTONYMS: unskillful, awkward, clumsy, stupid, unable

A **dexterous** typist is constantly in demand.

S

slant (v)

Something *slants* if it doesn't extend in a straight line up and down or in a straight line across. For instance, your handwriting *slants* when your letters do not go straight up and down. The roof of a barn *slants.* The legs of a stepladder *slant.*

slope

Slope is usually used in place of slant when you speak of the ground or land. *Slope* means slant gradually. A hill *slopes* toward its base. The winding path *sloped* toward the river.

lean

If something *leans,* it isn't standing or placed straight up. You might *lean* to one side if you lose your balance. But you wouldn't say you are slanting to one side. You can *lean* your back against a wall or *lean* a ladder against a building. Someone with a sprained ankle may *lean* against you to walk.

list

A boat *lists* when it leans in one direction. A sudden shift in the wind can make a sailboat *list.*

tip

Tip means slant or cause something to slant and possibly overturn. Maria *tipped* over the glass of water.

tilt

Tilt also means slant or cause to slant. A table will *tilt* if the legs are uneven. A seesaw *tilts* as it moves up and down.

incline

Incline means slant or bow, but it is more formal. The driveway *inclines* away from the house. You might say you *incline* your head when someone whispers in your ear.

slender

Slender describes something that is narrow and not wide. An arrow has a *slender* shaft. A *slender* person is not fat or stout.

thin

Thin can mean slender and not heavy or thick. Plywood is made by pressing and gluing *thin* sheets of wood together.

slim
slight

Slim and *slight* can mean slender and sometimes small and unimportant. You can keep *slim* by exercising. There is only a *slim* chance that it will snow. A *slight* person doesn't weigh much. I have a *slight* headache.

fine

Fine can mean very thin. I like to use a pen with a *fine* point.

tenuous

Tenuous can describe a long piece of rope or thread or wire that is or looks extremely thin. We watched breathlessly as the circus performer inched across the *tenuous* high wire.

See also *thin.*

ANTONYMS: wide, fat, stout, heavy, thick, coarse, broad

People watched breathlessly as the circus performer inched across the **tenuous** high wire.

S

sneak (v)

Sneak means go or move in a secret or sly way. He *sneaked* into the kitchen and ate a piece of cake when I wasn't looking.

slink

Slink means sneak away in order not to attract attention. I saw one boy *slink* around the corner as a crowd gathered in front of the broken window. The cat *slunk* through the front door and disappeared behind the sofa.

prowl

Prowl means sneak about looking for something. Wild animals *prowl* through the woods in search of food. The girls *prowled* around the Western ghost town.

lurk
skulk

Lurk and *skulk* can mean move in a secret way or try to keep out of sight. I thought I saw two figures *lurking* in the shadows. The fox *skulked* through the farmyard toward the chicken house.

slip

Slip can mean move quickly and quietly. You might *slip* in or *slip* out of a room without being noticed. They *slipped* quietly through the door. Karen *slipped* into line behind Donna without being seen.

sound (n)

A *sound* is something that you hear. It may be loud, like a jet taking off, or it may be as quiet as a whisper. Some *sounds* are pleasant—a bat hitting a ball (when your team is up), hot dogs sizzling over a fire, your dentist telling you that you have no cavities. There are unpleasant *sounds,* too—a siren, a growl, an alarm clock that wakes you. Did you hear that whirring *sound* coming from my bike?

- noise

Noise can be any sound, but especially it can be a loud and irritating sound. A vacuum cleaner makes a lot of *noise.* When people gather in large groups, they often make *noise.*

A vacuum cleaner makes a lot of **noise.**

- murmur

A *murmur* is a soft sound that is hard to hear. Often it is a continuous sound. You have to listen closely to hear the *murmur* of the trees on a windy day. *Murmur* can also be a low, grumbling complaint. The *murmur* of the crowd soon exploded into angry shouts.

- rumble

A sound that is low-pitched and continuous is called a *rumble.* Just one *rumble* of thunder sent my cousin Katie scurrying under the bed. A *rumble* of dissatisfaction spread through the audience when the singing group failed to appear.

- roar

A *roar* is the loud, deep cry of a wild animal such as a lion. People sometimes make sounds like *roars* when they are angry or in pain. Mr. Martinez's *roar* rang in our ears when he yelled at us for spilling paint on his lawn. A *roar* is also used to mean other loud, low sounds, as the *roar* of an engine or the *roar* of the wind.

ANTONYMS: quiet (n), silence

349

S

The witch **uttered** some magic words over her bubbling pot.

speak

Speak means make sounds, usually words, with your voice. You can *speak* loudly or in a whisper. Some people *speak* two languages. You can *speak* on a subject and *speak* to an audience. When you command a dog to *speak,* it usually barks.

utter

Utter means make a sound or speak. Herbert *uttered* a cry when his sister jumped out from behind a tree. The witch *uttered* some magic words over her bubbling pot.

express
voice

Express and *voice* mean say what you think or show your feelings. Carmella *expressed* her opinion in a letter to the editor of the magazine. The man's smile *expressed* his thanks. The chairperson asked if anyone wanted to *voice* an objection.

talk

Talk means utter words or speak. Usually you *talk* to someone who listens. People who are *talking* to each other are probably sharing opinions or information.

discuss

Discuss means talk about something in order to explore a subject or reach a decision. You talk about the points for and against some action—then decide on a solution. We *discussed* our plans for collecting bottles, cans, and newspapers.

See also *say.*

350

People speak of someone showing a **special** interest in music.

special	*Special* means different in some way from what is common, ordinary, or usual. We speak of someone having a *special* talent for art or of someone showing a *special* interest in music. Our *special* friends are the ones we like best.
individual particular	*Individual* and *particular* mean belonging to only one person or thing. This artist has an *individual* style of painting that identifies her work. Follow these *particular* directions for baking bread at high altitudes.
unique	Something *unique* is special because it is the only one of its kind. The Capitol is a *unique* building, though many other buildings are modeled after it.
exceptional extraordinary	*Exceptional* and *extraordinary* are used when someone or something is very special and out of the ordinary. He just ate an *exceptional* dessert. The solution to the crime in this mystery story is *extraordinary*.

See also *odd, precious, rare.*

ANTONYMS: common, ordinary, usual, general, average, familiar

S

A **splendid** display of colors and shapes can be seen in a kaleidoscope.

splendid

Splendid means outshining all others in excellence or beauty. A *splendid* display of colors and shapes can be seen in a kaleidoscope. The United States team made a *splendid* showing in the tennis match.

gorgeous

Gorgeous is a synonym for splendid, especially to describe a splendid display of color. It was a *gorgeous* sunset; fiery reds and yellows lit up the sky.

glorious

Glorious means splendid and delightful. A *glorious* morning is one that is crisp and clear, sunny and sparkling.

wonderful
magnificent

Wonderful can mean excellent or splendid or marvelous or astonishing. *Magnificent* means exceptionally fine and strikingly beautiful. Both are very tired words. They should be saved to describe things that are very good. I saw a *wonderful* display of dinosaur skeletons at the museum. Pascu thinks the new skyscraper is *magnificent.*

superb

Superb means of the highest possible degree of excellence. A *superb* book is one that is so beautifully written and so enjoyable that you hate to put it down.

ANTONYMS: dull, ordinary, plain (adj)

spot (n)

A *spot* is a small area that stands out from the things around it because of the way it is colored or the way it feels. Some dogs and cats have *spots.* People with measles have *spots* on their skin. Sometimes we think of a *spot* as something that doesn't belong on a surface. Artists wear smocks so they won't get *spots* on their clothes.

There were **blotches** of paint on the floor near the wall.

mark	A *mark* can be a spot. You can make scuff *marks* on a floor if you don't pick up your feet as you walk.
stain	A *stain* is a soiled spot. You can get grass *stains* on your clothes if you sit on the grass.
speck blotch	A *speck* is a small spot or mark. A *blotch* is larger than a speck. My glasses were covered with *specks* of dust. There were *blotches* of paint on the floor near the wall that had been painted.
smudge	A *smudge* is a blurry spot caused by smearing or rubbing. You're likely to get *smudges* on a piece of paper if your hands are dirty.
blot	We often use *blot* to mean an ink stain. A leaky pen will make *blots* on your paper.
flaw	A *flaw* is a small spot or weakness in something that may make it break. A bubble in a piece of glass could be a *flaw.* If you had a sweater made of yarn that was not twisted correctly in one place, there would be a *flaw.* If the weak part of the yarn broke, you would have a hole in the sweater.
blemish	A *blemish* is a spot or a flaw that shows on the surface of something but doesn't weaken the object or keep it from being used. A scratch on a table top is a *blemish.* A bruise on a peach is a *blemish,* but the peach can still be eaten. Some people who eat a lot of chocolate get *blemishes* on their skin.

S

start (v)

Start means begin. When you take the first step, you *start* walking. A telephone may *start* ringing just as you come in the door. School *starts* in the fall.

There are many words to use for the ways different things *start.*

spring
sprout

Spring and *sprout* mean start to grow. A stream may *spring* from a rock or from the side of a hill; it grows bigger until it becomes a river. A small town *has sprung* up where the two railroads meet. Buds *sprout* on trees; plants *sprout* from seeds in the ground.

A small town **has sprung** up where the two railroads meet.

launch

Launch means give something a start. A boat is *launched* when it is put into the water. A rocket is *launched* when it is pushed off the ground. A person can *launch* a new venture or career.

open

Open can mean begin something. The library *opened* a new branch on our street. The interviewer *opened* the conversation with a question. A new hamburger stand is *opening* tomorrow.

354

Companies **introduce** new products by giving away free samples.

introduce

Introduce can mean bring in or start something new. You *introduce* a new topic into a discussion when you change the subject. You *introduce* a new idea when you present it to other people to consider. Companies may *introduce* new products by giving away free samples.

establish
found

Establish and *found* mean bring into existence or start building something. Both words add the meaning of making something that will last for a long time. Schools and colleges are *established.* Plymouth Colony was *founded* by the Pilgrims in 1620.

commence
inaugurate
initiate

Commence, inaugurate, and *initiate* are all rather formal words that mean begin. You might *commence* exercising with twenty-five pushups. A football game *commences* with the playing of "The Star-Spangled Banner." *Inaugurate* adds the meaning of begin with some ceremony. The United States *inaugurates* a President every four years at the beginning of a term of office. The inauguration ceremony usually takes place on the steps of the Capitol. You *initiate* something when you take the first steps of an action and you expect the action to continue a long time. Ben Franklin *initiated* many improvements in Philadelphia's postal service.

See also *create.*

ANTONYMS: close (v), complete (v), conclude, end (v), finish (v), stop (v)

355

S

stop (v)

There are many, many ways to *stop* something.

In a story a Dutch boy *stopped* a hole in the dike by putting his finger in it. A truck can *stop* traffic by spilling a load of hay on the highway. You can *stop* your dog from running away by holding its leash. Mother *stops* the newspaper delivery when the family goes on vacation. One team *stops* another by winning the game.

People can *stop* doing something. I *stopped* running when the bus turned the corner. Please *stop* making me laugh. I *stopped* calling her "aunt" years ago.

Things can *stop* too. Rain *stops.* A train *stops.* A clock *stops.*

If you want to *stop* traffic, look up *block* (v).

If you want to *stop* a ball, look up *catch* (v).

If you want to *stop* the noise coming in through the window, look up *shut* (v). If you want to *stop* doing something, look up *end* (v).

story

A *story* is a series of events or incidents; it is written or told to entertain people. We usually think that *stories* tell about things that never happened, but authors do write *stories* about true events. Small children enjoy hearing bedtime *stories* before they go to sleep. Betty liked to read adventure *stories* like "Kon-Tiki."

There are many other kinds of *stories.*

• anecdote

Often **mysteries** tell of a
detective trying to solve a crime.

• romance

• mystery

• novel

An *anecdote* is a very short story that
usually tells of an amusing or interesting
event. There are many *anecdotes* in the life
of a famous person. The story of Benjamin
Franklin flying his kite is an *anecdote.*

A *romance* is a story about an imaginary
hero and the hero's heroic deeds and
adventures. A famous *romance* is the
story of King Arthur and his knights
of the Round Table.

A *mystery* is a story in which the ending is
uncertain or unknown. Often *mysteries* tell
of a detective trying to solve a crime.

A *novel* is a long story. There are usually
many characters and a lot of action in a
novel. Even when the people and situations
in a *novel* are imaginary, or fictitious, they
may seem very real to the reader.

See also *account* (n), *history, tale.*

strength

power

energy

If you have *strength,* you can do things that
are very hard and that require a lot of
effort. It takes *strength* to lift weights.

Power is another word for strength. A
football player needs *power* to run with the
ball and get past the tacklers.

Energy is the power to do something. With
a burst of *energy,* the runner crossed the
finish line.

strength continued on page 358 ▶

S

force
: *Force* is strength or energy to do something. The *force* of the wind nearly knocked me to the ground. The five of us used *force* to break down the door and rescue the cat. The great *force* of the water caused the dam to break.

vigor
: If you do something with *vigor,* you do it with all the force you have. Grace mowed the lawn and painted the fence with *vigor.* The candidate conducted the campaign with great *vigor.*

might
: *Might* is unusually great strength. There are many ancient myths about the *might* of Hercules. Roger pushed the stalled car with all his *might.* It took all my *might* to unscrew the lid from that jar.

    See also *endurance.*

    ANTONYM: weakness

strong
: *Strong* means having a lot of strength or power or force. It is the opposite of weak. A *strong* person is able to carry heavy objects. A *strong* wind can damage trees and homes. Someone who has been sick for a long time is not very *strong.* Sheryl's argument during the debate was so *strong* that I had to agree.

vigorous
: *Vigorous* means having or using much strength and energy. A *vigorous* person is strong and energetic. Someone with a *vigorous* mind thinks quickly and clearly. A *vigorous* plant is one that is growing well. *Vigorous* exercise can be tiring.

stable
sturdy

Stable and *sturdy* mean strong and firm. Something that is *stable* is not likely to break or give way. The workers made sure the scaffolding was *stable* before stepping on it. Something that is *sturdy* is firm and solid and well built. A *sturdy* chair or table will not wobble.

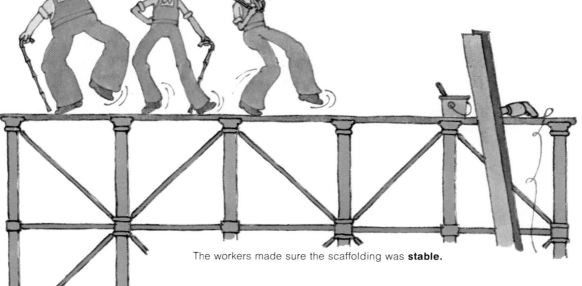

The workers made sure the scaffolding was **stable.**

sound

Something that is *sound* is in good condition. A toy is *sound* if it has not been damaged or broken. You are *sound* if you are healthy and well.

muscular
brawny

A *muscular* or *brawny* person has big, strong muscles. Wrestlers are usually *muscular* and *brawny.*

wiry

Wiry really means like wire. When you say people are *wiry,* you mean that they are thin but strong. Long-distance runners usually have a *wiry* build.

See also *powerful, tough.*

ANTONYMS: weak, flimsy, puny

S

substitute (v)   *Substitute* means put something in the place of something else. The recipe called for butter, but I *substituted* margarine. When our teacher was sick, another teacher *substituted* for him.

replace   *Replace* means fill or take the place of something. If you lose someone's pen, you should *replace* it with another one. The actor who *replaces* another actor in a play is called an understudy. I *replaced* the record I had broken.

change   *Change* can mean substitute. You can *change* wet clothes for dry ones. I *changed* places with Brett so that he could see better. Can you *change* a five-dollar bill for five one-dollar bills?

exchange   *Exchange* means trade or give something in return for something else. If you buy something on sale, most stores won't let you *exchange* it. You *exchange* letters with people when you write to them and they write back to you.

switch   *Switch* means change or substitute. The train *switched* to another track. I *switched* desserts with my little sister while she wasn't looking.

shift   *Shift* means change the position or direction of something. Drivers *shift* gears in their cars when they want to back up. If you're carrying a load of books in one arm and they become too heavy, you could *shift* them to your other arm. When the wind *shifted,* the clouds blew away.

succeed	*Succeed* is the opposite of fail. *Succeed* means do well or turn out well. Your plans for something *succeed* when nothing stops or interferes with them. My cousin *succeeded* in catching a large trout. Did the search for the lost dog *succeed?*
achieve	*Achieve* means succeed in doing or getting something that is very difficult or takes a lot of effort. She *achieved* her goal of becoming a doctor. Yoshio *achieved* fame as a writer.
prosper	*Prosper* can mean succeed financially or make lots of money. A company usually *prospers* if it has a product that people want to buy.
flourish thrive	Something *flourishes* or *thrives* when it succeeds or does well. Inez and Carl's vegetable garden is *flourishing.* My parents' business *flourished* after they started advertising their products. Most plants *thrive* if they get enough water and sunshine.

See also *win* (v).

ANTONYM: fail |

Inez and Carl's vegetable garden is **flourishing.**

S

sudden

Sudden means happening very fast. It is the opposite of gradual. We all fell forward when the bus came to a *sudden* stop. I was awakened by a *sudden* clap of thunder. Jack has had a *sudden* change of plans—he wants to leave tomorrow.

quick

Quick means fast. Some action that is *quick* may not last very long, like a *quick* trip to the store. I took a *quick* look at my notes before the test.

unexpected

Unexpected can mean sudden. Something that is *unexpected* also has not been thought of ahead of time or prepared for. Yesterday there was an *unexpected* drop in temperature. We had *unexpected* company, but we had enough food for everyone.

hasty

Hasty means quick and hurried. A *hasty* decision is not carefully thought out. Since we were going to be in Boston for only a weekend, we had to make a *hasty* tour of the Freedom Trail.

abrupt

Abrupt means sudden and often very unexpected. There was an *abrupt* end to our telephone conversation. Watch out for an *abrupt* bend in the road.

There was an **abrupt** end to our telephone conversation.

instant
immediate

Instant and *immediate* mean quick and without delay. It doesn't take long to prepare *instant* rice. There is an *immediate* need for more hospital volunteers.

See also *fast* (adj).

ANTONYMS: gradual, expected, deliberate, unhurried

362

suddenly

Suddenly tells how fast something happens or is done. The roller coaster stopped *suddenly.* The synonyms for *suddenly* have meanings similar to the meanings for the synonyms of sudden.

The roller coaster stopped **suddenly.**

unexpectedly	The phone rang *unexpectedly* in the middle of the night. I ran into Beth *unexpectedly.*
hastily	Linda didn't think about the question and answered *hastily.* You'll be sick if you eat too *hastily.*
abruptly	The road ends *abruptly. Abruptly* the judge banged the gavel and called for order.
instantly	They stopped talking *instantly.* The room was *instantly* silent.
immediately	Josh *immediately* volunteered to help paint the room. Come home *immediately* after the track meet.

See also *fast* (adv).

ANTONYMS: gradually, deliberately, unhurriedly

363

S

suffer

Suffer means have pain or grief or misfortune or loss. Ira is *suffering* from a cold. I don't think I can *suffer* another disappointment. A business will *suffer* if it is poorly managed.

• experience

Experience means go through or live through something. You *experience* many things—both pleasant and unpleasant. You may *experience* sadness when your best friend moves out of town. But you will *experience* happiness when your friend comes back for a visit.

undergo

Undergo means suffer or experience something, usually painful or unpleasant. It is not pleasant to *undergo* an operation. Pony Express riders *underwent* many hardships to deliver mail to Sacramento.

Pony Express riders **underwent** many hardships to deliver the mail.

bear
tolerate

Bear and *tolerate* can mean put up with something. It is hard to *bear* an insult. Jan *bore* her disappointments without complaining. The hotel manager would not *tolerate* any pets in the rooms.

364

endure

Endure means suffer or put up with for a long time without giving in. I can't *endure* this noise another moment!

See also *allow*.

suggest

Suggest means offer an idea or a thought. Mel *suggested* that we go swimming, and we all agreed. Emilio *suggested* hamburgers and potato salad for the picnic.

Suggest can also mean call to mind. Thunder and lightning *suggest* a storm. The color yellow *suggests* warmth and happiness to Russ.

hint

Hint means suggest something in an indirect way. The baby-sitter *hinted* that she was hungry by continually turning her eyes toward the refrigerator. I *hinted* that I wanted a catcher's mitt for my birthday.

Bev **hinted** that she wanted a new catcher's mitt for her birthday.

imply

Imply means suggest or mean something without saying it directly. George *implied* that I could have done better. Alice *implied* that I had been on the phone too long when she said, "Isn't your ear tired?"

insinuate

Insinuate means suggest something that is often unpleasant or unkind. Denise *insinuated* I wasn't telling the truth, but I really was. Joe *insinuated* I was a weakling just because I dropped the barbell.

propose

Propose means offer an idea or a plan for consideration. They *proposed* going horseback riding when the weather cleared up. Bill *proposed* marriage to my older sister.

S

suggestion   A *suggestion* is something mentioned for consideration. Every member of the family had a *suggestion* for the name of the sailboat. The motor club gave us several good *suggestions* for our trip. Jenny's *suggestion* is to use posters to advertise the school project.

proposal   A *proposal* is a suggestion to do something. The residents accepted the mayor's *proposal* to construct a new city hall.

hint   A *hint* is an indirect suggestion. Hal gave me a *hint* that helped me solve the riddle. The children begged me for a *hint* as to where the things for the treasure hunt were hidden.

implication   An *implication* is something suggested indirectly. I was not accused of cheating, but the *implication* was certainly there.

insinuation   An *insinuation* can be an unpleasant suggestion. Your *insinuation* that the election was dishonest is ridiculous! I refused to listen to the *insinuations* Norman was making about my friend.

advice   When you ask for people's *advice,* you want to know what they think about something or what they think you should do about something. The Cabinet gives *advice* to the President. The campers had problems because they didn't follow the ranger's *advice* about equipment.

support (v)	*Support* is used in many ways. It can mean hold something up. Steel beams or columns can be used to *support* the roof of a building. Your legs *support* you when you stand. *Support* also means help and assist. You should *support* your friends when they need you. You can *support* candidates for office by working in their campaigns.
prop	*Prop* means use an object to support something. You can *prop* a ladder against a wall or *prop* a rake against a fence. If you are tired, you might *prop* your head by putting your hand under your chin.
bear	*Bear* means support the weight of something. The walls of a house *bear* the weight of the roof. A person in a high position *bears* the burden of many responsibilities.
defend uphold	*Defend* and *uphold* mean support and fight or argue in favor of something. Soldiers *defend* their country. You *defend* a friend's reputation when you speak well of your friend. The Supreme Court *upheld* the decision of the lower courts.
maintain	*Maintain* means keep something in good condition. Jessie *maintained* the beautiful finish on her antique car by polishing it every weekend. *Maintain* also means support or uphold the claim that something is true. The suspects *maintained* that they had been at home the night of the robbery.

Jessie **maintained** the beautiful finish on her antique car by polishing it every weekend.

support (v) continued on page 368 ▶

S

confirm

Confirm means support the truth or claim of something. The X rays *confirm* that Lorie has broken her ankle. The freezing temperatures *confirmed* the weather forecast.

sustain

Sustain means keep or hold up or support. These elevators can *sustain* the weight of 3,500 pounds. Eating three good meals a day can help to *sustain* a person's health.

See also *help* (v), *protect.*

surprise (v)

Surprise means fill with wonder because of something unexpected. I was *surprised* to see my cousin from Chicago standing at our front door.

startle

Startle means suddenly frighten or make something or someone jump in surprise. Sirens always *startle* me. Kazumi is such a light sleeper that once a noisy goldfish *startled* him and woke him up.

Kazumi is such a light sleeper that once a noisy goldfish **startled** him and woke him up.

astonish

Astonish means surprise or suddenly fill with wonder. Receiving a thousand dollars by mail would certainly *astonish* you. What *astonished* me most was hearing my name mentioned on TV.

amaze

Amaze means astonish. It is overused and needs rest. Something that happens may *amaze* you if it is unexpected or if you felt it was not likely to happen. Seeing a six-legged giraffe would truly *amaze* you.

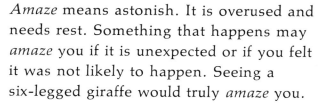

astound

Astound means confuse and fill with wonder. If something *astounds* you, it shocks you. The thought that there are billions of stars in the universe really *astounded* us. Olga's ability to add so many numbers in her head *astounded* the whole class.

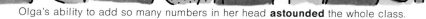

Olga's ability to add so many numbers in her head **astounded** the whole class.

flabbergast
dumfound
nonplus

Flabbergast, dumfound, and *nonplus* are all good, strong words to use when you mean surprise greatly. *Flabbergast* means overwhelm someone by surprising that person. I *flabbergasted* Sheila when I said she could use my brand-new bike. *Dumfound* means make someone speechless by surprising that person. The news that the city hall had burned down was so shocking that it *dumfounded* us for a moment. *Nonplus* means surprise someone so much that the person can't think. Having to answer ten questions at once was enough to *nonplus* Lewis.

369

ANTONYMS: hold (v), keep

surprise (n)   A *surprise* is an unexpected event. There are big *surprises* and little ones; pleasant

tale continued from page 373

- folk tale
- fairy tale

A long time ago *folk tales* were told in almost every country; they were passed on by word of mouth. Most people could not read or write, so the storytellers were popular figures who told tales to people of all ages. Sailors and traders carried these tales to many different countries. Stories of magical creatures, such as fairies and elves, became known as *fairy tales.*

- myth

Myths are tales that have come down to us from the ancient past. Many *myths* tried to explain certain facts of nature. One Greek *myth,* for example, explained the rising and setting of the sun as the god Apollo driving a fiery chariot across the sky.

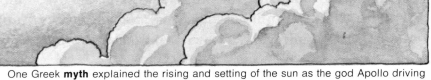

One Greek **myth** explained the rising and setting of the sun as the god Apollo driving a fiery chariot across the sky.

- legend

A *legend* is a tale that is usually based on something true. But it is probably exaggerated, and it cannot be proved. Stories about Davy Crockett are called *legends.*

- fable

A *fable* is a tale that teaches a lesson. In a *fable* animals often talk and act like human beings. "The Tortoise and the Hare" is a famous *fable* by Aesop.

See also *account* (n), *history, story.*

tame (adj)   *Tame* usually describes animals that are not wild or animals that have been trained to be gentle and obedient. Some of the animals that perform at a circus are *tame*. *Tame* also describes something that is not very exciting, lively, or spirited. A *tame* movie may not have much action.

domesticated   A *domesticated* animal is tame and used to living near people. Farm animals such as cows, horses, and pigs are *domesticated*. So are dogs, cats, and white mice.

docile   *Docile* means easily handled or managed. Farmers can drive *docile* cows home from the pasture. It is easy to saddle a *docile* horse. *Docile* people do what others ask or want them to do. Mrs. Ortiz never minds taking Miguel shopping with her because he is a *docile* baby.

quiet   A *quiet* person or animal is gentle. When it was sleeping, the fierce lion looked as *quiet* as a kitten.

subdued   *Subdued* means quiet or toned down. A *subdued* light or color is soft and not bright. When you speak in a *subdued* voice, you are not noisy or loud.

insipid   *Insipid* can mean tame, flat, and colorless. An *insipid* remark is not witty or clever. That book was *insipid,* and I feel I wasted my time reading it. Tasteless food is *insipid.*

ANTONYMS: wild, unruly, fierce, bright, noisy, loud, stubborn

T

task

A *task* is a certain amount of work that has to be done. Mowing the lawn is a *task;* so is washing the dishes. The girls helped their father with the *task* of putting up a new fence. Josh was given the *task* of cleaning the attic.

Painting something that is large can be quite a **job.**

job

A *job* can be any work you have to do. Painting something that is large can be quite a *job.* Betty was given the *job* of baby-sitting when her parents went out. My older sister was lucky to find a summer *job.*

chore

A *chore* is a regular task or job. Some *chores* may include setting the table, taking out the garbage, and making the beds every day. Some of Grandfather's *chores,* when he was young, was to chop wood, milk the cows, and collect eggs from the henhouse.

assignment

An *assignment* is a task assigned or given to do. Homework is an *assignment.* The story a reporter writes is an *assignment.* His *assignment* during the charity drive was to collect old clothes.

duty

A *duty* is a task that you should do or are required to do. A police officer has the *duty* of enforcing the laws. It is the *duty* of every citizen to pay taxes. It is also the *duty* of every citizen to keep the streets free from litter.

See also *work* (n).

tell

Here is a small word that *tells* a lot. *Tell* means give knowledge or information to someone else through speech. Of course, *tell* can be some way you communicate without speech too. The fingerprints will *tell* who did it. You can *tell* by the buds on the trees that spring is coming. Jill could *tell* by looking at us that we were having a good time. I can *tell* you don't believe a word I've said. My cousin has learned to *tell* time. The broken vase and my guilty look *told* the whole story.

In this book words for *tell* are grouped by the ways something can be *told*.

Ways to *tell* what has already happened are listed under *announce.*

Ways to *tell* what is going to happen are listed under *forecast* (v).

Ways to *tell* secrets or give out knowledge may be found under *inform.*

Ways to *tell* what someone wants to know or should know are under *answer* (v) and *explain.*

Ways to *tell* a story or *tell* how something happened are listed under *report* (v).

Ways to *tell* someone what to do are under *command* (v).

Ways to *tell* someone what you think, are listed under *advise* and *suggest.*

Ways to make words and sounds will be found under *say* and *speak.*

T

thin

Thin can describe both people and things. When *thin* is used to describe a person, it means the opposite of fat or plump. A *thin* person doesn't weigh much. When *thin* describes an object, it means the opposite of thick or heavy. It would be dangerous to skate on *thin* ice. This soup is very *thin.* This paper is so *thin* that you can almost see through it.

lean

Lean is the opposite of fat. It is often used to describe meat that has little or no fat. Even a piece of *lean* meat may have some fat around the edge.

A chick looks **scrawny** right after it leaves the shell.

skinny
scrawny

Skinny and *scrawny* mean too thin. A *skinny* person is usually underweight. We gave the *scrawny* dog a biscuit. Chicks look *scrawny* right after they leave the shell.

gaunt

Someone who has been sick for a long time may look *gaunt. Gaunt* means thin, pale, and feeble. Barry's face looked *gaunt* for weeks after he got out of the hospital.

emaciated

An *emaciated* person or animal is exceptionally thin and bony. By the end of the hard winter the buffaloes on the prairie were so *emaciated* that they could hardly stand.

weak
diluted

Weak and *diluted* mean made thinner by adding water or another liquid. *Weak* coffee doesn't have much flavor because it is too watery. If you put ice cubes in your milk, it will be *diluted* when they melt. Some canned soups are already *diluted,* so you don't have to add water.

flimsy

Flimsy means light and thin. It describes things, not people. It is the opposite of strong and firm. *Flimsy* can describe something that is poorly made or that will not stand up under wear. A piece of *flimsy* material is likely to tear easily.

See also *slender.*

ANTONYMS: fat, plump, thick, heavy, strong, firm (adj), husky, stout

think

Think means form an idea in your mind. There are different ways to *think.* You may sit back and relax and *think* about the marvelous time you had at a party or on a trip. Words for this kind of *thinking* are in the entry *remember.*

You may lean your chin on your hand and stare out the window and *think* about the moon and the stars and about what life would be like out there. This kind of *thinking* has synonyms under *imagine.*

Perhaps you are *thinking* hard about something you're going to do in the future. Look for this kind of word under *plan* (v).

If you have the hard kind of *thinking* to do before you can make up your mind about something, look up *decide.*

Words for the very hardest way to *think*—the *thinking* that wears you out because it is so important and serious—are listed under *consider.*

If you are sure about something and don't have to *think* at all, look up *know.*

Sending a get-well card to a
sick friend is a **thoughtful** thing
to do.

thoughtful

Thoughtful people think before they act.
When they act, they think of other people
first. They aren't selfish or thoughtless.
Sending a get-well card to a sick friend is a
thoughtful thing to do.

kind

A *kind* person cares about other people and
tries to make them happy. *Kind* is the
opposite of cruel and mean. She always has
a *kind* word to say about someone.

considerate

People who are *considerate* are thoughtful
of other people and their feelings. They are
not rude. Holding a door open for another
person is *considerate.*

sympathetic

Sympathetic means thoughtful and
understanding and knowing how someone
else feels. Often *sympathetic* people will
share your happiness, listen to your
troubles, and help you with your problems
if they can.

concerned

Concerned means showing care and interest
in someone or something. Several
concerned students organized a committee
to clean up the school grounds.

Concerned can also mean being troubled or
worried about something. The doctor was
concerned about the patient's health. Tomás
was *concerned* about getting to school
during the subway strike.

See also *serious.*

ANTONYMS: selfish, thoughtless, cruel,
mean (adj), rude, inconsiderate,
indifferent, unfriendly, unkind

380

thoughtless

Thoughtless means not concerned with others or their feelings. A *thoughtless* remark may hurt someone's feelings. Sometimes *thoughtless* means simply done without thinking. It was *thoughtless* of me to walk off with your pen; I automatically put it in my pocket after using it.

unthinking

Sometimes people are thoughtless because they are *unthinking* or not careful. They don't mean to be unkind.

inconsiderate

Inconsiderate means thoughtless of other people. The *inconsiderate* neighbors turned up the record player so loud that the whole apartment building could hear it.

heedless

Heedless means not thinking or noticing because you just don't care. Ann started arranging the sticks, *heedless* of the instructions that came with the kite.

careless
reckless

Careless and *reckless* mean not careful or cautious. *Careless* adding causes mistakes in math. You'd have to be *reckless* to talk back to the neighborhood bully.

scatterbrained

One meaning of scatter is fling or toss away carelessly. People who are *scatterbrained* act as though their brains were scattered around everywhere. They can't keep their minds on what they are doing. They start many projects but seldom finish them. Jason is so *scatterbrained* that he could never be trusted to keep track of the club dues.

ANTONYMS: careful, cautious, considerate, thoughtful

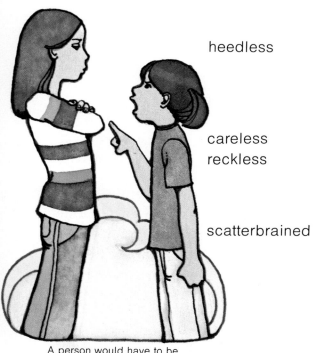

A person would have to be **reckless** to talk back to the neighborhood bully.

T

throw (v)

Throw means use your hand and arm to make something move through the air. In winter you might *throw* snowballs. Louella *threw* her books on the floor. Where have you *thrown* your coat?

Here are different ways to *throw*.

toss
cast

Toss and *cast* mean throw lightly. We *tossed* a coin to see who would go first. Please *toss* me my pencil. We say that a boat *tosses* when it is thrown about by waves. We *cast* our fishing lines into the water. Rudy *cast* a pebble at the lily pad.

pitch

Pitch means throw something at a target. Our neighbors like to *pitch* horseshoes. Nancy *pitched* a ball of paper into the wastebasket.

sling

Sling means throw something or swing something without letting go of it. You can *sling* stones. The skater *slung* a sweater over her shoulder.

fling
hurl

Fling and *hurl* mean throw forcefully, not always caring where the object goes. Lionel stormed into the room and *flung* his jacket on the floor. You would *hurl* things that weigh a lot. The laborers *hurled* the bags of cement to the ground as they unloaded the truck.

tough

Tough means strong or hard or difficult to pull apart. Something that is *tough* can be bent without being broken. It is not brittle. A rope can be *tough*. A *tough* steak is hard to cut and chew. It is not tender.

Tough also means able to endure great strain. People are *tough* if they are physically strong and healthy. The pioneers had to be *tough*.

Tough can also mean difficult to change or move or wear down. *Tough* opponents in a sport are hard to beat; you won't find them easy to face.

firm

Firm means steady and not easily moved. You should build a pier on *firm* supports. My mom was *firm* in her decision not to raise my allowance. The storekeeper said the price was *firm;* he couldn't let me have the baseball bat for less.

sturdy

Sturdy means strong and firmly built. It can be the opposite of fragile. It takes *sturdy* legs to walk ten miles. The roses in our garden look *sturdy* this year. Randy should wear *sturdy* shoes when he goes hiking through the woods.

durable

Durable describes something that can last a long time because it is tough or strong and doesn't change. Blue jeans are made of *durable* cloth. If you have a *durable* friendship, you are lucky.

stubborn

Stubborn means hard to change. *Stubborn* people seldom give up easily. Grandma wa stubborn in her demand that we all come her house.

See also *strong.*

ANTONYMS: brittle, tender, easy, fra
soft, weak

Blue jeans are made of **durable** cloth.

T

trade (v)   *Trade* means give something and receive something else in return. You *trade* at the stores where you buy things. You give your money and get something for it. Or you may *trade* something with a friend—like your goldfish for a tadpole. Countries *trade* with each other when each needs what the other one has.

barter   *Barter* means trade—but not with money. In the early days people did not need much money. Farmers would go to the general store and *barter* something they did not need for something they did need or could use. If they needed farm tools, they might *barter* some chickens for them—if the owner of the store wanted or needed chickens.

If she needed farm tools, she might **barter** some chickens for them.

deal   *Deal* can mean trade or do business. The owner of a department store *deals* in many products, but a baker may *deal* only in baked goods. People in town have always *dealt* with Mr. Pickett when they wanted to buy a new car.

bargain

Bargain means come to an agreement about the price or cost of an article. If you want to buy something that is too high priced, you offer a lower price. The seller could then lower the asking price a little. You might offer a little more than you did before. The two of you are *bargaining* until you finally agree on a price somewhere between the original price the seller wanted and the original price you were willing to pay.

exchange
swap

Exchange and *swap* mean trade. When customers discover that something they just bought is the wrong color or size, they may want to *exchange* it. Many people *exchange* birthday cards with friends and relatives. *Swap* is an informal word meaning exchange. You *swap* similar things with somebody. Luís and Molly *swapped* comic books.

See also *obtain.*

Luís and Molly **swapped** comic books.

training

Training is the things you do when you prepare for something. A swimmer's *training* might include swimming for many hours, trying out different strokes, learning to breathe correctly, and learning how to increase speed. A nurse's *training* is the period in which a nurse learns how to care for sick people, then actually cares for them as a student nurse.

Nancy can't play golf as well as she used to because she's out of **practice.**

• practice

Practice is the doing of something over and over again in order to do it easily or well. There is an old expression that *practice* makes perfect. It takes a lot of *practice* to play a musical instrument well. Nancy can't play golf as well as she used to because she's out of *practice.*

• exercise

Exercise is like practice. It is physical or mental training. Athletes need *exercise* in order to build strength and endurance.

• development

Development means a series of changes that take place during growth. *Development* of an athlete's muscles is most important. The railroads were responsible for much of the *development* of the United States.

• drill

Drill is training in doing something. Fire *drills* prepare you to act correctly in an emergency. A marching band goes through *drills* until it can carry out its formations without mistakes.

U

unclean

Unclean describes anything that is soiled, spotted, or stained. It is the opposite of clean and pure.

dirty

Dirty means covered with dirt, mud, grime, or dust. Please clean your *dirty* shoes and then polish them.

soiled

Something that is *soiled* is unclean and needs to be washed. A white shirt or blouse becomes *soiled* easily.

filthy

Filthy means very dirty. The boat was so *filthy* that she had to scrub it before she could paint it. The children's knees were *filthy* from playing.

The children's knees were **filthy** from playing.

slovenly
untidy

Slovenly and *untidy* mean not clean or neat. People who are *slovenly* don't care how sloppy and dirty their clothes are or how messy they look. Cary looked *slovenly* because his shirt was torn and dirty and his hair was uncombed. *Untidy* people are often careless and sloppy about their appearance and their work. An *untidy* room may have papers and toys and clothes scattered over the floor, with nothing in place.

U

urge

Urge means push someone into action or make someone do something. Our teacher *urged* us to see the science exhibit. I *urged* my dog to follow by pulling on its leash.

spur
goad

Spur and *goad* really mean urge an animal onward. You can *spur* a horse forward by poking it with your heels or with spurs attached to your boots. A farmer *goads* a mule into motion by hitting it with a stick or whip. *Spur* and *goad* can also be used to mean urge a person on. The thought of being late *spurred* Clarence to hurry. Angie *goaded* me into playing my guitar.

arouse
excite

Something *arouses* or *excites* you when it stirs up your feelings and causes you to do something. A speaker might *arouse* anger in an audience. Don't *excite* the dog.

prompt

Prompt means urge. The producer *prompted* the newscaster to finish the news report within two minutes. Whatever *prompted* you to say you'd sell tickets?

See also *force* (v).

The producer **prompted** the newscaster to finish the news report within two minutes.

useful

Useful means being of use. A compass is *useful* to a sailor. A pencil with a sharp point is *useful,* but one with a broken point is useless. Road maps are *useful* on a long trip. Scissors are *useful* for cutting paper. Gail's idea was *useful* to the people on the committee.

helpful

Helpful means being of help. A flashlight is *helpful* in the dark. With a weak battery, a flashlight is ineffectual. The truck driver was *helpful* in fixing my flat tire. I was helpless until he came along.

handy

Handy describes something that saves trouble and is easy to use. A dishwasher is *handy* when there are a lot of dishes to do. A can opener is a *handy* tool in the kitchen. The bus is *handy* to take to school because it stops right in front of my house.

serviceable

Serviceable describes something that is useful because it gives good service and does what it is expected, or supposed, to do. I don't care how old that car is, it is still *serviceable.* This old suit is out of style, but it is still *serviceable* for everyday wear.

He doesn't care how old that car is, it is still **serviceable.**

valuable

Valuable means serviceable and useful and desirable to have. A spare tire is *valuable* in case of a flat tire. Mrs. Inada would be a *valuable* worker in any politician's campaign. *Valuable* has the added meaning of worth. Gold, oil, and diamonds are considered to be *valuable.*

ANTONYMS: useless, ineffectual, helpless

V

visible

Visible means easily seen. Something that is *visible* is not hidden or concealed. The stars are *visible* on a clear night. Ice is *visible* on the flower.

noticeable

Noticeable describes something that attracts attention. There is a *noticeable* crack in that bowl. Something bright or colorful would be more *noticeable* than something dull and drab.

conspicuous

Conspicuous describes something so different or out of place that it attracts attention. A girl wearing a hoop skirt would be *conspicuous*. *Conspicuous* also means very easily seen. The No Smoking sign was put in a *conspicuous* place in the front of the bus.

apparent

Apparent means clearly visible, easy to understand, or obvious. The hole in that coat is very *apparent.* Toward the end of the game it became *apparent* that our team would win. *Apparent* can also describe something that seems to be real or true though it is not. The *apparent* size of a distant object may be about half its actual size.

evident

Evident means clearly visible and obvious. As the sky became darker, it became *evident* we were going to have rain.

See also *clear* (adj).

ANTONYMS: hidden, concealed, inconspicuous

Ice is **visible** on the flower.

W

walk (v)

Walk means move or go on foot. You *walk* when you raise one foot at a time and step forward. You always have one foot on the ground when you *walk.* You can *walk* at a slow pace or a fast pace, but never as fast as when you run.

Here are other words that describe how people *walk.*

stroll
saunter

Stroll and *saunter* mean walk slowly, leisurely, and happily. You may *saunter* along the beach. Or you may *stroll* through a park on a summer evening.

prance

Prance means walk with a springing movement. Horses often *prance* when they are in a parade. Little children sometimes *prance* when they're feeling happy and gay.

march

March means walk steadily with a certain rhythm, often in step with others. The band *marched* down the street. When the new toaster I'd bought wouldn't work, I *marched* right back to the store with it.

strut
swagger

Strut and *swagger* mean walk in a proud or boastful way, holding your head up high. The drum major *struts* in front of the band. The bully *swaggered* down the street because he knew we were watching.

shuffle

If you *shuffle,* you walk without raising your feet completely off the ground. You drag them. An extremely tired person may *shuffle* along the street.

walk (v) continued on page 392 ◗

W

stumble
trip

Stumble and *trip* can mean catch your foot against something and lose your balance. But these also are ways people walk. *Stumble* means walk unsteadily. A person could *stumble* along a stony path. *Trip* means walk or skip gaily with light, quick steps. In "The Wizard of Oz," Dorothy *tripped* down the yellow brick road.

hike

Hike means go for a long walk for fun or exercise. The backpackers *hiked* along the mountain path.

wade

Wade usually means walk in or through water.

tramp
tread
plod
trudge

Tramp, tread, plod, and *trudge,* all mean walk heavily. People have to *tramp* through a forest if there isn't a path to walk on. *Tread* means walk on or over, probably crushing what is beneath your feet. Dogs often *tread* on flowers. The cattle *trod* a path to the river. *Plod* means walk heavily and slowly. The old horse *plods* along the road. If you *trudge,* you walk with a lot of effort. You *trudge* through sand or heavy snow.

People have to **tramp** through a forest if there isn't a path to walk on.

Walk is also used in many idioms and phrases.

If you win a contest easily, you might *walk off with* a prize or trophy. If someone ignores your wishes and does whatever he or she wants, that person "is *walking* all over you."

wander

Wander means walk around without any special purpose. I *wandered* along the beach.

But *wander* is often used differently too. Your thoughts may *wander* if you are bored or can't concentrate on something. And if there are many things to look at, your eyes may *wander* from one thing to another. People who are talking may *wander* so far from the point that they actually forget what they started to talk about.

rove
roam

Rove and *roam* mean wander. Gypsies *rove* from place to place. They never stay in one place very long. We had fun *roaming* through the countryside.

range

Animals *range* when they wander and graze in fields and pastures. Large herds of buffaloes *ranged* on the plains in frontier days. We also say that prices *range* when they go up and down or vary from city to city and don't remain constant.

stray

Stray means wander so far out of your way that you may get lost. Puppies often *stray* from their neighborhood.

wander continued on page 394 ▶

W

wander continued from page 393

ramble   *Ramble* means move from place to place without any definite route or plan. We *rambled* from one spot to another until we came to a grassy place. Speakers *ramble* when they talk first about one thing and then about something else without any plan.

A wolf was caught **prowling** around the deserted farmhouse.

prowl   *Prowl* means wander about, searching or looking for something. Some wild animals *prowl* at night in search of food. A wolf was caught *prowling* around the deserted farmhouse.

meander   *Meander* means follow a winding course. We speak of a river *meandering* through a valley.

drift
float   *Drift* and *float* mean move freely or be carried along by something. Leaves *drift* through the air on a windy day. A boat will *float* out to the middle of a lake if it isn't anchored properly.

digress   *Digress* means wander from one subject to another when you are talking or writing. The speaker at my graduation frequently *digressed* to tell a funny story.

ANTONYMS: stay (v), remain

want (v)   If you *want* something, you would like to have or get it, or you would like to do it. You may *want* some candy or *want* a new bicycle or *want* to go swimming. Maybe you *want* to be President when you grow up. Everyone *wants* to have friends. Peter *wanted* the microscope he saw in the store window.

Want also means be without something. If a plant *wants* water and sunlight, it may die.

wish   *Wish* means want or hope for something. People sometimes *wish* for things they can't have or know they will never get. Al *wished* he had curly hair. Millie *wished* she hadn't lost her watch. My cousin *wished* she hadn't made that unkind remark. When you *wish* a person "Bon voyage," you are hoping that person has a good trip.

desire   *Desire* means want very much, but it is used more formally. People all over the world *desire* peace. What do you *desire* more than anything else in the world?

He **craves** ice cream and never seems to get enough of it.

crave   People *crave* a certain kind of food if they want it badly. He *craves* ice cream and never seems to get enough of it. People also *crave* affection and attention.

need   If you *need* something, you want it and may not be able to do without it easily. Sometimes you *need* something you don't want. Everyone *needs* plenty of sleep. Norene *needs* a haircut. I *need* another dollar before I can buy my brother that gift.

395

W

warning

A *warning* gives advance notice of something or tells of possible danger or harm. A *warning* enables people to prepare for or avoid something. A buoy in a channel is a *warning* to sailors of hidden rocks or shallow places. The weather bureau issued a storm *warning* early this evening.

A buoy in a channel is a **warning** of hidden rocks or shallow places.

advice

Advice is information that warns or helps a person in some way. You may seek your parents' *advice* when you're troubled or not sure about something. It is helpful to follow the *advice* of people who have solved the same problems you face.

admonition

An *admonition* is advice about something a person should do or about something a person has done incorrectly. The police officer gave the couple an *admonition* about crossing the street in the middle of the block.

forewarning A *forewarning* is a warning that is given well in advance. The early frost was a *forewarning* of a long winter.

hunch A *hunch* is a feeling or suspicion that something will happen or that something is true. Usually there is no real reason for having a *hunch*. I had a *hunch* it would rain on my birthday.

foreboding *Foreboding* is the feeling of something bad to come. It is a stronger feeling than a hunch. My sense of *foreboding* increased when the telephone rang at midnight.

sign A *sign* can be a warning. A No Trespassing *sign* warns people to stay off private property. The black clouds were a *sign* of an approaching storm.

signal A *signal* is something that puts a person on the alert, often for danger. A yellow light is a *signal* that the traffic light is going to change from green to red. The driver used the turn *signal* before turning the corner.

alarm An *alarm* is a warning of danger. Alonzo sounded the fire *alarm* when he saw smoke.

symptom A *symptom* can be a warning of some illness. Aching all over is sometimes the first *symptom* of the flu.

See also *sign* (n).

The driver used the turn **signal** before turning the corner.

watch (v)

Dad **watched** the spaghetti so that it wouldn't boil over.

Watch means look at something. You *watch* your favorite show on TV. Spectators *watch* a hockey game that has lots of action. *Watch* can also mean look for something or someone. You might *watch* for signs of rain if you're planning a picnic. I *watched* for the letter carrier.

Watch also means keep a close eye on something or someone. A baby-sitter *watches* young children while their parents are not at home. Dad *watched* the spaghetti so that it wouldn't boil over. I *watched* the time because I didn't want to be late.

observe

Observe means watch or look at closely. You can *observe* the stars through a telescope. The growth of a plant is easy to *observe*.

guard

Guard means watch and protect. Stores hire people to *guard* the merchandise against shoplifters. I was afraid of the huge collie that *guarded* our neighbor's house.

tend

Tend means watch over and care for. We say that a lioness *tends* her cubs when she protects them from dangerous animals. A nurse *tends* sick patients.

oversee

Oversee means watch and direct an activity. A supervisor *oversees* the work of employees.

See also *notice* (v), *protect*.

ANTONYMS: disregard, ignore, overlook

weak

Weak means lacking strength. You may feel *weak* if you haven't had breakfast. You could be *weak* if you've been sick for a while. A *weak* voice is not loud enough to be heard easily. A *weak* board is not strong or sturdy. A *weak* excuse is one that is not good or believable.

feeble

Feeble means lacking strength. Some people may become *feeble* as they get older. Barb made a *feeble* attempt to move the heavy chair.

flimsy

Flimsy means not strongly made or not well put together. This chair is very *flimsy;* it broke when I sat on it. A *flimsy* story doesn't have much of a plot.

frail

Frail means physically weak. A *frail* person can become ill easily. *Frail* also means easily broken. The smaller, *frail* blossoms were knocked off the tree during the hailstorm last week.

fragile
brittle

Fragile and *brittle* mean weak and easily broken. Something *fragile* is delicately made and must be handled with great care. A spider's web is *fragile,* but it is strong enough to trap a fly. Something *brittle* is easily broken, cracked, or snapped because it is not tough. It is stiff and cannot be bent. Icicles are *brittle.* Paper becomes *brittle* with age.

See also *powerless, thin.*

ANTONYMS: strong, sturdy, tough, healthy, husky, stout

W

Pirates' **treasure** is being discovered in sunken ships.

wealth

Wealth means a large amount or supply of something. *Wealth* is the opposite of poverty. People of *wealth* have many valuable possessions. *Wealth* includes a person's money and property. Natural resources are part of a country's *wealth*. An encyclopedia has a *wealth* of information.

money

Money is what is used in buying and selling. What something is worth may be measured in terms of how much *money* it costs or how much *money* someone is willing to pay for it.

property

Property is what a person owns. If you buy and pay for something, it becomes your *property*. A person's *property* may include a house and the land on which it is built, furniture, clothes, and money. People sometimes put up fences to keep strangers off their *property*.

riches

Riches is another word for wealth, though it is not so often used. The *riches* of our earth should be conserved.

treasure

Treasure is wealth that is stored up or collected. Pirates' buried *treasure* is being discovered in sunken ships in the Pacific Ocean.

abundance

An *abundance* is a great supply or quantity of something. Our cherry trees had an *abundance* of blossoms.

ANTONYM: poverty

400

wild

Wild, when it describes animals, means not tame or domesticated. Lions, giraffes, and elephants are *wild* animals. *Wild* also means not cared for or cultivated. *Wild* flowers grow in fields and forests. The explorers went into the *wild,* mountainous region. People who lose their tempers or become very angry sometimes act *wild.* You may say you are *wild* about something you like very much.

furious

Furious means wild and angry. You may be *furious* at yourself if you make a silly mistake. Mom and Dad were *furious* when they saw my sister scribbling on the wall. Wind that whips blinding snow ahead of it is *furious.*

violent

Violent means wild. The moose became *violent* when we surprised it as it was eating. *Violent* can also describe something that is strong or forceful—like a *violent* storm or a *violent* sea.

untamed

Untamed means not controlled or not tame. An *untamed* animal is hard to control. It hasn't been trained to be obedient or gentle.

savage
ferocious

A *savage* or *ferocious* animal is wild and fierce and dangerous. When the *savage* grizzly bear invaded the campsite, it ripped the tents. The *ferocious* lion tried to claw its trainer.

ANTONYMS: tame (adj), domesticated, timid, gentle, docile, harmless

401

W

win (v)

Win means gain victory or success. A bowling team *wins* when it has the highest score. Two dozen people entered the pie-baking contest, but Dick *won.*

succeed

You *succeed* when you do what you set out to do. The runner *succeeded* in jumping the hurdles without knocking any over. Mrs. Levine's new business is *succeeding.*

triumph

Triumph means gain a victory or rejoice after a victory has been won. The ancient Romans *triumphed* over the Greeks. The whole city *triumphed* when the home team won the pennant.

prevail

Prevail means win against great odds or because of greater strength. Jack *prevailed* against the giant.

See also *beat* (v), *conquer, defeat* (v), *obtain.*

ANTONYMS: lose, give

Jack **prevailed** against the giant.

wisdom

Very intelligent boys and girls of twelve may be called "wise beyond their years," but they do not possess *wisdom. Wisdom* is gained only after years and years of experience. People who have *wisdom* are intelligent and farsighted. They make good decisions based on what they know. They understand even the most complicated situations because of their broad experience and their ability to think things out. Grandmother displayed her *wisdom* when she advised me to get a good education.

These other words are related to *wisdom* but are not synonyms. They may have the precise meaning you're looking for in certain situations.

• insight

Insight is the power to look into a situation with understanding. People who have *insight* catch the real meaning or feeling of something. If something is bothering your brother, you might wish you had an *insight* into his problem so that you could help him. I told Mom I'd take the dog out for a walk before bedtime, but she had the *insight* to know I just wanted to avoid going to bed so early.

• sense

Sense is an ability to judge and make good decisions. It's also the ability to act appropriately in any situation. I hope you have enough *sense* to lock the cage after you feed the hamster.

wisdom continued on page 404 ▶

W

• judgment

Judgment adds training and experience to sense. You need *judgment* when you have to make a choice between two actions or objects. My *judgment* told me we wouldn't have time to see both Washington, D.C., and Jamestown on our vacation.

• knowledge

Knowledge is all the things you know or the state of knowing something well. To my *knowledge* he hasn't left the house all day. Because of Masumi's vast *knowledge* of science, everyone comes to her with questions.

• reason

Reason is the power to think things out in an orderly way. All my *reason* wasn't enough to figure out how Jane knew I'd borrowed her ring while she was away.

• understanding

Understanding is the ability to see things clearly and to see someone else's point of view. Mike's *understanding* of young people and their problems made him an ideal youth counselor.

ANTONYM: foolishness

wise

Wise means having knowledge or not foolish. It describes someone who understands people and situations well and uses good judgment in dealing with them. You would be *wise* to get plenty of sleep the night before a ten-mile hike.

• smart

Smart means alert, bright, or intelligent. It is the opposite of stupid. Rick was *smart* enough to figure out that we wanted him to buy us some pizza.

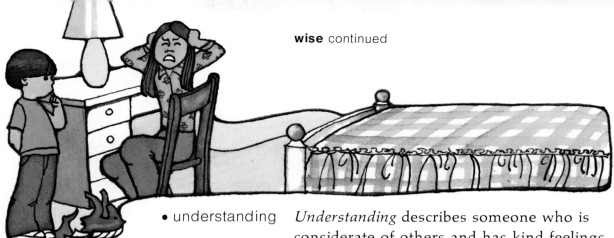

It is hard for Dottie to be **understanding** when her little brother breaks things.

- understanding

Understanding describes someone who is considerate of others and has kind feelings toward them and their problems. It is hard to be *understanding* when your little brother breaks things that belong to you.

- sensible

Sensible means having or using good sense or judgment. Some people are *sensible* almost all the time; others, not very often. Looking in both directions when crossing a street is *sensible.*

- levelheaded

Levelheaded means sensible and not easily upset. It is important to be *levelheaded* during an emergency.

- reasonable

A *reasonable* person is one who is sensible and not hard to get along with. If something is *reasonable,* it is fair and just. If a librarian asks you to be quiet in the library, she is making a *reasonable* request. An unreasonable request would be to ask you to make no noise at all.

Sometimes *reasonable* means not extreme. A *reasonable* price is one that is not too high. Paying fifty cents for a small package of gum is unreasonable.

ANTONYMS: foolish, unwise, stupid, unreasonable, absurd

405

W

work (n)   *Work* is the doing or accomplishing or making of something. It is sometimes the opposite of play. What some people think is *work* may be considered play by others. Washing windows is hard *work* for some people. It may take a lot of *work* to come up with an idea for my book report.

labor   *Labor* is strenuous work or work that takes a lot of strength. The piano movers were exhausted by their *labor*. Machines have taken much of the backbreaking *labor* out of farming.

toil   *Toil* is long and tiring work. After days of *toil*, the bird finally completed its nest.

drudgery   *Drudgery* is unpleasant or dull or very monotonous work. Practicing the piano is *drudgery* to Wanda because she has no interest in music. She thinks that taking out the trash every day is pure *drudgery*.

She thinks that taking out the trash every day is pure **drudgery**.

effort   *Effort* can mean demanding or difficult work. Sometimes it takes a lot of *effort* to get up in the morning. Eddie put a lot of *effort* into getting his model plane done in time for the contest.

activity

Activity can refer to work that is done over a long period of time. One *activity* of the committee is the planning of the new blood-donor program.

See also *action, task.*

work (v)

Work, when used as a verb, is sometimes the opposite of play. Mom *works* in a factory. When she comes home, she rests or relaxes. I *worked* hard all day.

Work can also mean run. Does your sewing machine *work?* It *works* well now that the parts have been oiled.

labor

Labor means work hard and long. The construction workers *labored* to complete the building on time.

toil

Toil means work even harder and longer. The farmers were completely exhausted after they had *toiled* in the field all day.

operate

Operate means work or make something run. My radio doesn't *operate* very well when the batteries are low. Dennis *operates* an elevator in the office building.

perform
function

Perform and *function* mean do or carry out something or act as something. Doctors *perform* operations. A rock can *function* as a hammer.

See also *act* (v).

W

worried

Worried means filled with fear or doubt about something. You may be *worried* about something that has happened or perhaps something you think might happen. If you're *worried* about someone, you fear that something bad may happen to that person. Elio was *worried* about making the swimming team. My grandmother is always *worried* when our family goes camping. She thinks camping is dangerous.

concerned

If you're *concerned* about something, you are interested in it and worried about it. My father is *concerned* about our local government. He's afraid the wrong person will be elected mayor.

troubled
disturbed

Troubled and *disturbed* mean upset or uneasy. After seeing a horror movie, you might fall into a *troubled* sleep. You might feel *disturbed* if you lost a friend's book.

nervous

Nervous means uneasy and even jumpy. If you're a *nervous* person, a loud noise may cause you to jump in your chair. *Nervous* people find it hard to relax.

A loud noise may cause a **nervous** person to jump.

anxious

Anxious means extremely uneasy or fearful. As early as September, settlers in the Northwest Territory became *anxious* about the coming of winter.

frantic

When people become *frantic,* they are so worried and excited that they do not think clearly. If a small child is lost in a store, the parents may become *frantic.* Instead of asking a clerk for help, they may run around the store calling the child's name.

See also *eager.*

ANTONYMS: calm (adj), easy, unconcerned, untroubled, undisturbed

worry (v)

One of the earliest meanings of *worry* was "snap at, tear, or bite, especially the throat." When a puppy grabs a slipper with its teeth, chews it, shakes it back and forth, and growls at it, the puppy is *worrying* the slipper. So *worry* means pull at something or disturb it or shake it over and over. Something that *worries* you shakes your thoughts and disturbs your mind continually. The problem of finding safe places to dump garbage *worries* the town council.

annoy

Annoy means worry or disturb someone over and over. Usually the things that *annoy* people are small and unimportant. What *annoys* me most about my little sister is that she asks so many questions.

worry (v) continued on page 410 ▶

W

bother

Bother means worry or disturb someone and cause that person to be nervous or impatient. Don't *bother* your mother while she's driving the car in heavy traffic.

irk
vex

Irk and *vex* both mean irritate and annoy. *Irk* is a good word to use when you mean irritate. It *irks* me to be weeding the garden while my friends are playing baseball. Use *vex* when you mean make angry. It has a stronger meaning than irritate. Nothing *vexes* me more than people who do not keep their promises.

tease

Tease means annoy by coaxing or bothering someone over and over again with jokes or tricks. People sometimes *tease* a dog by pretending to throw a stick and telling the dog to fetch it.

tantalize

Tantalize means tease by offering something but then keeping it just out of reach. This word comes from an ancient Greek myth. Tantalus, who was a king and a son of Zeus, was punished in a unique way. He was forced to stand chin-high in water, underneath trees filled with delicious-looking fruit. When he bent his head to drink, the water receded, or fell, so he could not touch it. When he reached for the fruit above, it moved higher, away from him. From his name came the word *tantalize.* Irene *tantalized* her dogs by holding food above their heads.

ANTONYMS: calm (v), please, soothe

Irene **tantalized** her dogs by holding food above their heads.

worth (n)　　The *worth* of something is determined by how excellent or important or useful it is, or by how much a person likes it or wants it. A real pearl has *worth* because it is rare and difficult to obtain. The natural resources of a country are of great *worth* to its people. Your *worth* can be measured by your deeds or by how kind and helpful you are. Sometimes the *worth* of an object is measured in terms of money. When we say we are getting our money's *worth* out of something, we mean we are satisfied with it and with the price we paid for it.

value　　*Value* is a close synonym of worth and is often used in place of it. A car has more *value* if its engine and body are not worn. Jewels have *value.* Education has great *value.*

importance　　Something has *importance* if it is of great worth or value, and if not having it makes you poorer in some way. Doctors speak of the *importance* of good health.

usefulness
utility　　Things have *usefulness* and *utility* when they are helpful and serve some purpose. No one can doubt the *usefulness* of modern machinery. A reaping machine has *utility* to a farmer, who needs help in cutting and harvesting grain.

benefit　　Something is to your *benefit* if it helps you. A long rest is of *benefit* to a tired person. A road map may be of *benefit* in planning a trip.

Y

yearning *Yearning* means the feeling of wanting or needing something. Have you ever had a *yearning* to join a circus?

desire A *desire* is a yearning or a wish for something. Sean has a *desire* to travel.

longing A *longing* is a deep desire or yearning for something presently out of your reach. I have a *longing* to live in Alaska.

craving A *craving* is usually a yearning for some kind of food. Do you ever get a *craving* for popcorn?

thirst *Thirst* can mean simply a desire for something, or it can mean a yearning for something to drink. Fern has a *thirst* for detective stories.

hankering *Hankering* is a perfectly good informal word to use when you have a mild yearning for something. Eleanor and Ron have a *hankering* for some deep-sea fishing.

liking If something is to your *liking,* it pleases you and you may want to have it—if you don't have it already. If you have a *liking* for horses, you probably read books about them and go to horse shows.

taste If something suits your *taste,* you like it. Many people have a *taste* for hot dogs.

• preference A *preference* is the liking of one thing better than another. Freda has a *preference* for foreign-made cars.

Fern has a **thirst** for detective stories.

yell (v)   *Yell* means speak loudly and forcefully. You may *yell* if you're in trouble and need help. You might also *yell* if you get excited over something or are furious at someone. People sometimes *yell* when they are hurt or frightened.

• call   *Call* and the rest of the words in this entry are related to yell but are not synonyms. *Call* means raise your voice so that someone who is far away can hear you. Golfers *call* "Fore" if they think a ball may hit another player. I *called* to Florence, but she didn't hear me.

• cry
• bawl   *Cry* and *bawl* can mean either call or weep loudly. The man *cried* "Help!" when his wallet was stolen in the crowd. The little boy *bawled* when he lost his family at the amusement park.

• exclaim   *Exclaim* can mean cry out in pleasure or surprise. "How good to see you again!" Aunt Marilyn *exclaimed* when she saw me getting off the train.

• howl   *Howl* means cry loudly for a long time. Coyotes *howl* at night. Nancy *howled* with laughter at the comedian.

• whine
• whimper   *Whine* and *whimper* mean speak in a low, complaining voice or make a low sound. Small children sometimes *whine* when they want their own way. Dogs *whine*. A puppy *whimpers*. Babies may *whimper* if they are sleepy.

yell (v) continued on page 414 ▶

Y

- shout

Shout means yell at the top of your voice. People *shout* when they're at a football game. Mary *shouted* "Fire!" when she saw the smoke in the hall. I *shouted* good-by to my friend as the train pulled out of the station.

- scream
- screech
- shriek

Scream, screech, and *shriek* are all good words to use for yell. They mean make a sharp, shrill sound. Some people *scream* when they see a snake. The tires of a car will *screech* if the car stops suddenly. They *shrieked* in fear when they visited a haunted house in the amusement park.

- clamor

Clamor means make a lot of noise. The zoo animals *clamor* for their food at feeding time.

- bellow
- roar

Bellow and *roar* can be used to mean make a loud, deep sound or noise. Wild animals *bellow* and *roar,* but we also say people and things *bellow* and *roar.* "Hurry up and help me clean the garage," Roscoe *bellowed.* The audience *roared* with laughter. The train *roared* out of the tunnel.

ANTONYM: whisper (v)

The train **roared** out of the tunnel.

Z

zone (n)

A *zone* is a particular part of something or a particular place. The earth's surface is divided into five parts or *zones.* Most of the United States is in the North Temperate *Zone.* Streets and highways are divided into traffic *zones.* The streets surrounding a school make up a school *zone.* You are not allowed to park in a no-parking *zone.* Zip Codes on letters and packages indicate the postal *zone* to which they are being sent.

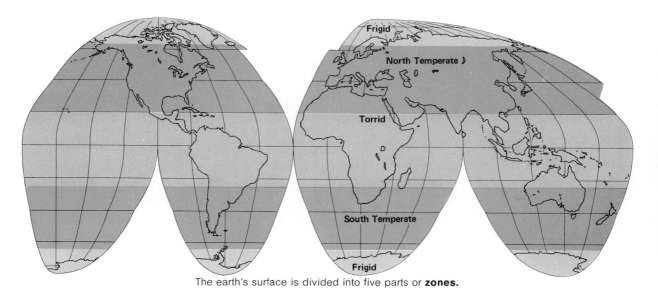

Frigid
North Temperate
Torrid
South Temperate
Frigid

The earth's surface is divided into five parts or **zones.**

• division

Division and the rest of the words in this entry are related to zone but are not synonyms. A *division* is one of the parts into which something can be divided. States, cities, and counties may all be called *divisions* within the United States. Some businesses have several *divisions.*

zone continued on page 416 ▶

Z

zone continued from page 415

• district

A *district* can be a division within a country or city. We speak of farming, mining, and business *districts*. There are also school *districts* and police *districts*.

• area

Area may mean the amount of ground space that something takes up. Or it may mean a place—either large or small, open or enclosed—that is set aside for a special purpose. A plain is a large *area* of level grass-covered land, usually used for farming or grazing. The room in your home where you eat dinner may be called a dining *area*. The space where cars can be left is called a parking *area*. A playground is an outside play *area*.

• region

A *region* is a large area. The area surrounding the North Pole is called the Arctic *region*. A desert is a barren *region*.

• belt

A *belt* can be a region where certain crops are raised. We speak of the South as being the cotton *belt* and of the Midwest as being the wheat *belt*.

• tract

A *tract* is a stretch of land. A prairie is a *tract* of level or rolling grassland. The factory bought a *tract* of land next to the railroad.

Index

A

abandon **leave** (v) 230
abandon **grasp** (v) 182
abbreviate **decrease** (v) 110
abdicate **surrender** (v) 371
ability 20
able **skillful** 345
abnormal **normal** 254
abrupt **sudden** 362
abruptly **suddenly** 363
abscond **run** (v) 315
absolute **perfect** (adj) 266
absurd **foolish** 166
absurd **wise** 404
abundance **wealth** 400
abundant **rare** 300
accelerate **advance** (v) 30
accelerate **decrease** (v) 110
acceptable **disagreeable** 120
accomplishment 21
account (n) 22
accumulate **gather** 173
accumulate **save** 321
accurate **correct** (adj) 97
achieve **obtain** 259
achieve **succeed** 361
achievement
　　accomplishment 21
achievement **conquest** 91
acquaint **inform** 214
act (v) 23
act (v) **pretend** 289
act (n) **action** 24
•act (n) **law** 229
action 24
action **battle** (n) 52
active 26
activity **action** 24
activity **work** (n) 406
actual **real** 301
actual **imaginary** 208

add **increase** (v) 213
add **decrease** (v) 110
•addition **branch** (n) 62
adjust **correct** (v) 98
admire 27
　　See also **love** (v) 241
admire **hate** (v) 194
admit **agree** 32
admit **allow** 36
admit **shut** (v) 340
admonish **advise** 31
admonition **warning** 396
adore 28
　　See also **love** (v) 241
adult (adj) 29
adult (adj) **new** 252
advance (v) 30
　　See also **move** 250
advance (v) **block** (v) 59
advertise **announce** 41
advice **suggestion** 366
advice **warning** 396
advise 31
　　See also **tell** 377
age (v) **grow** 186
agile **active** 26
agony **misery** 245
agree 32
agree **promise** (v) 290
agree **argue** 45
agree **object** (v) 257
agreeable **pleasant** 274
agreeable **disagreeable** 120
agreement 33
•agreement **pledge** (n) 276
agreement **objection** 258
agreement **quarrel** (n) 298

aid (v) **help** (v) 197
aid (v) **block** (v) 59
aid (n) **help** (n) 198
aim (n) **object** (n) 256
alarm (n) **fear** (n) 157
alarm (n) **warning** 396
alarm (v) **scare** (v) 325
alert (adj) 34
alibi **defense** 112
alien **foreign** 170
•alliance **club** (n) 80
allow 36
　　See also **give** 177
allow **block** (v) 59
almighty **powerful** 282
alter **change** (v) 75
amaze **surprise** (v) 368
amazement **surprise** (n) 370
ambush (v) **attack** (v) 48
amiable **friendly** 172
amplify **enlarge** 138
amuse 37
amusement 38
amusing **humorous** 205
ancient **new** 252
•anecdote **story** 356
anger 39
•annex (v) **increase** (v) 213
annex (v) **join** 222
announce 41
　　See also **tell** 377
annoy **worry** (v) 409
annoy **amuse** 37
•annoyance **difficulty** 116
answer (v) 42
　　See also **tell** 377
answer (v) **satisfy** 320
answer (v) **inquire** 216
answer (n) 43

NOTE: Each page listed in this Index is the page on which the entry begins.
•Identifies related word.

B

anticipate **forecast** (v) 168
antique (adj) **new** 252
anxiety **concern** (n) 86
anxious **eager** 130
anxious **worried** 408
appalling **dreadful** 127
apparent **visible** 390
•appear **come** 82
appease **satisfy** 320
appetizing **delicious** 114
•appliance **instrument** 219
appreciate **hate** (v) 194
•approach **come** 82
appropriate (adj) 44
   See also **right** 308
appropriate (adj) **correct**
  (adj) 97
•approval **agreement** 33
approval **objection** 258
approve **agree** 32
approve **object** (v) 257
•area **zone** (n) 415
argue 45
   See also **fight** (v) 158
argument **quarrel** (n) 298
arid **moist** 249
arouse **urge** 388
arrange **plan** (v) 272
arrange **put** 296
arrangement 46
arrest (v) **catch** (v) 72
arrest (v) **lengthen** 231
•arrive **come** 82
arrive **leave** (v) 230
•article **account** 22
article **object** (n) 256
artificial **real** 301
ascend **rise** (v) 309
ascend **fall** (v) 151
ascertain **find** (v) 160
ask **answer** (v) 42
ask about **inquire** 216

asleep **alert** (adj) 34
assemble **build** 68
assemble **gather** 173
•assembly **meeting** 244
assignment **task** 376
assist (v) **help** (v) 197
assistance **help** (n) 198
•association **club** (n) 80
assortment **mixture** 248
astonish **surprise** (v) 368
astonishment **confusion** 89
astonishment **surprise** (n) 370
astound **surprise** (v) 368
•attach **increase** (v) 213
attach **join** 222
attack (v) 48
   See also **fight** (v) 158
attack (n) **battle** (n) 52
attack (n) **defense** 112
attempt (v) 49
attractive **disagreeable** 120
authentic **real** 301
authority **power** 281
•autobiography **history** 200
average **special** 351
aversion **hate** (n) 194
avid **eager** 130
avoid **dodge** (v) 124
awake (adj) **alert** (adj) 34
award (v) **present** (v) 288
aware, be **know** 224
•awe **surprise** (n) 370
awful **dreadful** 127
awkward **clumsy** 81
awkward **skillful** 345

backbone **endurance** 136
bad **pleasant** 274
•badge **sign** (n) 341
baffle **confuse** 88
•band **party** 265
bankrupt **exhausted** 145
bankrupt **poor** 279
bankruptcy **failure** 147
bar (v) **block** (v) 59
bargain (v) **trade** (v) 384
•bargain **agreement** 33
•bargain **deal** (n) 107
barter **trade** (v) 384
bashful **shy** 341
basic 50
   See also **big** 58
basic **last** (adj) 227
battle (v) 51
   See also **fight** (v) 158
battle (n) 52
•bawl **yell** (v) 413
•beam **gleam** (n) 178
bear (v) **carry** 71
bear (v) **suffer** 364
bear (v) **support** (v) 367
beat (v) 53
beauteous **beautiful** 54
beautiful 54
•be aware **know** 224
becoming **appropriate** (adj) 44
be fond of **enjoy** 138
beg **request** (v) 306
begin **end** (v) 134
beginning 56
beginning (n) **end** (n) 136
beginning (n) **limit** (n) 235
beginning (adj) **last** (adj) 227
behave **act** (v) 23
behavior **action** 24

behold **notice** (v) 255
belief 57
belief **doubt** (n) 126
believe **imagine** 209
believe **doubt** (v) 125
•bellow **yell** (v) 413
•belt **zone** (n) 415
bend (v) **shape** (v) 334
benefit (v) **help** (v) 197
benefit (v) **harm** (v) 192
benefit (n) **help** (n) 198
benefit (n) **worth** (n) 411
benefit (n) **harm** (n) 191
bequeath **present** (v) 288
beseech **request** (v) 306
besiege (v) **battle** (v) 51
•be sure **know** 224
bewilder **confuse** 88
bewilderment **confusion** 89
biased **fair** (adj) 148
big 58
big **little** 236
bind **fasten** 155
•biography **history** 200
bit (n) **piece** 268
bitter **gentle** 176
blemish **spot** (n) 352
blend (v) **mix** (v) 247
blend (n) **mixture** 248
blessing **misfortune** 245
block (v) 59
    See also **stop** (v) 356
blockaded **enclosed** 134
blot (n) **spot** (n) 352
blotch (n) **spot** (n) 352
blue **sad** 317
•blueprint **plan** (n) 270

bluff (v) **fool** (v) 165
blurred **dim** (adj) 118
boast (v) **brag** 61
boisterous **silent** 343
boldness **bravery** 63
bombard **attack** (v) 48
boost (v) **lift** (v) 233
border (n) **edge** (n) 131
bore (v) **amuse** 37
bored **eager** 130
boredom **amusement** 38
boring **dull** 128
bother (v) **worry** (v) 409
•bough **branch** (n) 62
boundary **limit** (n) 235
brag 61
branch (n) 62
    See also **part** (n) 264
bravery 63
brawl (n) **battle** (n) 52
brawny **strong** 358
break (v) 64
break (v) **create** 100
break (v) **repair** (v) 304
break (n) 66
breakable 67
breakdown **failure** 147
•breed **group** 184
brief (adj) **little** 236
bright **dark** 106
bright **dim** (adj) 118
bright **dull** 128
bright **tame** (adj) 375
brilliant **dull** 128
bring **carry** 71
brink **edge** (n) 131
brittle **breakable** 67
brittle **weak** 399
brittle **elastic** 132
brittle **tough** 382

broad **slender** 347
broadcast (v) **announce** 41
broke (adj) **poor** 279
build 68
    See also **make** 243
build **ruin** (v) 314
bulky **large** 226
bull's eye **object** (n) 256
bully (v) **scare** (v) 325
bungling **clumsy** 81
burden (n) **load** (n) 238
businesslike **playful** 273
butt in **interfere** 220
buy **obtain** 259

C

•call **yell** (v) 413
calm (adj) 69
calm (adj) **worried** 408
calm (v) 70
calm (v) **scare** (v) 325
calm (v) **worry** (v) 409
calm (n) 71
calm (n) **anger** (n) 39
calm (n) **confusion** 89
calmness **fear** (n) 157
capable **skillful** 345
capture (v) **catch** (v) 72
care (n) **concern** (n) 86
careful **thoughtless** 381
careless **thoughtless** 381
cargo **load** (n) 238
carry 71
    See also **move** 250
    See also **take** (v) 373
carve **cut** (v) 103
cast (v) **throw** (v) 382
catch (v) 72
    See also **stop** (v) 356
    See also **take** (v) 373
•category **group** 184
cause (n) **reason** (n) 302
caution (v) **advise** 31
cautious **thoughtless** 381
cease **end** (v) 134
cement (v) **join** 222
center (n) 74
center (n) **edge** (n) 131
certain **confident** 88
chain (v) **fasten** 155
change (v) 75
    See also **make** 243
    See also **move** 250
change (v) **substitute** (v) 360
changeable 77

charge (v) **attack** (v) 48
charge (v) **command** (v) 85
charming **pleasant** 274
chase (v) **follow** 163
chat (n) **conversation** 95
cheap **precious** 285
cheat (v) **fool** (v) 165
check (v) **block** (v) 59
checkup (n) **inspection** 218
cheer (v) **amuse** 37
cheer (n) **amusement** 38
cheerful **comfortable** 84
cheerful **happy** 190
cheerful **pleasant** 274
cheerful **dark** 106
cheerful **sad** 317
cheery **comfortable** 84
cheery **pleasant** 274
cherished **precious** 285
chief (adj) **important** 211
childish **adult** (adj) 29
chisel (v) **cut** (v) 103
choose 78
    See also **take** (v) 373
chop (v) **cut** (v) 103
chore **task** 376
•chronicle **history** 200
chunk **piece** 268
circumstance **condition** 87
circumstance **event** 141
civilized **rude** 312
•clamor (v) **yell** (v) 413
clarify **explain** 146
clarify **confuse** 88
clasp (v) **grasp** (v) 182
•class (n) **group** 184
•classification **arrangement** 46
clean (adj) **unclean** 387
clear (adj) 79
clear (adj) **dark** 106
clear (adj) **dim** (adj) 118
clever **skillful** 345
clip (v) **cut** (v) 103

clog (v) **block** (v) 59
close (v) **end** (v) 134
close (v) **shut** (v) 340
close (v) **start** (v) 354
close (n) **end** (n) 136
•closing **last** (adj) 227
club (n) 80
    See also **gathering** 174
clumsy 81
clumsy **skillful** 345
clutch (v) **grasp** (v) 182
coarse **breakable** 67
coarse **slender** 347
coax **request** (v) 306
coerce **force** (v) 167
collapse (n) **failure** 147
collect **gather** 173
collect **scatter** 326
combat (v) **battle** (v) 51
combat (n) **battle** (n) 52
combination **mixture** 248
combine **join** 222
combine **mix** (v) 247
come 82
come **leave** (v) 230
comfort (v) **scare** (v) 325
comfortable 84
comfortable **convenient** 94
comical **humorous** 205
command (v) 85
    See also **tell** 377
command (v) **govern** 179
command (n) **power** (n) 281
commence **start** (v) 354
commence **end** (v) 134
comment (v) **say** 323
common **ordinary** 263
common **odd** 260
common **rare** 300
common **special** 351
commonplace **ordinary** 263
commonplace **rare** 300

communicate **announce** 41
•compact (n) **agreement** 33
•company **firm** (n) 163
compel **force** (v) 167
complain **object** (v) 257
complaint **objection** 258
complete (v) **end** (v) 134
complete (v) **start** (v) 354
complex **simple** 343
complicated **difficult** 115
complicated **simple** 343
comply **agree** 32
comply **command** (v) 85
compound **mixture** 248
compress (v) **shrink** 339
conceal **hide** (v) 199
conceal **announce** 41
conceal **inform** 214
conceal **show** (v) 337
concealed **visible** 390
conceited **proud** 292
conceited **shy** 341
concept **idea** 207
concern (n) 86
concerned **thoughtful** 380
concerned **worried** 408
conclude **end** (v) 134
conclude **start** (v) 354
•concluding **last** (adj) 227
conclusion **end** (n) 136
conclusion **opinion** 262
conclusion **beginning** 56
•conclusive **last** (adj) 227
condense **shrink** 339
condition 87
conduct (v) **direct** (v) 119
conduct (n) **action** 24
•conference **meeting** 244
confidence **belief** 57
confidence **doubt** (n) 126
confident 88
confident **shy** 341

confine **contain** 93
confine **limit** (v) 234
confine **shut** (v) 340
confirm **support** (v) 367
conflict (n) **battle** (n) 52
confuse 88
confuse **disturb** 122
confused **clear** (adj) 79
confusion 89
confusion **arrangement** 46
confusion **calm** (n) 71
congregate **gather** 173
connect **join** 222
conquer 90
conquest 91
consent (v) **agree** 32
consent (v) **argue** 45
consent (v) **object** (v) 257
consent (n) **permission** 268
consequence **result** (n) 307
conserve **save** 321
consider 92
   See also **think** 379
considerate **thoughtful** 380
considerate **thoughtless** 381
.conspicuous **visible** 390
construct **build** 68
construct **ruin** (v) 314
contain 93
contemplate **consider** 92
contemporary **new** 252
content (v) **satisfy** 320
contented **comfortable** 84
contented **happy** 190
contentment **happiness** 189
contentment **misery** 245
contest (n) **battle** (n) 52
continue **lengthen** 231

contract (v) **agree** 32
contract (v) **shrink** 339
contract (v) **enlarge** 138
•contract (n) **agreement** 33
contradict **agree** 32
contradiction **agreement** 33
contribute **present** (v) 288
contribution **present** (n) 287
control (v) **govern** 179
control (n) **power** (n) 281
convenient 94
•convention **meeting** 244
conversation 95
convert (v) **change** (v) 75
conviction **belief** 57
conviction **opinion** 262
cool (adj) **calm** (adj) 69
copy (n) 96
copy (v) **imitate** 210
core (n) **center** (n) 74
•corporation **firm** (n) 163
correct (adj) 97
   See also **right** 308
correct (v) 98
costly **precious** 285
•council **meeting** 244
counsel (v) **advise** 31
counterfeit (adj) **fake** (adj) 150
counterfeit (v) **imitate** 210
couple (v) **join** 222
courage **bravery** 63
courteous **polite** 278
courteous **rude** 312
cow (v) **scare** (v) 325
cowardice **bravery** 63
coy **shy** 341
cozy **comfortable** 84
craggy **rough** 310
crash (n) **failure** 147
crave **want** (v) 395
craving **yearning** 412

D

create 100
  See also **make** 243
- creation **invention** 220
- creek **branch** (n) 62
crisp **breakable** 67
crooked **dishonest** 121
cross-examine **inquire** 216
crow (v) **brag** 61
crowd (n) 101
  See also **gathering** 174
crude **rude** 312
cruel **friendly** 172
cruel **thoughtful** 380
- cry (v) **yell** (v) 413
cuff (v) **hit** (v) 202
cumbersome **heavy** 196
cunning **skillful** 345
curb (v) **govern** 179
curb (n) **edge** (n) 131
curious 102
curious **odd** 260
current (adj) **new** 252
custom **habit** 188
cut (v) 103
cut (v) **decrease** (v) 110
cut short **lengthen** 231

damage (v) **harm** (v) 192
damage (n) **harm** (n) 191
damp **moist** 249
danger 105
dangerous **safe** (adj) 319
daring (n) **bravery** 63
daring (adj) **shy** 341
dark 106
dark **shining** 336
- data **information** 215
dawdle **hurry** (v) 206
deadline **limit** (n) 235
deal (n) 107
deal (v) **trade** (v) 384
dear **precious** 285
debate (v) **argue** 45
deceit **honesty** 203
deceitful **dishonest** 121
deceive **fool** (v) 165
decide 108
  See also **think** 379
decide **choose** 78
decision 109
declare **say** 323
decline (v) **request** (v) 306
decrease (v) 110
  See also **make** 243
decrease (v) **increase** (v) 213
decrease (n) **growth** 186
deed **accomplishment** 21
defeat (v) 112
defeat (n) **conquest** 91
defective **perfect** (adj) 266
defend **protect** 290
defend **support** (v) 367
defend **attack** (v) 48
defense 112
defense **answer** (n) 43
defenseless **powerless** 284

definite **clear** (adj) 79
definite **dim** (adj) 118
deflate **shrink** 339
deflate **enlarge** 138
delay (v) **block** (v) 59
delay (v) **hurry** (v) 206
delectable **delicious** 114
deliberate **sudden** 362
deliberately **suddenly** 363
delicate **breakable** 67
delicate **delicious** 114
delicious 114
delight (v) **amuse** 37
delight (n) **amusement** 38
delight (n) **happiness** 189
delightful **delicious** 114
delightful **pleasant** 274
deliver **send** 328
demand (v) **command** (v) 85
demand (v) **request** (v) 306
demolish **ruin** (v) 314
demolish **build** 68
demonstrate **show** (v) 337
deny **allow** 36
depart **leave** (v) 230
depart **come** 82
dependable **dishonest** 121
depleted **exhausted** 145
depressed **sad** 317
descend **fall** (v) 151
descend **rise** (v) 309
describe **explain** 146
desert (v) **leave** (v) 230
design (v) **create** 100
- design (n) **plan** (n) 270
desire (v) **want** (v) 395
desire (n) **yearning** 412
despair (n) **sadness** 318
despair (n) **happiness** 189
despise **hate** (v) 194
destitute **poor** 279

destroy **ruin** (v) 314
destroy **build** 68
destroy **create** 100
destroy **repair** (v) 304
destroy **save** 321
detach **join** 222
detect **find** (v) 160
determine **decide** 108
determine **find** (v) 160
detest **hate** (v) 194
detest **enjoy** 138
develop **build** 68
develop **grow** 186
•develop **practice** (v) 284
development **growth** 186
•development **training** 386
•device **instrument** 219
devoted **loyal** 242
dexterity **ability** 20
dexterous **skillful** 345
dexterous **clumsy** 81
•diagram (n) **plan** (n) 270
dialogue **conversation** 95
•diary **history** 200
die **live** (v) 237
differ **agree** 32
difference **agreement** 33
difficult 115
difficult **convenient** 94
difficult **simple** 343
difficulty 116
•difficulty **misfortune** 245
digress **wander** 393
diluted **thin** 378
dim (adj) 118
dim (adj) **clear** (adj) 79
dim (adj) **shining** 336
diminish **decrease** (v) 110
diminish **increase** (v) 213

direct (v) 119
direct (v) **command** (v) 85
dirty **unclean** 387
disagree **argue** 45
disagree **object** (v) 257
disagree **agree** 32
disagreeable 120
disagreement **quarrel** (n) 298
disagreement **agreement** 33
disappear **come** 82
disapproval **objection** 258
disapproval **agreement** 33
disapprove **agree** 32
disarrange **disturb** 122
•disaster **misfortune** 245
disbelief **belief** 57
discard (v) **save** 321
•discern **know** 224
discontented **comfortable** 84
discourage **help** (v) 197
discourse **conversation** 95
discourteous **rude** 312
discover **find** (v) 160
•discovery **invention** 220
discuss **argue** 45
discuss **speak** 350
discussion **conversation** 95
disguise (v) **hide** (v) 199
disgust (n) **hate** (n) 194
dishonest 121
dishonesty **honesty** 203
dishonor (v) **admire** 27
dishonor (n) **honesty** 203
dishonorable **dishonest** 121
dislike (v) **hate** (v) 194
dislike (v) **enjoy** 138
dislike (n) **hate** (n) 194
disloyal **loyal** 242
disorder **arrangement** 46
disorderly **neat** 252
dispatch (v) **send** 328
dispel **scatter** 326

disperse **scatter** 326
disperse **gather** 173
displace **disturb** 122
display (v) **show** (v) 337
display (n) **show** (n) 338
displeasing **pleasant** 274
displeasure **amusement** 38
dispute (v) **argue** 45
dispute (v) **agree** 32
dispute (n) **quarrel** (n) 298
dispute (n) **agreement** 33
disregard **admire** 27
disregard **consider** 92
disregard **watch** (v) 398
disrespectful **rude** 312
dissension **agreement** 33
dissent (v) **agree** 32
distaste **hate** (n) 194
distasteful **delicious** 114
distinct **dim** (adj) 118
•distinguish **know** 224
distinguished **famous** 152
distract **disturb** 122
distress (n) **misery** 245
•distress (n) **misfortune** 245
•district **zone** (n) 415
distrust (v) **doubt** (v) 125
distrust (n) **doubt** (n) 126
disturb 122
    See also **move** 250
disturb **amuse** 37
disturb **calm** (v) 70
disturbed **worried** 408
disturbed **calm** (adj) 69
diversion **amusement** 38
divert **amuse** 37
divide **decrease** (v) 110
divide **increase** (v) 213
divide **join** 222

E

•division **zone** (n) 415
•divulge **report** (v) 305
docile **tame** (adj) 375
docile **wild** 401
dodge (v) 124
domesticated **tame** (adj) 375
domesticated **wild** 401
dominion **power** 281
donate **present** (v) 288
donation **present** (n) 287
dote on **enjoy** 138
doubt (v) 125
doubt (n) 126
doubt (n) **belief** 57
doubtful **clear** (adj) 79
doubtful **confident** 88
downcast **sad** 317
downcast **happy** 190
•draft (n) **plan** (n) 270
drag (v) **pull** (v) 293
draw (v) **pull** (v) 293
draw out **lengthen** 231
dread (n) **fear** (n) 157
dreadful 127
dreary **dark** 106
drift (v) **wander** 393
•drill (n) **training** 386
drill (v) **practice** (v) 284
drive (v) **push** (v) 295
drive (v) **send** 328
drop (v) **fall** (v) 151
drop (v) **carry** 71
drowsy **alert** (adj) 34
drudgery **work** (n) 406
dry (adj) **moist** 249
duck (v) **dodge** (v) 124
duel (n) **battle** (n) 52

dull 128
dull **alert** (adj) 34
dull **clear** (adj) 79
dull **shining** 336
dull **splendid** 352
dumb **silent** 343
dumfound **confuse** 88
dumfound **surprise** (v) 368
•duplicate (n) **copy** (n) 96
duplicate (v) **imitate** 210
durable **tough** 382
dusky **dark** 106
duty **task** 376
dwell **live** (v) 237
•dwelling **shelter** (n) 335
dwindle **decrease** (v) 110

eager 130
earliest **last** (adj) 227
earn **obtain** 259
earnest **serious** 329
easy **comfortable** 84
easy **convenient** 94
easy **simple** 343
easy **difficult** 115
easy **tough** 382
easy **worried** 408
eccentric **odd** 260
economize **save** 321
edge (n) 131
effect (n) **result** (n) 307
effective **powerful** 282
effort **work** (n) 406
effortless **simple** 343
egotistical **proud** 292
eject **push** (v) 295
elastic 132
elect **choose** 78
element **portion** (n) 280
elevate **lift** (v) 233
emaciated **thin** 378
emancipate **free** (v) 171
•emancipation **liberty** 232
•emblem **sign** (n) 341
•emergency **difficulty** 116
eminent **famous** 152
enchanting **pleasant** 274
encircle **surround** 372
enclose **contain** 93
enclose **surround** 372
enclosed 134
encompass **surround** 372
encourage **help** (v) 197

end (v) 134
   See also **stop** (v) 356
end (v) **start** (v) 354
end (n) 136
end (n) **limit** (n) 235
end (n) **object** (n) 256
end (n) **result** (n) 307
end (n) **beginning** 56
endanger **protect** 290
endeavor (v) **attempt** (v) 49
endorsement **objection** 258
endurance 136
•endure **allow** 36
endure **suffer** 364
energetic **active** 26
energy **strength** 357
engrave **cut** (v) 103
enjoy 138
   See also **love** (v) 241
enjoy **hate** (v) 194
enlarge 138
   See also **make** 243
enlarge **decrease** (v) 110
enlargement **growth** 186
enormous **large** 226
enormous **little** 236
enter 140
entertain **amuse** 37
entertainment **amusement** 38
episode **event** 141
equal **fair** (adj) 148
escape (v) **run** (v) 315
essential **basic** 50
establish **create** 100
establish **start** (v) 354
evade **dodge** (v) 124
even **rough** 310
event 141
•eventual **last** (adj) 227

everyday **ordinary** 263
evident **clear** (adj) 79
evident **visible** 390
evolve **grow** 186
exact **correct** (adj) 97
exalt **adore** 28
exalted **grand** 180
examination **inspection** 218
examine 142
   See also **see** 327
example 143
exasperation **anger** 39
excellent **perfect** (adj) 266
exception **habit** 188
exceptional **special** 351
exceptional **ordinary** 263
excessive **gentle** 176
exchange (v) **change** (v) 75
exchange (v) **substitute** (v) 360
exchange (v) **trade** (v) 384
•exchange (n) **deal** (n) 107
excite **urge** 388
excite **calm** (v) 70
excited **calm** (adj) 69
excited **sad** 317
exciting **dull** 128
•exclaim **yell** (v) 413
exclude **shut** (v) 340
exclude **contain** 93
excuse (n) **defense** 112
exercise (v) **practice** (v) 284
exercise (n) **action** 24
•exercise (n) **training** 386
exhausted 145
exhibit (v) **show** (v) 337
exhibit (n) **show** (n) 338
exhibition **show** (n) 338
expand **enlarge** 138
expand **shrink** 339
expandable **elastic** 132
expansion **growth** 186
expectation **sadness** 318
expected **sudden** 362

expel **push** (v) 295
expensive **precious** 285
•experience (v) **suffer** 364
expert (adj) **perfect** (adj) 266
explain 146
   See also **tell** 377
exploit (n) **accomplishment** 21
explore **examine** 142
expose **protect** 290
exposition **show** (n) 338
express (v) **speak** 350
exquisite **beautiful** 54
•extend **come** 82
extend **increase** (v) 213
extend **lengthen** 231
extend **decrease** (v) 110
•extension **branch** (n) 62
extensive **large** 226
external **foreign** 170
extraneous **foreign** 170
extraordinary **special** 351
extraordinary **ordinary** 263

F

•fable **tale** 373
fabricate **build** 68
•fabrication **invention** 220
fail **fall** (v) 151
fail **succeed** 361
failure 147
failure **accomplishment** 21
failure **conquest** 91
fair (adj) 148
   See also **right** 308
fair (adj) **beautiful** 54
•fairy tale **tale** 373
faith **belief** 57
faith **doubt** (n) 126
faithful **loyal** 242
faithless **loyal** 242
fake (adj) 150
fake (adj) **real** 301
fall (v) 151
   See also **go** 179
fall (v) **rise** (v) 309
fall back **advance** (v) 30
false **fake** (adj) 150
false **correct** (adj) 97
false **loyal** 242
false **real** 301
famed **famous** 152
familiar **ordinary** 263
familiar **odd** 260
familiar **special** 351
famous 152
fanciful **imaginary** 208
fancy (v) **imagine** 209
fantastic **imaginary** 208
fashion (v) **create** 100
fast (adj) 153
fast (adv) 154

fasten 155
fasten **break** (v) 64
fat **slender** 347
fat **thin** 378
fatigued **exhausted** 145
favor (n) **present** (n) 287
fear (n) 157
fearlessness **fear** (n) 157
feat **accomplishment** 21
federation **club** (n) 80
feeble **weak** 399
feign **pretend** 289
fence (v) **limit** (v) 234
fenced **enclosed** 134
ferocious **fierce** 158
ferocious **wild** 401
fetch **carry** 71
fiasco **failure** 147
fickle **changeable** 77
fickle **loyal** 242
fictitious **imaginary** 208
fierce 158
fierce **tame** (adj) 375
fight (v) 158
fight (n) **battle** (n) 52
figure (n) **shape** (n) 333
•final **last** (adj) 228
find (v) 160
find (v) **hide** (v) 199
•finding (n) **invention** 220
fine **slender** 347
finish (v) **end** (v) 134
finish (v) **start** (v) 354
finish (n) **end** (n) 136
finish (n) **beginning** 56
firm (adj) 161
firm (adj) **tough** 382
firm (adj) **thin** 378
firm (n) 163
   See also **gathering** 174

first **basic** 50
first **last** (adj) 227
fit (adj) **appropriate** (adj) 44
fit (v) **join** 222
fit (v) **shape** (v) 334
fitting (adj) **appropriate** (adj) 44
fix (v) **repair** (v) 304
fix (v) **break** (v) 64
fix (v) **ruin** (v) 314
fizzle (n) **failure** 147
flabbergast **surprise** (v) 368
flabby **firm** (adj) 161
•flash (n) **gleam** (n) 178
flaw (n) **spot** (n) 352
flawless **perfect** (adj) 266
flee **run** (v) 315
fleet (adj) **fast** (adj) 153
fleetly **fast** (adv) 154
flexible **elastic** 132
flexible **firm** (adj) 161
•flicker (n) **gleam** (n) 178
flighty **serious** 329
flimsy **thin** 378
flimsy **weak** 399
flimsy **strong** 358
fling (v) **throw** (v) 382
float (v) **wander** 393
flog **beat** (v) 53
flourish **succeed** 361
flow (v) **run** (v) 315
fluctuating **changeable** 77
fluster **disturb** 122
•folk tale **tale** 373
follow 163
   See also **go** 179
follow **imitate** 210
fondness **hate** (n) 194
fond of, be **enjoy** 138

fool (v) 165
foolish 166
foolish wise 404
foolishness wisdom 403
forbid allow 36
force (v) 167
   See also move 250
force (n) strength 357
forceful powerful 282
foreboding (n) warning 396
forecast (v) 168
   See also tell 377
forecast (n) 169
foreign 170
foresee forecast (v) 168
foretell forecast (v) 168
forewarn forecast (v) 168
forewarning (n) warning 396
forge (v) shape (v) 334
forged real 301
forget find (v) 160
forget remember 304
forgo obtain 259
form (n) shape (n) 333
form (v) create 100
form (v) shape (v) 334
forsake leave (v) 230
fortitude endurance 136
found start (v) 354
fracas quarrel (n) 298
fraction portion (n) 280
fracture (v) break (v) 64
fragile breakable 67
fragile weak 399
fragile tough 382
fragment piece 268
•fragrant delicious 114
frail weak 399
frame (n) edge (n) 131
frantic worried 408

free (v) 171
free (v) catch (v) 72
free (v) fasten 155
•freedom liberty 232
freight load (n) 238
frequent rare 300
friendly 172
fright fear (n) 157
frighten scare (v) 325
frightful dreadful 127
frisky playful 273
frivolous serious 329
frolicsome playful 273
frontier limit (n) 235
frustrated happy 190
fun amusement 38
function (v) act (v) 23
function (v) work (v) 407
fundamental basic 50
funny foolish 166
funny humorous 205
funny odd 260
furious wild 401
further (v) advance (v) 30
fury anger 39
fuse (v) mix (v) 247
fusion mixture 248
fuss (n) quarrel (n) 298

G

gallantry bravery 63
gallop (v) run (v) 315
•gang party 265
gather 173
gather scatter 326
gathering 174
gaunt thin 378
gawky clumsy 81
gay sad 317
gaze (v) look (v) 240
general rare 300
general special 351
genial friendly 172
genial rude 312
gentle 176
gentle fierce 158
gentle harsh 193
gentle rude 312
gentle wild 401
genuine real 301
genuine fake (adj) 150
•gesture (n) sign (n) 341
get present (v) 288
get send 328
gift present (n) 287
gigantic large 226
give 177
give obtain 259
give win (v) 402
give up attempt (v) 49
give up obtain 259
glad sad 317
gladness sadness 318
glance (v) look (v) 240
glare (v) look (v) 240
gleam (n) 178
glimmering shining 336
•glint (n) gleam (n) 178
gloat brag 61
gloom sadness 318
gloomy dark 106
gloomy sad 317
gloomy happy 190
gloomy pleasant 274

H

glorious **splendid** 352
•glow (n) **gleam** (n) 178
glue (v) **join** 222
go 179
go **come** 82
goad (v) **urge** 388
goal **object** (n) 256
go away **come** 82
good **fair** (adj) 148
gorgeous **beautiful** 54
gorgeous **splendid** 352
govern 179
grab **grasp** (v) 182
graceful **beautiful** 54
graceful **clumsy** 81
gradual **sudden** 362
gradually **suddenly** 363
grand 180
grant (v) **present** (v) 288
grant (n) **present** (n) 287
grapple **battle** (v) 51
grasp (v) 182
  See also **take** (v) 373
gratify **satisfy** 320
grave (adj) **serious** 329
grave (adj) **humorous** 205
great 183
  See also **big** 58
green **adult** (adj) 29
grip (v) **grasp** (v) 182
group 184
  See also **gathering** 174
•group **party** 265
grow 186
grown-up (adj) **adult** (adj) 29
growth 186
gruff **harsh** 193
•guarantee (n) **pledge** (n) 276
guard (v) **protect** 290
guard (v) **watch** (v) 398
guard (v) **attack** (v) 48
guess (v) **imagine** 209
guide (v) **direct** (v) 119

habit 188
halt (v) **end** (v) 134
handsome **beautiful** 54
handy **convenient** 94
handy **skillful** 345
handy **useful** 389
handy **clumsy** 81
hankering **yearning** 412
•happen **come** 82
happening **event** 141
happiness 189
happiness **misfortune** 245
happiness **misery** 245
happiness **sadness** 318
happy 190
happy **sad** 317
harbor (v) **protect** 290
•harbor (n) **shelter** (n) 335
hard **difficult** 115
hard **firm** (adj) 161
hard **convenient** 94
hard **gentle** 176
hard **simple** 343
•hardship **difficulty** 116
•hardship **misfortune** 245
harm (v) 192
harm (n) 191
harm (n) **help** (n) 198
harmless **safe** (adj) 319
harmless **fierce** 158
harmless **wild** 401
harsh 193
harsh **gentle** 176
harvest (v) **gather** 173
hasten **hurry** (v) 206
hastily **suddenly** 363
hasty **sudden** 362

hatch (v) **plan** (v) 272
hate (v) 194
hate (v) **enjoy** 138
hate (n) 194
hatred **hate** (n) 194
haughty **proud** 292
haughty **humble** (adj) 204
haul (v) **pull** (v) 293
hazard **danger** 105
hazardous **safe** (adj) 319
healthy **powerless** 284
healthy **weak** 399
heart **center** (n) 74
heave **lift** (v) 233
heavy 196
heavy **slender** 347
heavy **thin** 378
heedless **thoughtless** 381
heedless **alert** (adj) 34
help (v) 197
help (v) **block** (v) 59
help (n) 198
help (n) **misfortune** 245
helpful **useful** 389
helpless **powerless** 284
helpless **powerful** 282
helpless **useful** 389
herald (v) **announce** 41
heroism **bravery** 63
hidden **visible** 390
hide (v) 199
hide (v) **announce** 41
hide (v) **find** (v) 160
hide (v) **show** (v) 337
hideous **beautiful** 54
hike (v) **walk** (v) 391
hinder **block** (v) 59
hinder **advance** (v) 30
hinder **help** (v) 197
hinder **hurry** (v) 206
hindrance **help** (n) 198

I

hint (v) **suggest** 365
hint (n) **suggestion** 366
history 200
hit (v) 202
hitch (v) **fasten** 155
hoarse **harsh** 193
hoist (v) **lift** (v) 233
hold (v) **contain** 93
hold (v) **surrender** (v) 371
hollow **firm** (adj) 161
homely **beautiful** 54
honest dishonest 121
honesty 203
honor (v) **admire** 27
honor (n) **honesty** 203
honorable **dishonest** 121
hoodwink **fool** (v) 165
hope (n) **sadness** 318
hopefulness **sadness** 318
horde **crowd** (n) 101
horrible **disagreeable** 120
horrid **disagreeable** 120
horrid **beautiful** 54
•howl (v) **yell** (v) 413
hub **center** (n) 74
huge **large** 226
huge **little** 236
humble (adj) 204
humble (adj) **grand** 180
humble (adj) **proud** 292
humid **moist** 249
humorous 205
hunch **warning** 396
hunk **piece** 268
hunt (v) **follow** 163
hurl **throw** (v) 382
hurry (v) 206
hurt (v) **harm** (v) 192
husky **harsh** 193
husky **thin** 378
husky **weak** 399
hustle (v) **hurry** (v) 206

idea 207
ideal (adj) **perfect** (adj) 266
ideal (n) **example** 143
idiotic **foolish** 166
idle **active** 26
idleness **action** 24
idolize **adore** 28
ignore **consider** 92
ignore **notice** (v) 255
ignore **watch** (v) 398
ill-mannered **rude** 312
illustrate **show** (v) 337
illustration **example** 143
illustrious **great** 183
•image **copy** (n) 96
imaginary 208
imaginary **real** 301
imagine 209
See also **think** 379
imitate 210
imitation (adj) **fake** (adj) 150
•imitation **copy** (n) 96
immature **adult** (adj) 29
immediate **fast** (adj) 153
immediate **sudden** 362
immediately **fast** (adv) 154
immediately **suddenly** 363
immense **large** 226
immense **little** 236
immodest **humble** (adj) 204
immovable **firm** (adj) 161
impart **inform** 214
impartial **fair** (adj) 148
impatient **eager** 130
imperfect **perfect** (adj) 266
impersonate **imitate** 210
impish **playful** 273
•implement (n) **instrument** 219
implication **suggestion** 366
implore **request** (v) 306

imply **suggest** 365
impolite **rude** 312
impolite **polite** 278
importance **worth** (n) 411
important 211
See also **big** 58
important **serious** 329
important **little** 236
imposing **grand** 180
impression **idea** 207
imprison **contain** 93
improper **appropriate** (adj) 44
improve **correct** (v) 98
improve **help** (v) 197
inability **ability** 20
inaccurate **correct** (adj) 97
inactive **active** 26
inactivity **action** 24
inappropriate **appropriate** (adj) 44
inappropriate **correct** (adj) 97
inaugurate **start** (v) 354
incident **event** 141
incline (v) **slant** (v) 346
include **contain** 93
include **shut** (v) 340
inconsiderate **thoughtless** 381
inconsiderate **thoughtful** 380
inconspicuous **visible** 390
inconvenient **convenient** 94
incorrect **correct** (adj) 97
increase (v) 213
See also **make** 243
increase (v) **decrease** (v) 110
increase (n) **growth** 186
indefinite **clear** (adj) 79
•independence **liberty** 232
indifference **concern** (n) 86
indifferent **eager** 130
indifferent **thoughtful** 380
indistinct **dim** (adj) 118
individual **special** 351

P

pacific **calm** (adj) 69
pacify **calm** (v) 70
pack (n) **load** (n) 238
•pact **agreement** 33
•palatable **delicious** 114
panic (n) **fear** (n) 157
parched **moist** 249
parley (n) **conversation** 95
part (n) 264
partial **fair** (adj) 148
particle **piece** 268
particular **special** 351
•partnership **firm** (n) 163
party 265
　　See also **gathering** 174
passive **active** 26
paste (v) **join** 222
patch (v) **repair** (v) 304
pattern (n) **example** 143
pause (n) **break** (n) 66
peace **calm** (n) 71
peaceful **calm** (adj) 69
peculiar **odd** 260
peek (v) **look** (v) 240
peer (v) **look** (v) 240
penetrate **enter** 140
penniless **poor** 279
peppy **active** 26
perfect (adj) 266
　　See also **right** 308
perform **act** (v) 23
perform **work** (v) 407
performance **action** 24
performance **show** (n) 338
peril **danger** 105
permission 268
permit (v) **allow** 36
permit (v) **block** (v) 59
permit (n) **permission** 268
perplex **confuse** 88
perplexity **confusion** 89

petty **little** 236
petty **grand** 180
petty **great** 183
pick (v) **choose** 78
pick (v) **pull** (v) 293
•picture (n) **copy** (n) 96
piece 268
　　See also **part** (n) 264
pierce **enter** 140
pitch (v) **throw** (v) 382
place (v) **put** 296
placid **calm** (adj) 69
plain (adj) **clear** (adj) 79
plain (adj) **simple** 343
plain (adj) **dim** (adj) 118
plain (adj) **splendid** 352
plan (v) 272
　　See also **think** 379
plan (n) 270
•plan (n) **arrangement** 46
play (v) **pretend** 289
play (v) **work** (v) 407
play (n) **work** (n) 406
playful 273
plead **request** (v) 306
pleasant 274
pleasant **disagreeable** 120
please **satisfy** 320
please **worry** (v) 409
pleased **happy** 190
pleased **sad** 317
pleasing **pleasant** 274
pleasure **amusement** 38
pleasure **anger** 39
pleasure **misery** 245
pleasure **misfortune** 245
pledge (v) **promise** (v) 290
pledge (n) 276
plentiful **rare** 300
plod (v) **walk** (v) 391
plot (v) **plan** (v) 272
•plot (n) **plan** (n) 270
pluck (v) **pull** (v) 293
plump **thin** 378

point (n) **location** 239
poisonous **safe** (adj) 319
poke (v) **push** (v) 295
poky **fast** (adj) 153
polite 278
polite **harsh** 193
polite **rude** 312
ponder **consider** 92
ponderous **heavy** 196
poor 279
popular **ordinary** 263
portion (n) 280
　　See also **part** (n) 264
•portrait **copy** (n) 96
portray **explain** 146
position **location** 239
positive **confident** 88
potent **powerful** 282
poverty **wealth** 400
power 281
power **strength** 357
powerful 282
powerful **powerless** 284
powerless 284
powerless **powerful** 282
practice (v) 284
practice (n) **habit** 188
•practice (n) **training** 386
prance (v) **walk** (v) 391
precarious **safe** (adj) 319
precede **follow** 163
precious 285
precise **correct** (adj) 97
•predicament **difficulty** 116
predict **forecast** (v) 168
prediction **forecast** (n) 169
prefer **choose** 78
•preference **yearning** 412
•preparation **arrangement** 46
present (v) 288
　　See also **give** 177
present (n) 287

Q

preserve (v) **save** 321
pretend 289
pretty **beautiful** 54
prevail **win** (v) 402
prevent **block** (v) 59
prevent **allow** 36
priceless **precious** 285
primary **basic** 50
primary **last** (adj) 227
principal **important** 211
prized **precious** 285
probe (n) **inspection** 218
problem **mystery** 251
problem **answer** (n) 43
proceed **advance** (v) 30
process **action** 24
prod (v) **push** (v) 295
produce (v) **create** 100
• production **invention** 220
profess **say** 323
• profile **shape** (n) 333
prognostication **forecast** (n) 169
program (v) **plan** (v) 272
progress (v) **advance** (v) 30
prohibit **block** (v) 59
prohibit **allow** 36
• project (n) **plan** (n) 270
prolong **lengthen** 231
promise (v) 290
• promise (n) **pledge** (n) 276
promote **advance** (v) 30
promote **block** (v) 59
prompt (v) **urge** 388
pronounce **say** 323
prop (v) **support** (v) 367
propel **force** (v) 167
proper **appropriate** (adj) 44
property **wealth** 400

prophecy **forecast** (n) 169
prophesy **forecast** (v) 168
proposal **suggestion** 366
propose **suggest** 365
prosper **succeed** 361
prosperity **misfortune** 245
protect 290
protect **attack** (v) 48
protected **safe** (adj) 319
protection **defense** 112
• protection **shelter** (n) 335
protest (v) **object** (v) 257
protest (v) **agree** 32
protest (n) **objection** 258
proud 292
proud **humble** (adj) 204
prowl **sneak** (v) 348
prowl **wander** 393
prune (v) **cut** (v) 103
prying **curious** 102
publish **announce** 41
pull (v) 293
   See also **move** 250
pull (v) **push** (v) 295
pummel **beat** (v) 53
punch (v) **hit** (v) 202
punish **correct** (v) 98
• puny **little** 236
puny **strong** 358
purchase (v) **obtain** 259
• purchase (n) **deal** (n) 107
pure **perfect** (adj) 266
pure **unclean** 387
purpose (n) **object** (n) 256
pursue **follow** 163
push (v) 295
   See also **move** 250
push (v) **pull** (v) 293
put 296
   See also **move** 250
puzzle (v) **confuse** 88
puzzle (n) **mystery** 251
puzzling **difficult** 115

quaint **odd** 260
quake (v) **shake** (v) 331
qualified **appropriate** (adj) 44
quarrel (n) 298
quarrel (v) **argue** 45
quarrelsome **friendly** 172
queer **odd** 260
query **answer** (n) 43
question (n) **answer** (n) 43
question (v) **doubt** (v) 125
question (v) **inquire** 216
question (v) **answer** (v) 42
quick **alert** (adj) 34
quick **fast** (adj) 153
quick **sudden** 362
quickly **fast** (adv) 154
quiet (adj) **calm** (adj) 69
quiet (adj) **silent** 343
quiet (adj) **tame** (adj) 375
quiet (v) **calm** (v) 70
quiet (v) **scare** (v) 325
quiet (n) **calm** (n) 71
quiet (n) **sound** (n) 348
quit **leave** (v) 230
quit **attempt** (v) 49
quit **come** 82
quiver (v) **shake** (v) 331

R

race (v) **run** (v) 315
radiant **shining** 336
rage (n) **anger** 39
raging **fierce** 158
rainy **moist** 249
raise (v) **lift** (v) 233
ramble (v) **wander** 393
range (v) **wander** 393
ransom (v) **free** (v) 171
rapid **fast** (adj) 153
rapidly **fast** (adv) 154
rare 300
raspy **harsh** 193
rattle (v) **disturb** 122
ready **alert** (adj) 34
real 301
   See also **right** 308
real **fake** (adj) 150
real **imaginary** 208
realize **imagine** 209
•realize **know** 224
reason (v) **consider** 92
reason (n) 302
•reason (n) **wisdom** 403
•reasonable **wise** 404
reasonable **foolish** 166
recall **remember** 303
recede **advance** (v) 30
receive **obtain** 259
receive **present** (v) 288
receive **send** 328
recent **new** 252
recess (n) **break** (n) 66
•recite **report** (v) 305
reckless **thoughtless** 381
•recognize **know** 224
recognize **remember** 303
recollect **remember** 303
•record (n) **history** 200
recreation **amusement** 38
reduce **decrease** (v) 110
reduce **enlarge** 138
refined **rude** 312

•reflect **remember** 303
reform (v) **correct** (v) 98
refreshing **pleasant** 274
•refuge **shelter** (n) 335
refuse (v) **choose** 78
refuse (v) **request** (v) 306
regard (v) **admire** 27
•region **zone** (n) 415
regular **normal** 254
regular **odd** 260
regulate **govern** 179
•regulation **law** 229
reign (v) **govern** 179
reject (v) **choose** 78
•relate **report** (v) 305
relax **work** (v) 407
release (v) **free** (v) 171
release (v) **catch** (v) 72
release (v) **contain** 93
release (v) **grasp** (v) 182
reliable **changeable** 77
reliable **dishonest** 121
relief **help** (n) 198
relinquish **surrender** (v) 371
relinquish **obtain** 259
remain **leave** (v) 230
remain **wander** 393
remedy (v) **correct** (v) 98
remember 303
   See also **think** 379
remind **remember** 303
remove **put** 296
renounce **surrender** (v) 371
renowned **famous** 152
repair (v) 304
repair (v) **break** (v) 64
repair (v) **harm** (v) 192
repair (v) **ruin** (v) 314
•repeat **practice** (v) 284
repeat **say** 323

replace **substitute** (v) 360
reply (v) **answer** (v) 42
reply (v) **inquire** 216
reply (n) **answer** (n) 43
report (v) 305
   See also **tell** 377
•report (n) **account** (n) 22
repulsive **disagreeable** 120
repulsive **pleasant** 274
request (v) 306
request (v) **answer** (v) 42
require **force** (v) 167
rescue (v) **free** (v) 171
rescue (v) **save** 321
•resemblance **copy** (n) 96
reside **live** (v) 237
resign **surrender** (v) 371
resilient **elastic** 132
resolution **decision** 109
resolve **decide** 108
respect (v) **admire** 27
respectful **rude** 312
respond **answer** (v) 42
respond **inquire** 216
response **answer** (n) 43
rest (v) **work** (v) 407
rest (n) **action** 24
rest (n) **work** (n) 406
restless **calm** (adj) 69
restless **silent** 343
restore **repair** (v) 304
restrain **block** (v) 59
restrict **limit** (v) 234
restricted **enclosed** 134
restriction **limit** (n) 235
result (n) 307
result (n) **beginning** 56
retort (v) **answer** (v) 42
retort (n) **answer** (n) 43
•reveal **report** (v) 305
reveal **show** (v) 337
reveal **hide** (v) 199

S

reversible **changeable** 77
rich **poor** 279
riches **wealth** 400
riddle **mystery** 251
ridiculous **foolish** 166
right 308
rigid **firm** (adj) 161
rigid **elastic** 132
rim **edge** (n) 131
rip (v) **break** (v) 64
ripe **adult** (adj) 29
ripen **grow** 186
rise (v) 309
　　See also **go** 179
rise (v) **fall** (v) 151
risky **safe** (adj) 319
roam **wander** 393
•roar (v) **yell** (v) 413
•roar (n) **sound** (n) 348
rock (v) **shake** (v) 331
•romance **story** 356
root **beginning** 56
rough 310
rough **rude** 312
rough **gentle** 176
rout (v) **conquer** 90
routine **normal** 254
rove **wander** 393
rude 312
rude **polite** 278
rude **thoughtful** 380
rugged **rough** 310
ruin (v) 314
•ruin (n) **misfortune** 245
rule (v) **decide** 108
rule (v) **govern** 179
rule (n) **habit** 188
•rule (n) **law** 229
ruling **decision** 109
•rumble **sound** (n) 348
run (v) 315
　　See also **move** 250
rush (v) **hurry** (v) 206

sacrifice (v) **surrender** (v) 371
sad 317
sad **happy** 190
sad **pleasant** 274
sadness 318
sadness **amusement** 38
sadness **happiness** 189
safe (adj) 319
safety **danger** 105
•sale **deal** (n) 107
sample (n) **example** 143
•sanctuary **shelter** (n) 335
satisfaction **happiness** 189
satisfied **comfortable** 84
satisfied **happy** 190
satisfy 320
satisfying **pleasant** 274
saunter (v) **walk** (v) 391
savage **fierce** 158
savage **wild** 401
save 321
savory **delicious** 114
say 323
　　See also **tell** 377
•scarce **rare** 300
scare (v) 325
scatter 326
scatter **gather** 173
scatter **mix** (v) 247
scatterbrained **thoughtless** 381
scheme (v) **plan** (v) 272
•scheme (n) **plan** (n) 270
scorn (v) **hate** (v) 194
scrawny **thin** 378
•scream (v) **yell** (v) 413
•screech (v) **yell** (v) 413
screen (v) **protect** 290

scrutinize **examine** 142
scrutiny **inspection** 218
secret (n) **mystery** 251
section (n) **portion** (n) 280
secure (adj) **safe** (adj) 319
secure (v) **fasten** 155
•security **pledge** (n) 276
security **danger** 105
see 327
see **look** (v) 240
segment **portion** (n) 280
seize **catch** (v) 72
seize **grasp** (v) 182
select (v) **choose** 78
self-control **anger** 39
selfish **thoughtful** 380
self-reliant **confident** 88
send 328
　　See also **move** 250
send **obtain** 259
•sense **wisdom** 403
•sensible **wise** 404
sensible **foolish** 166
separate (v) **fasten** 155
separate (v) **gather** 173
separate (v) **join** 222
separate (v) **mix** (v) 247
separation **mixture** 248
serene **calm** (adj) 69
serenity **calm** (n) 71
serious 329
serious **humorous** 205
serious **playful** 273
service (n) **help** (n) 198
serviceable **useful** 389
set (v) **put** 296
set (v) **rise** (v) 309
•set (n) **group** 184
settle **decide** 108
settlement **decision** 109

sever **fasten** 155
shadowy **dim** (adj) 118
shake (v) 331
shape (v) 334
   See also **make** 243
shape (v) **create** 100
shape (n) 333
share (n) **portion** (n) 280
sharp **dim** (adj) 118
sharp **dull** 128
sharp **gentle** 176
shatter **break** (v) 64
shelter (v) **protect** 290
shelter (n) 335
shield (v) **protect** 290
shield (n) **defense** 112
•shield (n) **shelter** (n) 335
shift (v) **change** (v) 75
shift (v) **substitute** (v) 360
shimmering **shining** 336
shining 336
ship (v) **send** 328
shipshape **neat** 252
shiver (v) **shake** (v) 331
•shoot (n) **branch** (n) 62
short **little** 236
shorten **decrease** (v) 110
shorten **lengthen** 231
•shout (v) **yell** (v) 413
shove (v) **push** (v) 295
shove (v) **pull** (v) 293
show (v) 337
show (v) **hide** (v) 199
show (n) 338
•shriek (v) **yell** (v) 413
shrink 339
   See also **make** 243
shrink **enlarge** 138
shrivel **shrink** 339
shudder (v) **shake** (v) 331
shuffle (v) **walk** (v) 391
shut (v) 340
   See also **stop** (v) 356

shy 341
sign (n) 341
sign (n) **warning** 396
•signal (n) **sign** (n) 341
signal (n) **warning** 396
significant **important** 211
signify **show** (v) 337
silence **sound** (n) 348
silent 343
silhouette **shape** (n) 333
silly **foolish** 166
simple 343
simple **difficult** 115
simulate **pretend** 289
sincerity **honesty** 203
sink (v) **fall** (v) 151
site **location** 239
situation **condition** 87
situation **location** 239
skepticism **doubt** (n) 126
•sketch (n) **plan** (n) 270
skill **ability** 20
skillful 345
skillful **clumsy** 81
skinny **thin** 378
skirmish **battle** (n) 52
skulk **sneak** (v) 348
slant (v) 346
slap (v) **hit** (v) 202
slash (v) **cut** (v) 103
slender 347
slice (v) **cut** (v) 103
slight (adj) **little** 236
slight (adj) **slender** 347
slight (adj) **heavy** 196
slight (adj) **large** 226
slim **slender** 347
sling (v) **throw** (v) 382
slink (v) **sneak** (v) 348

slip (v) **sneak** (v) 348
slit (v) **cut** (v) 103
slope (v) **slant** (v) 346
sloppy **neat** 252
slovenly **unclean** 387
slow (adj) **active** 26
slow (adj) **alert** (adj) 34
slow (adj) **fast** (adj) 153
slow (adv) **fast** (adv) 154
slow (v) **advance** (v) 30
slow down **hurry** (v) 206
slowly **fast** (adv) 154
slug (v) **hit** (v) 202
sluggish **alert** (adj) 34
sluggish **fast** (adj) 153
sluggishly **fast** (adv) 154
small **little** 236
small **grand** 180
small **great** 183
small **large** 226
•smart **wise** 404
smash (v) **break** (v) 64
smooth **harsh** 193
smooth **rough** 310
smudge (n) **spot** (n) 352
smug **proud** 292
snare (v) **catch** (v) 72
snatch **catch** (v) 72
snatch **grasp** (v) 182
sneak (v) 348
   See also **go** 179
snoopy **curious** 102
snug **comfortable** 84
snug **safe** (adj) 319
soar **rise** (v) 309
sober **serious** 329
sociable **friendly** 172
•society **club** (n) 80
soft **gentle** 176
soft **firm** (adj) 161
soft **rough** 310
soft **tough** 382

soiled **unclean** 387
solemn **serious** 329
solemn **playful** 273
solid **firm** (adj) 161
solution **answer** (n) 43
solve **answer** (v) 42
solve **explain** 146
soothe **calm** (v) 70
soothe **scare** (v) 325
soothe **worry** (v) 409
soothing **gentle** 176
sorrow **sadness** 318
sorrow **happiness** 189
sorrowful **sad** 317
sort (v) **mix** (v) 247
sound (adj) **strong** 358
sound (n) 348
source **beginning** 56
spank (v) **beat** (v) 53
sparkling **shining** 336
spat (n) **quarrel** (n) 298
speak 350
　See also **tell** 377
special 351
special **ordinary** 263
specimen **example** 143
speck **spot** (n) 352
spectacle **show** (n) 338
speechless **silent** 343
speed (v) **hurry** (v) 206
speedily **fast** (adv) 154
speedy **fast** (adj) 153
spend **save** 321
spirited **active** 26
splendid 352
splinter (v) **break** (v) 64
split (v) **break** (v) 64
spoil (v) **ruin** (v) 314
spot 352
spot (n) **location** 239
spread (v) **scatter** 326

spring (v) **start** (v) 354
springy **elastic** 132
sprint (v) **run** (v) 315
sprout (v) **grow** 186
sprout (v) **start** (v) 354
spry **active** 26
spur (v) **urge** 388
spur (n) **reason** (n) 302
squabble (n) **quarrel** (n) 298
squander **scatter** 326
squander **save** 321
stable (adj) **strong** 358
stable (adj) **changeable** 77
stain (n) **spot** (n) 352
stamina **endurance** 136
stare (v) **look** (v) 240
start (v) 354
　See also **make** 243
start (v) **end** (v) 134
start (n) **beginning** 56
start (n) **end** (n) 136
startle **scare** (v) 325
startle **surprise** (v) 368
state (v) **say** 323
state (n) **condition** 87
stately **grand** 180
status **condition** 87
stay (v) **advance** (v) 30
stay (v) **leave** 230
stay (v) **wander** 393
steady (adj) **firm** (adj) 161
steer (v) **direct** (v) 119
stiff **firm** (adj) 161
stiff **elastic** 132
still (adj) **calm** (adj) 69
still (adj) **silent** 343
stillness **calm** (n) 71
stillness **action** 24

stir up **calm** (v) 70
stop (v) 356
stop (v) **advance** (v) 30
stop (v) **lengthen** 231
stop (v) **start** (v) 354
store (v) **save** 321
storm (v) **attack** (v) 48
stormy **rough** 310
stormy **calm** (adj) 69
story 356
•story **account** (n) 22
stout **slender** 347
stout **thin** 378
stout **weak** 399
straight **dishonest** 121
straight **rough** 310
straighten **shape** (v) 334
strange **odd** 260
stray (v) **wander** 393
strength 357
strenuous **active** 26
stretch (v) **lengthen** 231
stretchable **elastic** 132
strew **scatter** 326
strike (v) **hit** (v) 202
strive **attempt** (v) 49
stroll (v) **walk** (v) 391
strong 358
strong **powerless** 284
strong **thin** 378
strong **weak** 399
struggle (v) **battle** (v) 51
strut (v) **walk** (v) 391
stubborn **tough** 382
stubborn **tame** (adj) 375
study (v) **consider** 92
stumble (v) **walk** (v) 391
stupid **skillful** 345
stupid **wise** 404
sturdy **tough** 382
sturdy **weak** 399

T

subdue **conquer** 90
subdued **tame** (adj) 375
submit **surrender** (v) 371
submit **conquer** 90
substitute (v) 360
subtract **decrease** (v) 110
subtract **increase** (v) 213
succeed 361
succeed **win** (v) 402
success **conquest** 91
success **failure** 147
success **misfortune** 246
succulent **moist** 249
sudden 362
suddenly 363
suffer 364
suffering **misery** 245
suggest 365
   See also **tell** 377
suggestion 366
suitable **appropriate** (adj) 44
suitable **convenient** 94
sunny **dark** 106
superb **splendid** 352
superior **great** 183
support (v) 367
support (n) **help** (n) 198
suppose **imagine** 209
suppress **announce** 41
supreme **great** 183
sure **confident** 88
sure, be **know** 224
surpass **defeat** (v) 112
surprise (v) 368
surprise (n) 370
surrender (v) 371
   See also **give** 177
surrender (v) **conquer** 90

surround 372
surrounded **enclosed** 134
suspect (v) **doubt** (v) 125
suspend **shut** (v) 340
suspicion **doubt** (n) 126
sustain **support** (v) 367
swagger (v) **walk** (v) 391
swap (v) **trade** (v) 384
swat (v) **hit** (v) 202
sway (v) **shake** (v) 331
swear **promise** (v) 290
swear **say** 323
swell (v) **enlarge** 138
swell (v) **shrink** 339
swift **fast** (adj) 153
swiftly **fast** (adv) 154
switch (v) **change** (v) 75
switch (v) **substitute** (v) 360
swoop **fall** (v) 151
•symbol **sign** (n) 341
sympathetic **thoughtful** 380
•symptom **sign** (n) 341
symptom **warning** 396
•system **arrangement** 46
•system **habit** 188

•tactful **polite** 278
tactless **polite** 278
take (v) 373
take **carry** 71
take away **put** 296
take back **present** (v) 288
tale 373
talent **ability** 20
talk (v) **speak** 350
talkative **silent** 343
tame (adj) 375
tame (adj) **fierce** 158
tame (adj) **wild** 401
tantalize **worry** (v) 409
target **object** (n) 256
task 376
taste (n) **yearning** 412
tasty **delicious** 114
teach **inform** 214
•team **party** 265
tear (v) **break** (v) 64
tear (v) **repair** (v) 304
tear down **build** 68
tease (v) **worry** (v) 409
tedious **dull** 128
tell 377
tend **watch** (v) 398
tender **gentle** 176
tender **tough** 382
tenuous **slender** 347
terminate **end** (v) 134
terminate **lengthen** 231
termination **end** (n) 136
terrible **dreadful** 127
terrify **scare** (v) 325
terror **fear** (n) 157
terrorize **scare** (v) 325
test (v) **examine** 142
tether (v) **fasten** 155
thick **heavy** 196
thick **slender** 347
thick **thin** 378

thin 378
thin **slender** 347
thin **heavy** 196
thing **object** (n) 256
think 379
thirst (n) **yearning** 412
thought (n) **idea** 207
thought (n) **opinion** 262
thoughtful 380
thoughtful **serious** 329
thoughtful **thoughtless** 381
thoughtless 381
thoughtless **thoughtful** 380
thrash **beat** (v) 53
threat **danger** 105
thrive **succeed** 361
throng (n) **crowd** (n) 101
throw (v) 382
   See also **move** 250
throw away **save** 321
thrust (v) **push** (v) 295
thump **beat** (v) 53
tidy **neat** 252
tidy **unclean** 387
tie (v) **fasten** 155
tilt (v) **slant** (v) 346
timid **wild** 401
timidity **bravery** 63
tiny **little** 236
tiny **large** 226
tip (v) **slant** (v) 346
tire (v) **amuse** 37
tired **exhausted** 145
tiresome **dull** 128
toil (v) **work** (v) 407
toil (n) **work** (n) 406

•token **sign** (n) 341
•tolerate **allow** 36
tolerate **suffer** 364
•tool **instrument** 219
torment (n) **misery** 245
toss (v) **throw** (v) 382
tough 382
tough **breakable** 67
tough **gentle** 176
tough **weak** 399
tow (v) **pull** (v) 293
trace (v) **imitate** 210
track (v) **follow** 163
•tract **zone** (n) 415
trade (v) 384
•trade (n) **deal** (n) 107
trail (v) **follow** 163
•train (v) **practice** (v) 284
training 386
traitorous **loyal** 242
tramp (v) **walk** (v) 391
tranquil **calm** (adj) 69
tranquilize **calm** (v) 70
tranquillity **calm** (n) 71
•transaction **deal** (n) 107
transfer (v) **change** (v) 75
transform **change** (v) 75
transmit **send** 328
transparent **clear** (adj) 79
transport (v) **carry** (v) 71
trap (v) **catch** (v) 72
treacherous **loyal** 242
tread (v) **walk** (v) 391
treasure **wealth** 400
•treaty **agreement** 33
tremble **shake** (v) 331
tremendous **large** 226
•tributary **branch** (n) 62
trick (v) **fool** (v) 165
trim (adj) **neat** 252
trip (v) **walk** (v) 391

triumph (v) **win** (v) 402
triumph (n) **conquest** 91
trivial **little** 236
trivial **basic** 50
trivial **grand** 180
trivial **great** 183
trivial **heavy** 196
trivial **important** 211
trivial **serious** 329
•troop (n) **party** 265
trot (v) **run** (v) 315
trouble (v) **disturb** 122
•trouble (n) **difficulty** 116
trouble (n) **misfortune** 245
troubled **worried** 408
trounce **beat** (v) 53
•troupe **party** 265
truck (v) **send** 328
trudge (v) **walk** (v) 391
true **loyal** 242
true **real** 301
true **changeable** 77
true **fake** (adj) 150
true **imaginary** 208
trust (v) **doubt** (v) 125
trust (n) **belief** 57
trust (n) **doubt** (n) 126
trustworthy **loyal** 242
trustworthy **dishonest** 121
truthful **dishonest** 121
truthfulness **honesty** 203
try (v) **attempt** (v) 49
tug (v) **pull** (v) 293
turn (v) **change** (v) 75
twinkling **shining** 336
typical **normal** 254

U

ugly **beautiful** 54

•ultimate **last** (adj) 227

unable **skillful** 345

unappetizing **delicious** 114

unbiased **fair** (adj) 148

unbind **fasten** 155

unbreakable **breakable** 67

uncertain **confident** 88

unchangeable **changeable** 77

uncivilized **rude** 312

unclean 387

uncomfortable **comfortable** 84

uncomfortable **convenient** 94

•uncommon **rare** 300

uncommon **ordinary** 263

uncomplicated **simple** 343

uncomplicated **difficult** 115

unconcern **concern** (n) 86

unconcerned **worried** 408

undergo **suffer** 364

•understand **know** 224

•understanding (adj) **wise** 404

•understanding (n)
  agreement 33

•understanding (n) **wisdom** 403

undertake **attempt** (v) 49

undisturbed **worried** 408

uneasy **comfortable** 84

uneasy **confident** 88

uneven **rough** 310

unexpected **sudden** 362

unexpected **ordinary** 263

unexpectedly **suddenly** 363

unfair **fair** (adj) 148

unfit **appropriate** (adj) 44

unfold **enlarge** 138

unfriendly **friendly** 172

unfriendly **thoughtful** 380

ungainly **clumsy** 81

unhappiness **misery** 245

unhappiness **happiness** 189

unhappy **sad** 317

unhappy **happy** 190

unhurried **sudden** 362

unhurriedly **suddenly** 363

unimportant **important** 211

uninterested **curious** 102

uninterested **eager** 130

uninteresting **dull** 128

•union **club** (n) 80

union **mixture** 248

•unique **rare** 300

unique **special** 351

unit **portion** (n) 280

unite **join** 222

unite **break** (v) 64

unjust **fair** (adj) 148

unkind **friendly** 172

unkind **thoughtful** 380

unknown **famous** 152

unknown **great** 183

unlimited **enclosed** 134

unmannerly **rude** 312

unmask **hide** (v) 199

unnatural **normal** 254

unnecessary **basic** 50

unpalatable **delicious** 114

unpleasant **disagreeable** 120

unpleasant **pleasant** 274

unreal **fake** (adj) 150

unreal **imaginary** 208

unreal **real** 301

unreasonable **wise** 404

unreliable **changeable** 77

unrestricted **enclosed** 134

unripe **adult** (adj) 29

unruly **tame** (adj) 375

unsafe **safe** (adj) 319

unsatisfied **comfortable** 84

unsavory **delicious** 114

unshaken **firm** (adj) 161

unskillful **skillful** 345

unsoiled **unclean** 387

unstable **changeable** 77

unsteady **changeable** 77

unsteady **firm** (adj) 161

unsuitable **appropriate** (adj) 44

unsuitable **convenient** 94

unsure **confident** 88

untamed **wild** 401

unthinking **thoughtless** 381

untidy **unclean** 387

untidy **neat** 252

untie **fasten** 155

untroubled **worried** 408

untrue **fake** (adj) 150

untrustworthy **dishonest** 121

untruthful **dishonest** 121

untruthfulness **honesty** 203

unusual **odd** 260

•unusual **rare** 300

unusual **ordinary** 263

unveil **hide** (v) 199

unwise **wise** 404

uphold **support** (v) 367

uplift (v) **lift** (v) 233

upright **dishonest** 121

upset (v) **disturb** 122

up-to-date **new** 252

urge 388
  See also **move** 250

usage **habit** 188

useful 389

usefulness **worth** (n) 411

useless **useful** 389

usual **ordinary** 263

usual **odd** 260

usual **rare** 300

usual **special** 351

•utensil **instrument** 219

utility **worth** (n) 411

utter **speak** 350

V

vacate **leave** (v) 230
vacation **break** (n) 66
vague **dim** (adj) 118
vague **clear** (adj) 79
vain **proud** 292
vain **shy** 341
valor **bravery** 63
valuable **precious** 285
valuable **useful** 389
value **worth** (n) 411
vanish **come** 82
varied **dull** 128
vary **change** (v) 75
vast **large** 226
vast **little** 236
veil (v) **hide** (v) 199
verdict **decision** 109
•version **account** (n) 22
vex **worry** (v) 409
vexation **anger** 39
vibrate **shake** (v) 331
victory **conquest** 91
view (v) **notice** (v) 255
view (n) **opinion** 262
vigilant **alert** (adj) 34
vigor **strength** 357
vigorous **active** 26
vigorous **strong** 358
violent **fierce** 158
violent **wild** 401
visible 390
vital **basic** 50
voice (v) **speak** (v) 350
vow (v) **promise** (v) 290
•vow (n) **pledge** (n) 276

W

wade **walk** (v) 391
walk (v) 391
　　See also **move** 250
wander 393
　　See also **go** 179
want (v) 395
warn **advise** 31
warn **forecast** (v) 168
warning 396
watch (v) 398
　　See also **see** 327
watchful **alert** (adj) 34
watery **moist** 249
weak 399
weak **powerless** 284
weak **thin** 378
weak **powerful** 282
weak **strong** 358
weak **tough** 382
weakness **endurance** 136
weakness **strength** 357
wealth 400
wealthy **poor** 279
weary **exhausted** 145
weigh **consider** 92
weight **load** (n) 238
weighty **heavy** 196
weighty **important** 211
well-mannered **polite** 278
well-to-do **poor** 279
•whimper (v) **yell** (v) 413
•whine (v) **yell** (v) 413
whisper (v) **yell** (v) 413
wide **slender** 347
widen **enlarge** 138
wild 401
wild **tame** (adj) 375
win (v) 402
win (v) **defeat** (v) 112
win (v) **obtain** 259
•wing (n) **branch** (n) 62
wiry **strong** 358
wisdom 403

wise 404
wise **foolish** 166
wish (v) **want** (v) 395
withdraw **come** 82
withdraw **present** (v) 288
withhold **announce** 41
withhold **present** (v) 288
witty **humorous** 205
woe **sadness** 318
wonder (n) **surprise** (n) 370
wonderful **splendid** 352
•word **pledge** (n) 276
work (v) 407
work (n) 406
work (n) **action** 24
work (n) **amusement** 38
worried 408
worry (v) 409
worry (n) **concern** (n) 86
worship (v) **adore** 28
worth (n) 411
wrath **anger** 39
wreck (v) **ruin** (v) 314
wrestle **battle** (v) 51
wrong (adj) **correct** (adj) 97

Y

yank (v) **pull** (v) 293
yearning 412
yell (v) 413
yield (v) **surrender** (v) 371
young **new** 252

Z

zone (n) 415
 See also **part** (n) 264

Answers to questions on pages 7–18

Entries

(page 7)

1. **increase**
2. *increase*
3. They tell you what *increase* means. It means become or make larger or more. It is the opposite of decrease.
4. They show you how *increase* can be used in different sentences.
5. *add, multiply, extend*
6. The paragraphs tell what each synonym means and show how each synonym can be used in a sentence.
7. *attach* and *annex*
8. They are not real synonyms for *increase.*
9. There are black dots in front of them.
10. See also *enlarge.* (Look up *enlarge.*)
11. if the synonyms listed in the entry are not the best ones that you can use
12. at the end of the entry

(page 8)

13. decrease, diminish, divide, subtract
14. They are printed in blue.
15. She is putting leaves into an album.
16. the sentence under the picture
17. *added*
18. in the paragraph next to *add*

19. page 36—cross-reference, picture, illustrative sentence
    page 97—synonyms, cross-reference
    page 119—related words, antonyms
    page 124—cross-reference, antonyms

Synonyms

(page 9)

1. *race, sprint*
2. No. A river doesn't *gallop;* a calculator doesn't *jog;* a person doesn't *flee* at a certain time every morning; a horse doesn't *operate;* a person doesn't *flow* when he or she is running away from something.
3. The Mississippi River *flows* into the Gulf of Mexico.
   Sandy's new calculator *operates* on batteries.
   I *jog* around the block at 6:00 every morning.
   I don't like to ride a horse when it *gallops.*
   Rudy dreamed that he was trying to *flee* from a riderless motorcycle.

(page 10)

4. *dislike*
5. *loathe*
6. *scorn, detest* or *despise, loathe*

(page 11)

7. There are black dots in front of them.

8. Possible related words to use are:
   exclaimed—called, cried, shouted, screamed, bellowed, roared, shrieked, screeched
   roared—howled, shrieked
   whines—whimpers, cries

Antonyms

(page 12)

1. false, artificial, made-up, fake, forged, imaginary, unreal

2. false, artificial, fake, unreal

Tired Words

(page 13)

1. It does not have synonyms listed in a column under the entry word. Related words and antonyms are also not included in this entry.

2. **large, great, important, basic**

Idioms

(page 13)

1. *Act* means to do something or cause something to happen.
   Act for means do something in place of someone else.

Act on means follow through on something.
Act up means disobey or not act properly.

2. No. The idioms have different meanings than the word *acted.*

3. *Honor* means honest and fair.
   "Hold in *honor*" means to greatly respect a person or thing.
   "Uphold the *honor*" means to defend the good reputation of a person or thing.

Formal and Informal Words

(page 14)

1. "I *bought* some roller skates."
   Answers may vary.

2. *Adults* $2.50
   Children $1.00
   Answers may vary.

(page 15)

3. *mob*—informal
   commenced—formal
   desire—formal
   swap—informal

continued on page 448 ▶

447

Parts of Speech

(page 16)

1. three

2. No one could *calm* Melvin. . . .
   calm (v); *quiet, soothe, pacify*
   It was hard for Leona to feel
   calm. . . . **calm** (adj); *cool,*
   tranquil, serene
   Calm can be felt in the
   air. . . . **calm** (n); *quiet, stillness*

Index

(page 17)

1. synonym
2. **leave** (v)
3. page 230
4. Each page listed in this Index is the
   page on which an entry begins.
5. No. Some entries are more than
   one page long, so a synonym may
   be on a different page than the
   entry word.
6. the black dots in front of the words
7. abandon
   It is printed in blue.

(page 18)

8. **grasp** (v)
9. **ability**
10. eight